Ageing, Crime and Society

edited by

Azrini Wahidin
and
Maureen Cain

WILLAN
PUBLISHING

Published by

Willan Publishing
Culmcott House
Mill Street, Uffculme
Cullompton, Devon
EX15 3AT, UK
Tel: +44(0)1884 840337
Fax: +44(0)1884 840251
e-mail: info@willanpublishing.co.uk
website: www.willanpublishing.co.uk

Published simultaneously in the USA and Canada by

Willan Publishing
c/o ISBS, 920 NE 58th Ave, Suite 300
Portland, Oregon 97213-3786, USA
Tel: +001(0)503 287 3093
Fax: +001(0)503 280 8832
e-mail: info@isbs.com
website: www.isbs.com

Paperback
ISBN-13: 978-1-84392-152-3
ISBN-10: 1-84392-152-9

Hardback
ISBN-13: 978-1-84392-153-0
ISBN-10: 1-84392-153-7

British Library Cataloguing-in-Publication Data

A catalogue record for this book is available from the British Library

Typeset by GCS, Leighton Buzzard, Beds
Project management by Deer Park Productions, Tavistock, Devon
Printed and bound by T.J. International, Padstow, Cornwall

Contents

Notes on contributors

Ronald H. Aday received his PhD in Sociology from Oklahoma State University in 1976 with an emphasis in Gerontology and Crime and Corrections. He is a professor and current Chair of the Department of Sociology and Anthropology at Middle Tennessee State University. He also served as Director of Aging from 1980–2005. Current research is focusing on the Social, Emotional, and Health Care Needs of Aging Female Prisoners in the Southern States. Publications include: Wahidin, A. and Aday, R.H. (2005) 'The Needs of Older Men and Women in the Criminal Justice System: An International Perspective', *Prison Service Journal*, 160, 13–22; Aday, R.H. *Aging Prisoners: Crisis in American Corrections* (Praeger Press, 2003); Aday, R.H. 'Aging Prisoners' Concerns Toward Dying in Prison', *Omega: Journal of Death and Dying* (in press).

Gaynor Bramhall is a Principal Lecturer in Criminology and Criminal Justice at the University of Central Lancashire, Preston. Following a Social Sciences degree at Manchester Polytechnic she went on to take an MA in Social Work at the University of Nottingham as a Home Office sponsored student, qualifying as a social worker at the same time. She has previously worked as a Probation Officer in a range of community and court settings. Her research and teaching interests are in issues of diversity, criminal justice, media representations of offenders and community penalties. Her recent chapters and articles include an article with Professor Barbara Hudson entitled 'Assessing the "Other": constructions of "Asianness" in risk assessments by probation officers', *British Journal of Criminology*, Vol. 45, No. 5,

September 2005. She has also written with Helen Codd on 'Older Offenders and Probation: A Challenge for the Future', *Probation Journal*, Vol 49, No 1, pp. 27–34.

Mike Brogden is Honorary Professor in the Department of Applied Social Sciences, University of Lancaster. He recently retired from the Chair of Criminal Justice at Queen's University, Belfast. While most of his books are within the field of socio-legal studies, he has written two texts on elder abuse – *Crime, Abuse, and the Elderly* (with P. Nijhar), Willan Publishing, Cullompton (2000) and *Geronticide: Killing the Elderly*, Jessica Kingsley Publishers, London (2001).

Alan Burnett, senior policy officer with Help the Aged since 2000, was previously a principal lecturer at the University of Portsmouth, where he researched and taught courses in urban geography, geography of crime, and locational conflicts. Earlier in his career he taught Metropolitan Police cadets, was a British Council scholar in Romania and worked for the Scottish Office. He was a local Justice of the Peace for a decade in Portsmouth. During the last five years he has studied and published on crime, fear of crime and older people, and is currently conducting a joint research project on ways of combating anxiety about crime and anti-social behaviour on the part of senior citizens in the East Midlands and North Yorkshire with HtA and the Suzy Lamplugh Trust. He has collaborated with the Home Office on issues relating to crime and older people and has been involved in training with neighbourhood wardens' schemes in a number of cities.

Maureen Cain studied sociology at the London School of Economics, and was awarded a BA in 1959 and a PhD in 1969. After brief research posts at LSE and Manchester, Maureen taught at Brunel University for twelve years until she left as a senior lecturer in 1979. After a few years of short-term posts abroad and in this country (UK), including the Institute of Criminology in Cambridge which obligingly served as base camp, Maureen took the Chair of Sociology at the University of the West Indies, Trinidad campus, where she served from 1987–1995. This changed her life spiritually and intellectually. Maureen returned to the UK in 1995 for personal reasons, and has since worked at the University of Birmingham. In 1988 the American Society of Criminology presented her with the Sellin Clueck Award for Contributions to International Criminology, and from 2003–2006 she served as President of the British Society of Criminology. Maureen's main publications include *Society and the*

Policeman's Role, Routledge, 1969; *Marx and Engels on Law* (with Alan Hunt), Academic Press, 1979; *Growing Up Good: Policing the Behaviour of Girls in Europe* (ed.), Sage, 1989; and *For a Caribbean Criminology* (ed.), special double issue of *Caribbean Quarterly* (Mona, University of the West Indies Press, 1996).

Mervyn Eastman began his career in the late 1960s as a welfare assistant in East London. In the early 1970s he trained and worked in social care relating to the needs of older people. In 1995 he co-founded the Practitioner Alliance Against Abuse of Vulnerable Adults (PAVA) which he chairs. Following early retirement as Director of Social Services in a north London borough, he became Director of 'Better Government for Older People (BGOP)' in 2001. In 1999 he was one of four recipients of Action on Elder Abuse's Five Year Anniversary Awards for a significant contribution to raising awareness of elder abuse in the UK and in the same year an Honorary Doctorate was conferred on him by Middlesex University for his work with older people. He continues to challenge the way professionals, organisations and society generally view older people, and considers that public services will only radically change once older people are fully engaged at all levels of decision making and are seen as a resource not a health and social care drain.

Gary Fitzgerald has been with Action on Elder Abuse since 2001 and was appointed Chief Executive on 2 April 2002. AEA is a charity that provides information and guidance on the prevention of elder abuse. It has sought to influence social policy to facilitate the protection of older people and other vulnerable adults and to ensure that action is taken when abuse is identified. AEA provides comprehensive free-standing training packs and also a specialist cascade programme which was developed in conjunction with Comic Relief.

Thomas Görgen has been with the Criminological Research Institute of Lower Saxony (KFN) in Hanover (Germany) since 2002. He is a psychologist and has been doing empirical research in the field of elder abuse and criminal victimisation of the elderly since 1998. Following a psychology degree at the University of Trier, he worked as a criminological researcher at the universities of Trier and Giessen before joining KFN. He gained a PhD in psychology from Giessen University. He is among the German representatives of the International Network for the Prevention of Elder Abuse (INPEA). Thomas is currently doing a federally-funded study on 'Crime and violence in older people's lives'. He has published on different aspects of elderly victimisation, including elder sexual abuse, abuse in residential settings and domestic violence in old age.

Debby Jaques is currently Head of Healthcare at HMP and YOI Norwich. She has a degree in Nursing Practice and has over 25 years' experience in the NHS, working mainly in Acute Trusts. She has a special interest in the care of older prisoners.

Stuart Lister is a lecturer in criminal justice at the Centre for Criminal Justice Studies in the School of Law, University of Leeds. Before joining the University of Leeds, he worked as a researcher at the universities of Oxford, Keele, and Durham. His research has largely focused on public and private forms of policing and crime prevention. He recently co-directed (with Adam Crawford, 2005) a series of linked projects into visible forms of policing, including a Nuffield-funded study of the 'extended policing family'. His books and reports include: *Bouncers: Violence and Governance in the Night-time Economy* (with D. Hobbs, P. Hadfield and S. Winlow, Oxford University Press, 2003); *Evaluation of the Leeds Distraction Burglary Project* (with D. Wall, Home Office, 2004); and *Plural Policing: the Mixed Economy of Visible Security Patrols* (with A. Crawford, S. Blackburn and J. Burnett, Policy Press, 2005). He recently received (with T. Seddon and E. Wincup) a Joseph Rowntree Foundation award to study the street policing of problem drug users.

Jill Manthorpe is Professor of Social Work at King's College London and co-director of the Social Care Workforce Research Unit. She has been a trustee of Action on Elder Abuse and chairs the Adult Protection Committee of Hull and the East Riding of Yorkshire. She has written widely on the subject of adult protection, with books including *Institutional Abuse* (eds Stanley, Manthorpe and Penhale, Routledge) and *The Age of the Inquiry* (eds Stanley and Manthorpe, Routledge) and is working on a study of partnership and regulation in adult protection and on the Comic Relief/Department of Health funded study of the prevalence of elder abuse being undertaken by NatCen and King's College London.

Preeti Nijhar is a Lecturer in the Centre for Comparative Criminology and Criminal Justice at the University of Wales, Bangor and an Associate Lecturer at the Open University. She was a research fellow at the Institute of Criminology and Criminal Justice, Queen's University,

Belfast and has also worked in South Africa and India. While most of her work engages with a range of critical approaches to law, crime and criminology, especially socio-legal studies and postcolonial theory, her research also crosses traditional disciplinary boundaries and challenges distinctions between 'private' and 'public' transgressions and abuses in their new 'global' forms. Recent publications include *Community Policing: International Models and Approaches* (2005) with M. Brogden; 'Abuse of Adult Males in Intimate Partner Relationships in Northern Ireland' for the Office of the First Minister and Deputy First Minister, Equality Directorate, Belfast (2004) with M. Brogden; and *Crime, Abuse, and the Elderly* (2000) with M. Brogden.

Bridget Penhale is currently Senior Lecturer in the Department of Community, Ageing, and Rehabilitation (CAR) at the University of Sheffield. With a first degree in psychology, she has been qualified as a social worker since 1981. Bridget has specialised in work with older people since 1983, and has worked in urban, rural and city areas in addition to hospitals. Bridget has published extensively on elder abuse. Her research interests include elder abuse, adult protection, domestic violence; mental health of older people; bereavement in later life and intergenerational relationships. She is currently the Principal Investigator in a Department of Health-funded research project on Adult Protection (2004–2007) and is in collaboration with a University of Geneva/World Health Organisation project on developing global responses to elder abuse.

Judith Phillips is Professor of Social Work and Gerontology at the University of Wales, Swansea. She is a qualified social worker and has worked in statutory residential and field settings, specialising in work with older adults. Following a geography degree at the University of Wales, Aberystwyth, Judith went on to study at Stockholm University and Oxford University (MSc. and CQSW) and at UEA, Norwich, where she gained a PhD in social work. She worked at UEA and the University of Keele before moving to Swansea in 2004. Her research interests are in social work and social care and include housing and retirement communities, family and kinship networks, care work and older offenders. Judith also directs the Older People and Ageing Research and Development Network in Wales. Publications include: *Women Ageing* (Routledge, 2000); *The Family and Community Life of Older People* (Routledge, 1999); *The Social Policy of Old Age* (Centre for Policy on Ageing, 2000) and *Juggling Work and Care for Older People* (JRF with Policy Press, 2003).

Jason L. Powell, Lecturer in Sociology, University of Liverpool. Previously, Jason was Senior Lecturer at MMU and was appointed Associate Head of School and Director of Admissions at the University of Salford. Jason also serves on nine editorial boards and has given invited papers in the UK and the US. Jason has published over 70 papers and his book *Social Theory and Aging* (2005) is part of Charles Lemert's *New Discursive Formations* series for Rowman and Littlefield. His other publications include 'Theorizing Gerontology: The Case of Old Age, Professional Power and Social Policy in the United Kingdom', *Journal of Aging and Identity*, 6(3); Powell, J.L. and Wahidin, A. 'Ageing in the Risk Society', *International Journal of Sociology and Social Policy*, 25(8), 2005; Cook, I. and Powell, J.L. 'China, Ageing and Social Policy: The Influence and Limitations of the Bio-Medical Paradigm', *Journal of Societal and Social Policy*, 4(2), 71–89, 2005.

Azrini Wahidin is a Reader in Criminology and Criminal Justice at the Centre for Criminal Justice Policy and Research (CCJPR) at the University of Central England in Birmingham. She is also a visiting Professor in the Department of Sociology and Anthropology at Middle Tennessee State University. She has been a trustee of The Howard League for Penal Reform and chairs the Older Prisoners Research Forum for Age Concern England. She has written widely on the subject of older offenders, prison staff experiences of managing the needs of older offenders, crime in later life, women in prison and the prison estate. She is currently working on a research project with Professor Ron Aday. Publications include: *Older Women in the Criminal Justice System: Running Out of Time* (Jessica Kingsley, 2004); *Foucault and Ageing* (Nova Press, 2006); co-editor of *Criminology* (Oxford University Press, 2005).

David S. Wall is Professor of Criminal Justice and Head of the School of Law at the University of Leeds, where he also conducts research and teaches in the fields of criminal justice and information technology, policing and cyberlaw. Formerly the Director of the Centre for Criminal Justice Studies, David's specialist area of research is criminal justice and information technology, an area in which he has conducted many research projects and published a wide range of articles and books. His books include *Cybercrimes* (Polity, 2007, forthcoming); *Policy Networks in Criminal Justice* (ed. with M. Ryan and S. Savage, Palgrave, 2001), *The Chief Constables of England and Wales* (Ashgate/Dartmouth, 1998).

Acknowledgements

We would like to thank the British Society of Criminology and Better Government for Older People who co-sponsored the conference from which this book emerged, and Paul Kiff and Emma Hodgkinson who organised it for us with considerable skill and good humour. In editing this volume our biggest debt, of course, is to our contributors. Given the level of commitment it is not surprising that the process was more time-consuming than our original schedule proposed. It is sometimes hard to know who feels guiltier in this process: editors for nagging people about deadlines or contributors for missing them. The end product which is this book, makes it worthwhile. We are grateful to Brian Willan and his team at Willan Publishing for having confidence in the project from the very beginning and to Alison Wagstaff who prepared the manuscript for publication. We would like to thank the participants in the workshop, most particularly the BGOP members who, by sharing their experiences of being unyoung, challenged accepted academic accounts, and contributed to the critical approach adopted in this book.

Foreword
by Lord Ramsbotham
H.M. Chief Inspector of Prisons, 1995–2001

It is always an honour to be invited to write a foreword to a book, particularly by people whose commitment to an important subject you have admired for a number of years. My sole qualification for being so honoured is that, for a short time, I was privileged to be a 'bit player' on the same stage that the contributors to this erudite and focused volume have occupied for much longer. For five and a half years I was Her Majesty's Chief Inspector of Prisons for England and Wales, the holder of which post is required to inspect the treatment and conditions of all those held in prison and report on them, to Parliament and the public, through the Home Secretary. They included a growing number of those described as ageing.

The Chief Inspector of Prisons is a Crown official, not a civil servant, which enables him or her to remain independent of the Prison Service and speak directly to anyone and everyone – Ministers, officials, staff, prisoners and the general public – without having to go through a third party. His principal weapon is observed facts, something that those who prefer to deal in spin find extremely uncomfortable. This legally enshrined independence can be used to disclose situations to Ministers and the public that might otherwise remain hidden behind official obfuscation.

However, at the time of writing this foreword, that independence is under threat. Extraordinarily, following no study of whether or not they were effective, the Chancellor announced, in his budget speech, that the existing thirteen inspectorates of public services were to be merged into four large ones. No longer will the Chief Inspector of Prisons be an independent Crown official, but subordinate to a Chief

Inspector of Justice and Community Safety, together with the Chief Inspectors of Courts, Police and Probation. In future he or she will not be able to speak directly to the public, only through someone who has to work to an agenda agreed with Ministers. What a travesty, that the government which introduced the Human Rights Bill should deliberately stifle a unique jewel in the crown of the criminal justice system of this country – only Scotland and Western Australia also have independent Chief Inspectors of Prisons – independent quality assurance, of the way that the human rights of prisoners are preserved in their treatment and conditions.

I mention this because, in many ways, this book performs the same function as the Chief Inspector. However its contributors understand the issues of ageing, in crime and society, far more deeply than an inspectorate. Its timing is fortunate, because it follows the publication of two important government documents, *Opportunity Age*, published by the Home Office, and *Vision for the Future of Social Care for Adult Services*, by the Department of Health, both in 2005. It also follows a thematic review, *No Problems – Old and Quiet*, published by my successor, Anne Owers, in 2004. In the concluding chapter of this book, Mervyn Eastman draws the lessons of these, together with those from the other contributors, into what is, for me, the heart of the whole publication – a strategic framework that is a perspective of a whole system citizenship approach to older prisoners. This is evidence-based, comprehensive, powerful and persuasive, so why should I be so concerned about its future?

We are all prisoners of our experience. My experience, of trying to persuade the very government that is now seeking to stifle independent quality assurance, that the treatment of and conditions for older prisoners were, currently, totally unacceptable in a civilised society, was unfortunate. My recommendations were airbrushed – which is how uncomfortable revelations are treated – so what hope that a group of independent experts, voicing practical advice based on years of study and observation, will be listened to? There is something of a Greek tragedy about this, because Mervyn Eastman also wrote the ignored recommendations that I put forward six years ago.

I became aware that the Prison Service was extraordinarily bad at dealing with anyone who was not a young, adult male, during the very first prison inspection in which I took part, that of HMP Holloway, then the largest women's prison in the country. It was neither structured nor organised to look after other types of prisoners particularly those with different characteristics and needs. Management was all about money, not identifying and tackling what it was that had prevented an offender from leading a useful and law-abiding life.

With the sole exception of High Security prisons – and then only following a commissioned report on an escape, deemed so embarrassing for the Home Secretary that he sacked the Director General of the Prison Service – no-one was – or is – responsible and accountable for any one group of prisoners – women, children, young offenders, older prisoners, unsentenced prisoners, prisoners in training prisons, prisoners in resettlement prisons, mentally disordered prisoners, lifers, sex offenders, foreign nationals, asylum seekers or immigration detainees. Combinations of almost all of these can be held in any prison, making it virtually impossible for its Governor to treat them all appropriately. Treatment of and conditions for prisoners remains a lottery, depending on the inclination and will of the governor of whichever prison in which a prisoner is held and the amount of money allocated to it by its area manager.

To my amazement I also learned that, alone in the country, the Prison Service was not part of the NHS; only 10 per cent of prison doctors were qualified to be NHS GPs; no-one was responsible for any of the groups who needed special consideration – such as the mentally disordered, the disabled and older prisoners – all of whom were denied access to what is theirs by right in the community.

As a result I decided to conduct a series of thematic reviews of different aspects of imprisonment, making recommendations for improvement. Having examined healthcare, women prisoners, young prisoners, lifers, suicide prevention, unsentenced prisoners and the most difficult and dangerous prisoners in the system, I turned my attention to those whose treatment was unequal, which is where my association with Mervyn Eastman began.

'Inequalities' was designed to examine the treatment of 'cultural diversity', 'gender and sexuality', the mentally disordered, the disabled and the elderly. In the case of the growing numbers of prisoners over the age of 60, with the honourable exception of the Governor of HMP Kingston who, on his own initiative, was trying bravely to introduce a suitable unit for elderly prisoners without official help or recognition, the Prison Service was doing nothing to cater for their particular needs.

My chosen method was to engage with the organisation responsible for policy or community provision, while my inspectors did the field work. I contended then, as I contend now, that the root cause of the problem was poor management, starting with inadequate direction and financial provision from Ministers, down through inappropriate management structures within the Prison Service to inconsistent or non-existent practice on the ground.

I asked Mervyn Eastwood, then Director of Social Services responsible for the elderly, to join and guide us in the venture. The report that he wrote for me was alarming in what it revealed and positive in its approach. He recommended that, rather than try to develop an internal organisation, the Prison Service should sub-contract the Social Services to provide the same cover for the elderly in prison that they did in the community. Had his advice been acted upon I suggest that this book might not have been written.

But in my enthusiasm I had not counted on government. One day the then Prisons Minister, Mr Paul Boateng, told me that he did not want me to do race – that was for the CRE. In vain did I and the then Director of the CRE explain that we were working together, which co-operation would enable the CRE to be much more precise about what aspects needed their full attention. Mr Boateng remained adamant, and so I called the whole exercise off, on the grounds that it would be unthinkable to review the treatment of inequalities, without including cultural diversity.

However, I could not let Mervyn's work die. I therefore attached his report as an annex to an inspection report on HMP Kingston and sent it to the then Director General of the Prison Service. I commended it is as an excellent and timely piece of work on which I hoped that he would act, because it contained practical advice which would help him to solve an increasing problem.

However nothing happened.

That is why I regard this excellent book as a further attempt to persuade the authorities to take practical advice from expert practitioners. It is particularly valuable because it covers so many aspects of ageing, as well as the particular issue of ageing prisoners.

On 20 July 1910, the then Home Secretary, Winston Churchill, told the House of Commons that the way in which it treated crime and criminals was the most unfailing test of the civilisation of any country. In 2006 this country fails that test as far as the treatment of ageing criminals is concerned. I hope that, despite their chosen way with independent, constructive criticism, those responsible for the unacceptable way in which ageing prisoners are currently held, will read, mark and accept the wise advice of Azrini Wahidin, Mervyn Eastwood and all the other contributors. I hope then that, in their shame, they will ensure the introduction of appropriate, dignified and humane treatment and conditions.

Lord Ramsbotham GCB CBE
June 2006

Chapter 1

Ageing, crime, and society: an invitation to a criminology

Azrini Wahidin and Maureen Cain

How did it happen?

Age has been a key variable in the study of 'conventional' criminality and in criminological theorising at least since the Chicago School focused attention on migration, socialisation, and the young offender. Young people still predominate among those caught for conventional offending in the west, and the young were for many years the most popular subjects of ethnographic work. In spite of this, age has remained under-theorised in criminology, a last bastion, perhaps, of positivist categorisation (Cain 2003), long after 'race', 'gender', and 'sex' have all earned their postmodern quotation marks. Ageing as duration has been studied in relation to rates of desistance, but age as a social construction and ageing as a social process have played little part in our understanding of the phenomena of victimisation, crime, and punishment. Thus, in order to begin to theorise the relation of older people or 'elders' to these processes we have first had to recognise that for the 'old' as well as the 'young' very little is pre-given. We and our contributors have had to suspend our common sense upon the subject. Once this suspension is achieved, the relationship of older people to crime emerges as complex and varied, and as amenable to explanation in terms of what are by now normal post-modern theoretical categories such as subjectivity, identity construction, agency, and risk, as well as the interplay between these categories and what Powell and Wahidin (this book, pp. 17–34) have called the political economy of ageing. Before going deeper into our argument let us just point out that while domestic violence against elderly women (aged 65–74 and 75 years+) is reportedly less than it is for younger women, the rate is still higher than the rate for men in those age groups (Simmons *et al.* 2002): victimisation of the aged remains gendered. Also, there is an increasing number of both older women and older men in prison (aged 50 years+) with the vast majority being men (Wahidin this book, pp. 171–93), and a disproportionate number of the older women are black (Phillips, in this book, pp. 53–70): imprisonment of the aged is both sexed and raced. There are reasons why understanding older people may need a particular elaboration of theory, but there are also many instances where the social patterns for older people do not require a different theorisation from the patterns for the rest of us.

These have been our theoretical starting points, but before we discovered these understandings we travelled separate, more personal routes to a recognition that criminology needs to engage in a more theoretical and less demeaning way with the victimisation, crime, and punishment of the elderly.

Maureen's starting point was the long dying of her mother in what Brogden (2001) has described as a 'death hastening institution' (p. 43).[1] It was this, coupled with the development of a new section for her undergraduate course called 'Crime and the Body', which led her to recognition of structural grounds for hostility to and disregard for the aged. In less than a week of residence, her mother was given clothes to wear which were not her own, in spite of hours of bedside sewing in of labels. But at least Maureen was now able to add anger to her guilt, and the seeds were sown of the course of action that became this book.

As to the teaching, well, it gave Maureen something to talk about when, while chairing the Advisory Committee of the British Society of Criminology, she first made contact with Azrini. She brought to the table a concern with victims, while Azrini brought a recently published doctoral thesis on 'Older Women in the Criminal Justice System' (Wahidin 2004).

Azrini's story began, and perhaps remains, in a more academic place, in particular with her mentors at Keele University[2] where, having completed a PGCE, she registered for a Master's and then a PhD in criminology. She became involved with the NGOs *Justice for Women* and *Women in Prison*, and also ran a series of classes at HMP Drake Hall. Here she realised that elderly women who were serving lengthy prison sentences were forgotten, neglected in a system at breaking point, and institutionally maligned in a system catering for the able bodied, mainly those aged 20–40. Here too, she became involved in two miscarriage of justice campaigns, meeting and corresponding with Sheila Bowler and Sue May. Both women found themselves, in their mid-sixties, serving a life sentence for the first time. In both cases their convictions were eventually quashed, but not before Sheila had spent 4 years in prison, and Sue 12 years. The injustice they suffered was particular to each woman, but also through listening to them Azrini learned to notice the plight of all older people in prison, and the degree of institutional abuse and neglect they endured – but do not become used to – on a daily basis.

The prisons Azrini worked in then and as a researcher did not vary their regimes: she noticed, now, that aged prisoners are subject to the same lack of facilities, same timetables, same physical plan as the men and women in their 20s and 30s who formed the majority. Later, when she started formal research, there were people she interviewed who have subsequently died in prison; there were many suffering from incontinence, Alzheimer's, arthritis, Parkinson's. She learnt that fellow prisoners helped clean the incontinent when staff did not. She began to wonder why criminologists (like the prison staff) did not regard research on the elderly as quite so worthwhile as on subjects such as the core, the mainstream, the still under 40 (and certainly under 50). On raising these issues, as an interested young researcher, she was told 'the prison estate has more pressing concerns'. Colleagues responded to her interest in the aged with incredulity. She realised that the journey she had embarked on might be a lonely one. Yet each time she saw an older woman in preventable pain, because 'arthritis' (the catch all term) is 'normal' for her age, her sense of injustice burned stronger and deeper. The rest of her journey to this point will be known to our readers: it continues.

What Azrini and Maureen shared was an understanding of the parallels between reactions in the 1970s to academics who wanted to write about violence against women (VAW) and reactions to us as people who wanted to write about violence against the aged (VAA). When Maureen took our proposal for a one-day conference on *Ageing, Crime, and Society* to the BSC's executive committee, there was at least one snickering remark to the effect that it was understandable that she in particular should want to do this. Of course it was! She was already 66! But how reminiscent of the responses to those feminist proposals 30 years ago! In those days VAW was most likely a minority male activity, but the presumptions of dominance which made it possible were pervasive. Similar presumptions about the lesser humanity of the aged create a social space in which VAA may be condoned.

(Though perhaps granny bashing was never quite so funny as wife beating once was thought to be: 'have you stopped beating your wife', ha! ha!). The response was a foretaste of responses to ageing which has been immensely helpful to Maureen professionally: she was alerted to the relevance of feminist theory to an understanding of what is going on and also to how to deal with such responses without losing her cool (too often). More importantly, it has helped us both to realise that to change the culture of legitimation which refuses to name abuse as crime, a political movement is required: a movement by older people with the support of younger people, most particularly active researchers and those in positions of authority. Already there are NGOs established through which we can work, some of which have contributed to the event and to this book (see Burnett, pp. 124–38; Eastman, pp. 249–64; Fitzgerald, pp. 90–106).

Criminology and crimes against the aged

Please note that in this text we intentionally change our terminology: elders, elderly, aged, older people. Similarly, we do not suggest a chronological moment when one or another of these terms should come into effect. In our view, rather than an empirical cut off point we need a theorised concept of those who are getting on a bit, getting past it, surprisingly alert for their age, and so on. The concept we propose will undoubtedly be refined by the further research and campaigning which we hope will result from this book. In the meantime we offer, as above, empirically interchangeable terms which broadly connote the women and men with whom we are concerned. Beyond that, we propose a concept indicative of the socially constructed nature of the aged. This concept denotes those characterised as *unyoung* as the concept of the deviant denotes the unconforming. The unyoung, being presumed to be beyond the norm(al) (the able bodied, the well remembering, the workers, the sexually active) are exposed to the censure of being beyond the fully human and the protections which recognition of that condition ensures. Can human rights extend to those beyond the full and archetypal status of human? In law, yes. What happens in practice is the subject of this collection.

Unlike deviants, the unyoung are not objects of official censure, although this may soon be the case for those who are physically capable of work but do not. Rather, the unyoung are deemed beyond the pale of the human because of their perceived frailties, their perceived dependence, their perceived failure to be contributing members of the society. Those who have money and own property challenge the view that only those who work 'deserve' a reasonable standard of living. The many in poverty are a 'drain' on the national resources. A Catch 22 situation. What the unyoung share with the deviant is an outsider status, and it is this which leaves them vulnerable.

The forms of abuse resulting from this vulnerability have been ably categorised as physical abuse, psychological abuse, financial or material abuse, unsatisfactory living environments, and violation of individual or constitutional rights (Boudreau 1993). An earlier taxonomy by Hudson (1991) supplies further distinctions in relation to a very similar basic classification, namely between different kinds of relationship based on trust, i.e. personal/social or professional/ business; between abuse and neglect; and between intentional and unintentional behaviour. In the intervening decade these complex descriptors have had no impact within criminology. This leads us to believe that in spite of important contributions relating to abuse such as those of Brogden (2001), Brogden and Nijhar (2000), Decalmer and Glendenning (1993), Manthorpe, Penhale, and Stanley (1999) and Pillemer and Suiter (1988), and on older people in custody (Wahidin 2004), there has been remarkably little theoretical engagement with the plight of the unyoung within criminology. The lack of a concept denoting the subject area to be studied has been one problem. Another may have been the low status of the subject area: dealing with the aged is largely women's work after all. A third reason may have been criminology's historic problem of boundary definition. Here our mentors have been Howe (1987), Hillyard *et al.* (2004), Brogden and Nijhar (this book) and above all Edwin Sutherland (1949) who argued forcefully that there are two criteria for inclusion within the subject matter of criminology, the first being 'the legal description of an act as socially harmful' (p. 31), which he explicitly does not restrict to those 'descriptions' contained in the criminal law, and the second being 'the legal provision of a penalty' (*ibid.*, p. 31). Once again, his text makes it clear that he does not restrict this concept either to sanctions imposed by the criminal law. Indeed, he offers as one example of what would be sufficient to bring the initial behaviour within his definition the possibility of contempt sanctions for those failing to comply with a court order. Tortious neglect would also fall within his definition. Ten years after his work was published Sutherland was criticised for an 'anything goes' approach to criminology (Tappan 1960). In fact he restricted the field of criminology to what we might call the post-political moment, to the time after a law of some kind has been put in place using harm language and indicating the possibility, at some stage, of punishment if there is no reparative action in relation to the harm caused. This definition may still be too restrictive for many. Indeed, since the emergence of deviance and conflict theories in the 1960s and 1970s, and with some impetus from the feminist concern with VAW, contemporary criminology has also analysed social and political struggles leading to or inhibiting criminalisation, precisely the political moment, the contest about the form of social order, itself. However, we are spared that debate on this occasion as crime, abuse, and neglect of the unyoung, as identified in the literature on institutionalised age in particular, fall well within what should by now be the conventional parameters of the discipline, having been established by Sutherland almost 60 years ago.

In saying this we are not arguing for a punitive response to harassed carers. In the home there may be wild emotions at play, sometimes perhaps scores to settle, often tiredness and resentment at being tied. In care homes there is evidence that untrained staff are more likely to abuse than the qualified (Görgen, this volume). Punishing individuals for being untrained is unlikely to produce the widespread changes in practice we are looking for. Arguing that a problem falls within the discipline of criminology simply means that documenting, interpreting, and theorising these problems, and making recommendations based on this empirico–theoretical work, is an appropriate task for a criminologist. We would go further than this, arguing that the theoretical understanding of social relations and the compendium of research strategies and techniques that criminology can bring to bear mean that it is a special responsibility of criminology as a discipline to engage with these issues.

Beyond the understandable personal issues, as several contributions to this volume have indicated, there are structural factors at play in the generation of crime and abuse against the unyoung. There is a political economy of both abuse and conventional crime, and similar factors affect the availability of appropriate penalties and conditions in the prison environment. Here we briefly disentangle some strands in this argument, drawing on papers in this book as well as the wider literature, before turning to a more particular discussion of the individual contributions in the final section of this introduction to our book.

Aged people, the unyoung, often control resources that the next two generations need (Brogden 2001). In our society this may well be the family home. Does this connect with the 'death hastening' character of unyoung residential care? Does the cost to the state of quality care make a difference? These are crude and shocking questions. We can address them by realising that most of us would not take that decision for our parents, but perhaps many of us are too ready to take the death-in-care of those who are already 'a good age' for granted. Why no demand for published league tables of dying in care, so that we can have the debate? So, indeed, that we can form a waiting list for the best homes, and have our personal choices opened to scrutiny.

Care at home also costs money, unseen money in lost earnings and reduced pensions, local authority resources. Social workers have made sure that these issues are widely understood, as Manthorpe (this book) makes plain. But do criminologists not have anything to add, after 35 years' sustained work on domestic violence? There are challenges here: the challenge of methodology, always a problem when a dominant co-resident is present at interview: more of a problem when the respondent has a short attention span, a failing memory, or a deep fear of reprisal; there is the challenge of theory, because VAW theories will not do for VAA. In the VAA situation the assaulter may stand to gain more than the victim by being set free. Does this increase the risk for the unyoung? The fact that as yet we have no solutions to these methodological and theoretical questions does not detract from the argumental criminology as a discipline is, by virtue of its history, well positioned to address them.

The political economy of care homes, of local authority versus private provision, of the limited resources of many clients is not a new topic either, but the evidence that (expensive) trained staff provide better care (Görgen, this book, pp. 71–89) can no longer be evaded. Training programmes falling short of full qualification may help with the training versus wage cost dilemma. Higher levels of supervision of the untrained could also be useful. This is old knowledge, and these are not new proposals. Manthorpe (this book) discusses a landmark initiative from the Department of Health (2000) which at local level brings together those concerned with social and individual care work and those traditionally concerned with conventional crime such as the police and the Crown Prosecution Service. She describes the availability of confidential legal advice as a welcome new resource. The aim of this book is not only to disseminate such useful models of practice, but also to raise the question of whether theory can catch up with and contribute to this new liaison between care work and crime work in protecting the unyoung and other vulnerable adults.

Can criminology then help in conjunction with nursing and social work, i.e. do yet more research (it usually takes several studies

7

before the results are officially 'heard', possibly even replications by those more socially 'entitled' to make knowledge), and assist in the development of a viable social and legal framework in support of quality care? We believe that criminology can help with these intractable problems precisely because of its capacity to theorise at the level of the political/economic as well as at the cultural and the interpersonal levels. On methodological grounds too, criminology as a discipline has much to offer, from a strong code of ethics governing research practice (BSC 2004) to technical expertise in assisting those victimised in the domestic sphere to remember and represent their abusive experiences, sometimes in ways that can be quantified for epidemiological purposes (Mirrlees-Black 1998); always in ways that reveal the depths and extent of the victims' pain (for example Kelly 1988; Mooney 1993; 2000). Criminologists are also familiar with the problems of changing deeply embedded cultures which support deviant behaviour (as in policing) and with the equally intractable problems of desistance from habitual patterns of crime and abuse. The cultures in elder care establishments are smaller and weaker than those of the police, the visibility of the outcomes, potentially at least, is higher; good management, particularly at the very top, and the substitution of a professional ethos for a workaday one, could help with desistance. Not rocket science, but not *spiel* either, given the political economic climate, including the cultural climate, in which these changes would need to take place.

And the unyoung in conventional criminology?

Once again there are similarities between the experiences of the 'unyoung' and women, for in the early British Crime Surveys both were deemed to have irrational fears of crime (Hough and Mayhew 1985), prompting a debate which rumbled on for a decade or more. What is now clear is that the aged take precautions to avoid anticipated vulnerability, and that, as in the case of women, if vulnerability from relatives and carers were to be included then their fear level would be less unrealistic. Moreover, fear relates to a longer past than the cut off point of the surveys. To date, victim studies specifically focused on the aged have not been undertaken to investigate the 'ever experienced' dimension, as has been the case for women. In addition, most people approaching their 70s will have lived through the ageing of their parents, and will know first hand about the vulnerability of the aged to the actions of their carers. We need to understand the remembered pasts and anticipated futures of the aged before we can comment at all upon the well or unfounded nature of their fears.

As regards victimisation from conventional crime, Lister and Wall (this book, pp. 107–23) reinforces earlier findings concerning the correlation between age and vulnerability, demonstrating in addition that distraction burglary is an age-of-victim specific offence, and that those aged 75+ are at greatest risk.

Moreover, women and men in later life also commit crimes, and as with younger people, some are arrested, some are convicted, some are sent to prison, and some grow old in prison. How they get there, however, is one of criminology's great silences, for we know nothing about policing or adjudication in relation to the aged, nothing about their relationships with the legal profession, or how any of these encounters are compounded by issues of race or class. Indeed, age is such a dominant category that data about the unyoung are very rarely analysed by race and class, although they may be analysed by sex and, increasingly, by further subdivisions of agedness.

Information about elderly offenders and their experiences with the criminal justice system therefore remains scarce. This dovetails neatly with the denial of agency to the unyoung which is one facet of their less than fully human status. In criminology, no one has felt the need to ask them about their own crimes. And according to Bramhall (this book pp. 231–48) for several years no one has seen the need to study the use and effectiveness of community penalties in relation to the aged. Community sentences imply agency and the possibility of change: to study the aged in this context would perhaps challenge too many deeply held ideologies and cosy stereotypes. But we are going too far beyond Bramhall here. Instead we throw out a challenge: the work is there to do.

When attention turns to older prisoners, to the unyoung behind bars, the number of people over 50 arrested for serious or violent crime on both sides of the Atlantic has been going up (Aday 2003; Wahidin 2002), and this has led to an increased number of older offenders in the prison population. As early as 1989, the American Department of Justice predicted with prescience that by 2005 16 per cent of federal prisoners would be over 50 (cited in James 1992). So work in this area has begun, as the chapters by Wahidin (pp. 211–30), Jaques (pp. 171–93), and Aday (pp. 194–210) (this book) testify. However, Wahidin's work on older women reveals that not all the rights of prisoners as established by the United Nations apply to unyoung female offenders, *viz* that 'the treatment will be such as will encourage their self respect and develop their sense of responsibility' (Rule 65, United Nations Standard Minimum Rules for the Treatment of Prisoners 1977). Sadly enough, this rightlessness almost certainly extends to older men as well.

Making a start

In preparing the conference and this book we, as criminologists, have been above all mindful of the gaping hole in criminology where research and analysis of the victimisation, crime, and punishment of the growing numbers of the unyoung should be. But we have also been mindful that in nursing, social work, and gerontology attention *has* been paid, both in theory and in practice, to the issues of abuse and neglect. In arguing for criminological attention to these areas, we have, of course, emphasised what the discipline of criminology can bring to the table, and the fact that this contribution cannot be replicated by other disciplines. Here, in this final section of our introduction, we wish to emphasise instead the role that can be played by *interdisciplinary* work, and the contribution that has already been made by scholars from the other social sciences. Azrini in particular has found their theories and their insights invaluable in relation to her own research on older women in prison. Indeed, without them she would have been bereft of colleagues in her field. Because of this recognition of criminology's dependence on prior work in other fields we convened an expressly interdisciplinary conference and the resultant collection reflects this intention. It is our belief that criminologically trained readers will benefit as we have from the research of academics in related fields and the experiences of intrepid campaigners for the unyoung. We are grateful to them for what we have learnt from them, and for the developments in criminology itself that we have been able to make and propose as a result of their pioneering work.

The structure of the book

Our book opens with three programmatic papers, identifying directions for a criminology of ageing or the unyoung. Jason Powell and Azrini Wahidin, in pointing to a lack of theory, wonder why the criminological imagination has so far been unable to (re)conceive the aged. They identify starting points for a theorisation in political economy, in gender studies, and in post-modernism. These influences are also apparent, we hope, in our introduction. They point to discrepancies between embodied subjectivities and identities and the body as interpreted in specific cultures, not least the Anglo-Saxon cultures. This connects with the massive surveillance to which aged bodies are subjected, a veritable denial of a private and personal identity.

Mike Brogden and Preeti Nijhar, too, point to the need to re-conceive the aged as having agency, pointing out that the concept of harm transcends the dichotomy between crime and abuse. Importantly, they argue that in so doing it provides the foundation for interdisciplinary work and alliances between social work and criminology in particular. We are pleased to find this note struck early in the collection: the prospect of criminology and other disciplines competing for the right to interpret the unyoung body is a truly appalling one, and the opposite of what we as editors intend. Brogden and Nijhar have effectively steered us away from this deep pitfall, towards the possibility of a constructive dialogue.

The first section is concluded by Judith Phillips' comprehensive survey of current research and theorising. She points to empirical findings on the overrepresentation of minority ethnic groups among the older as well as younger age groups in the prisons; to the premature dependency encouraged by lack of appropriate health care and facilities; to the lack of flexibility such that there is no grasp of the fact that relationships with grandchildren might be important for both the well-being and the rehabilitation of the aged. The carceral denial of identity, and the struggle of critical gerontology against it, emerges as a central theme.

Abuse and crime are brought together in the section on perpetrators and victims, for, as we have argued, we do not find the distinction helpful. Indeed, insofar as it draws a distinction between 'understandable' and 'unacceptable' harms, it is a distinction to be avoided at all costs.

Thomas Görgen presents the results of a study of the victimisation of older people in nursing homes, based on triangulated qualititative and quantitative data collected from both residents and staff in a wide range of institutions. Discrepancies between the priorities of front line nurses (security) and management (autonomy) are revealed, as are some very stark results: 'In most nursing homes there appears to be permanent neglect in the psycho-social field.' Agency? What agency? On the other hand, Görgen's work yields one finding which offers a clear guide to action: a rare and precious gem of a finding. His quantitative analysis reveals that a high *proportion* of qualified nurses reduces the risks to residents, and that this makes more difference than increasing the numbers on the wards. Qualified nurses are expensive, so clear evidence of this kind will be of inestimable value to campaigning groups taking on cash strapped providers.

Gary Fitzgerald directs one such campaigning group, which among other projects runs a help line. His analysis is based on calls to Action on Elder Abuse. Pointing out that 62 per cent of the reported abuse is by paid staff, he argues that culture change in institutions and the training of staff is the key to protecting the residents: individual 'detection' of incidents will not produce a generalised effect. In the home, male abusers are more likely to be family members, whereas the ratio is roughly 50/50 for female abusers – a reflection of the higher proportion of female workers and volunteers in domestic care.

The final two chapters in this section deal with conventional crime. Lister and Wall's work on distraction burglary breaks new ground. Not all old people are equally vulnerable: most at risk are those who are aged 75+, female, white, and living alone. The authors suggest that rather than 'naturalising' the problem in terms of ostensibly self evident 'vulnerabilities' of the aged in general, help can be effectively targeted to those now known to be most vulnerable to these professional thieves.

Alan Burnett discusses the policy and practice of Help the Aged in relation to fear of crime, and in particular emphasises the need for more data about violence by carers and loved ones. This is surely where criminology could assist, for the professional concern of care workers has not typically been with the production of aggregate data, whereas such data, brought to life by qualitative work, have been a mainstay of criminological research on VAW. Sensitive policing and reassurance are also crucial, but supplementation and re-focusing are required.

Jill Manthorpe's contribution reveals that improvements in this area are under-resourced, but also possible. On the basis of her experience as Chair of an Adult Protection Committee, she emphasises the importance of pragmatic local arrangements in relation both to resource generation from the multiple agencies involved and to service delivery. She is able to report improvement among the previously weaker providers, and a wider recognition and use of specialist skills such as 'court craft' and long-term therapeutic support for victims. The service is not age restricted but available to all 'vulnerable' adults, a better term to guide practice, although our concept of the unyoung is of greater value in theorising the objects of social and cultural ideologies of ageing, and the ideological problematisation of ageing processes. This emergent theory, we hope, may assist diverse practitioners in understanding and therefore in preventing the harms of conventional crime, 'abuse', and neglect.

Bridget Penhale produces heartening evidence of workable policies in relation to elder abuse being developed throughout both 'old' and 'new' Europe, as well as in Israel[3] many sparked off by a conference of the British Geriatric Society in 1988. National and local interventions include helpline networks, the training of community-based listeners and of counsellors within institutions, research and evaluation, and quality assurance developments in nursing care. Nonetheless, a prevalence rate of 5 per cent remains cross nationally: the problem is serious, but at least it is being taken seriously.

In discussing the problems of 'growing old in prison', Azrini Wahidin argues that gerontology has used social theory to greater effect than criminology, in which the latter discipline has failed to understand ageing as a (social) process. The chapter is not only informative, but also a spur to theoretical action and an incentive to undertake more inter-disciplinary work. The horrors of growing old in prison remain largely unaddressed and misunderstood.

A ray of hope is offered by Debbie Jaques' discussion of the high level of care offered to the aged in the special unit at Norwich prison. Demand for places is high, and the criterion for admission to this 'nursing home' standard facility is health, not age or even disability. 93 per cent of those admitted have multiple health problems, yet despite this within the prison community they are probably regarded as the lucky ones! Perhaps it goes without saying that the facility is unable to admit women.

More positive reporting is offered by Ron Aday. After surveying provision in the US, where the best as well as the worst facilities can be found, he focuses on the range of programmes made available to older prisoners by the Ohio Department of Rehabilitation and Corrections: from managing memory loss through medication; education to exercise classes; from assertiveness training to grandparenting; the appropriateness and inventiveness of these initiatives is impressive. Prison workers and NGOs delivering services to prisons will find a rich seam of ideas to mine in this upbeat contribution.

We discussed Gaynor Bramhall's chapter in our introduction, and we return to it again now. She fears that appraisal of elders is on the basis of their age rather than of their individual characteristics, and points out that the absence of the aged from the literature on community penalties results from their lack of voice – further evidence of denial of agency to the aged. Are the aged also omitted from the training of those who administer community penalties? That too could explain why they remain unseen and unheard. Are the aged deemed beyond rehabilitation, and if so upon what grounds? Bramhall's chapter provokes these questions, identifying another huge gap in basic information as far as the unyoung are concerned.

Our work is concluded with a view from the Director of another NGO, Mervyn Eastman from Better Government for Older People (BGOP). This organisation co-hosted the conference that gave rise to this book, and has a long experience of working with and for aged prisoners. BGOP makes two major recommendations: first, that there should be a senior manager in large penal institutions with a designated responsibility for older prisoners; secondly that a 'whole systems' approach to citizenship should govern policy, linking individuals with NGOs, with the NHS, the local authority, legal services, community care, and the prison. Too often these institutions function in isolation. And far too often the aged offender or ex-prisoner is not regarded as a citizen at all. BGOP exists to change all that. It is in close touch with its clientele. Policymakers would be well advised to hear it.

By further disturbing the silence surrounding the unyoung we have begun, as a group of contributors, to explore the hidden places of the criminological enterprise. By questioning the naturalisation of abuse and the purpose and nature of imprisonment for the unyoung we have taken a step in the direction of theoretical understanding and the development of effective policies. We believe that alternatives to the contradiction of abusive care and equally abusive punishment are lurking in the depths of our consciousness, collectively and as concerned individuals. Alluding to the title of Ignazio Silone's novel *The Seed Beneath the Snow* (1943), Colin Ward indicated that such earth shatteringly wholesome and liberatory thoughts are:

> ... always in existence like a seed beneath the snow, buried under the weight of the state and its bureaucracy, capitalism and its waste, privilege and its injustices. (Ward 1973, p.11)

By letting our imaginations and our knowledge play with alternatives we can move on from the one size fits all model that our present theories – just like the prison service of England and Wales – employ. Only by breaking the silence surrounding the diversity of needs and experiences of the unyoung – as victims, as perpetrators, as 'cases' as 'prisoners', as wives, husbands, singles, granddads, grandmas, friends, widowers and aunties, consumers, football fans, cigarette smokers, bibliophiles, brass band lovers, movie lovers, reggae lovers, rememberers, forgetters, fish and chips eaters (if we could afford it), dog lovers, humanists, religious observers, and, ultimately, as human beings – can we reduce abuse and crime within and without the criminal justice system. Unyoung offenders, unyoung victims, older prisoners and older carers, the people they love and the people who love them, deserve no less. And then, surely, the policy makers will hear our new noise.

Notes

1 See also Brogden (2001) chapter 5 for a more complete discussion.
2 Azrini wishes to thank in particular Nickolas Rose, Vikki Bell, Caroline Ramazanoglu, Pat Carlen, Anne Worrall, and Judith Phillips for generating an interest which has, by now, become her obsession.
3 Israel is a guest member of the European conference from those members Penhale derives her data.

References

Aday, R. (2003) *Aging Prisoners: Crisis in American Corrections*. Westport, CT: Praeger Publishers.

Boudreau, F.A. (1993) 'Elder Abuse' in R. Hampton, T.P. Gullota, G.R. Adams, E.H. Potter and R.P. Weissberg (eds), *Family Violence: Prevention and Treatment*. London: Sage.

British Society of Criminology (2004) *Code of Ethics*. London: BSC.

Brogden, M. and Nijhar, P. (2000) *Crime, Abuse and the Elderly*. Cullompton: Willan Publishing.

Brogden, M. (2001) *Geronticide: Killing the Elderly*. London: Jessica Kingsley.

Cain, M. (2000) 'Orientalism, Occidentalism, and the Sociology of Crime', *British Journal of Criminology*, 40 (2): 239–60.

Decalmer, P. and Glendenning, F. (eds) (1993) *The Mistreatment of Elder People*. London: Sage.

Department of Health (2000) *No Secrets, Guidance on Developing Multi-agency Practice and Procedures to Protect Vulnerable Adults from Abuse*. London: HMSO.

Hillyard, P. *et al.* (eds) (2004) *Taking Harm Seriously*. London: Pluto Press.

Hough, M. and Mayhew, P. (1985) *Taking account of Crime: Key Findings from the Second British Crime Survey*. London; HMSO.

Howe, A. (1987) '"Social Injury" Revisited: Towards a Feminist Theory of Social Justice', *International Journal of the Sociology of Law*, 15 (4): 423–38.

Hudson, M. (1991) 'Elder Mistreatment: A Taxonomy with Definitions by Delphi', *Journal of Elder Abuse and Neglect*, 3 (2): 14.

James, M. (1992) 'Sentencing of Elderly Criminals', *American Criminal Law Review*, 29: 1025–1044.

Kelly, L. (1988) *Surviving Sexual Violence*. Cambridge: Polity.

Manthorpe, J., Penhale, B. and Stanley, N. (eds) (1999) *Institutional Abuse: Perspectives Across the Life Course*. Cambridge: CUP.

Mirrlees-Black, C. (1998) *Domestic Violence: Findings from a New British Self Completion Questionnaire*. London: HORDS, Research Study No. 91.

Mooney, J. (1993) *The Hidden Figure: Domestic Violence in North London*. London University, Centre of Criminology, unpublished paper.

Mooney, J. (2000) 'Family Violence in North London' in J. Hanmer *et al.* (eds) *Home Truths About Domestic Violence: Police, Criminal Justice and Victims*. Oxford: Oxford University Press.

Pillemer, K. and Suiter, J. (1998) 'Elder abuse' in V. van Hasselt *et al.* (eds) *Handbook of Family Violence*. New York: Plenum Press, pp. 25–40.

Simmons, J. *et al.* (2002)' Crime in England and Wales 2001/02', July, London. Home Office Statistical Bulletin.

Sutherland, E. (1949/1961) *White Collar Crime*. New York: Holt Rinehart and Winston.

Tappan, P. (1960) *Crime, Justice, and Corrections*. New York: McGraw Hill.

United Nations (1977) *Standard Minimum Rules for the Treatment of Prisoners* (resolutions 663C (XXIV) 31/07/1957 and 2076 (LXII) of 13/05/1977). Geneva: Office of the High Commissioner for Human Rights.

Wahidin, A. (2002), 'Reconfiguring Older Bodies in the Prison Time Machine', *Journal of Aging and Identity*, 7 (3): 117–93.

Wahidin, A. (2004) *Older Women in the Criminal Justice System: Running Out of Time*. London: Jessica Kingsley.

Ward, C. (1973) *Anarchy in Action*. London: Allen & Unwin.

Chapter 2

Rethinking criminology: the case of 'ageing studies'

Jason L. Powell and Azrini Wahidin

Introduction

This chapter explores how ageing has been overlooked by perspectives within criminology and by criminological researchers, particularly when compared to the consideration which has been given to class, 'race', gender and sexuality. Our aim is to demonstrate that researchers studying the relationship between older people and crime would benefit from a more careful conceptualisation of 'age', one which focuses on the ways in which 'old age' itself is socially constructed, is represented and used by particular interest groups.

Criminal behaviour and criminological studies have focused predominantly on young people's activities. While young people have for long been associated with crime, it appears that, as is the case with social class, different age groups commit different types of crime. Yet many theories deal almost exclusively with juvenile delinquency. It has been stated that '[o]ne of the few facts agreed on in criminology is the age distribution of crime' (Hirschi and Gottfredson 1983, p. 552). A series of 'moral panics' have, 'demonised' young people, from the teddy boys, mods and rockers of the 1960s, through to punks, skinheads, muggers, joyriders, "rat" boys (Curtis 1999, p. 28), girl gangs, and mobile phone snatchers of 2000 (see for example, Cohen 1973; Pearson 1983). However, the assumption that crime is overwhelmingly a young person's activity must be called into question (for a further discussion, see Wahidin 2005).

As already hinted at, until the 1990s, the dominant criminological triumvirate of 'race', class and gender were seen as major vehicles that mobilised major research funding opportunities. Not only was age subsumed under 'race', class and gender, but the dominant explanatory framework concerning ageing came from outside of criminology: bio-medicine. The medical model was and is a global influence that perceive(s) old age, in particular, as related to physical, psychological and biological 'problems'. Such 'problems' of old age were tied to very narrow individualistic explanations, whereupon ageing bodies and minds 'decay' and 'decline'. Coupled with this, the rise and consolidation of functionalist accounts of old age compounded such medical discourses (Powell 2001). For functionalists in the USA during the 1950s and 1960s, the purpose of old age was for older people to disengage from work roles and prepare for the ultimate disengagement: death (Powell 2001). Old age then took on a problem focus. These perspectives encapsulated dominant ideas that helped shape and legitimise policies of retirement and subsequent inequality.

Indeed, 'old age' throughout the twentieth century was seen as a social and medical *problem* and this predominant perspective is evident through the language used by policy makers, mass media and the general public. A significant contribution of criminology as a discipline has been to highlight how individual lives and behaviours which were thought to be determined solely by biological, medical and psychological factors, are, in fact, heavily influenced by social environments in which people live. However, it is quite astonishing that given the range and explosion of such sociological ideas that there was not, until recently, much consideration and application of such critical ideas to 'ageing'.

Throughout this chapter we will argue that *criminology* would benefit from 'ageing studies' (Powell 2001) in understanding the relationship between crime and later life. Pain, suggests that 'age':

> ... has largely been overlooked by criminologists, the debate so far being located mainly in medical and social welfare disciplines (Pain 1997, p. 18).

To this end, we will map out four dimensions of analysis: 'political economy of old age'; 'gender and ageing'; 'ageing and postmodernism'; and 'ageing and surveillance'. These areas may have overlapped with certain theories of crime and deviance, but what makes this particularly illuminating and important to criminology is the rich tapestry of ideas that deconstruct ageing as a discursive, symbolic, experiential, material, and existential subject/object of power.

We begin by questioning the nature of criminology and then we go on to unravel theoretical schisms such as: left idealism; left realism and the culture of crime control. We then suggest that these theories have omitted representations of ageing in their analyses and alternatively we suggest that drawing on insights from social gerontology will provide an epistemologically informed and ontologically flexible account of age, crime and society.

Early criminology: past and present

... had it not been for the rise of Nazism in Germany, and the appointment of the three distinguished European émigrés, Hermann Mannheim, Max Grünhut and Leon Radzinowicz, to academic posts at elite British Universities, British criminology might never have developed sufficient academic impetus to have become an independent discipline. (Garland 2002, p. 39)

Leon Radzinowicz was the founder of the first Institute of Criminology to be established in a British university (Cambridge) in 1959 (Radzinowicz 1988; 1999). Much earlier contributions were made by Hermann Mannheim at the London School of Economics and Max Grünhut at Oxford. Together they brought to the discipline a humanistic conception of the value of scientific effort in the field of criminology. Their writings reveal that they were neither positivists nor doctrinaire in their approach (Hood 2004). The discipline has moved on from the time in the 1930s when criminology was 'a subject which does not attract a great deal of academic attention' (Chorley to ACC, 2 February 1934, Ms SPSL 270/2, f.78 cited in Hood 2004). Compounding this, Hillyard *et al.* (2004), observe that recent trends of the last 10 years in criminology have been shaped by the thirst for 'evidence-led policy' research – a demand that has translated itself in the criminological context as a 'revival of number crunching, schematic and instrumental positivism' (2004, p. 34). In retrospect, the decade of the 1970s appears as a watershed, in which the intellectual, institutional and political assumptions of modern criminology were challenged, often in the name of a more radical social politics. It was during this decade that there arose a more critical and reflexive style of criminology, and a more explicit questioning of criminology's relation to the state, to criminal justice, and to the disciplinary processes of welfare capitalism. Criminology focused on broader themes of social thought and over time became more critical of criminal justice practice. In these years, criminology's centre of gravity shifted a little, becoming more reflexive, more critical and more theoretical. 'As it happens, this was a short-lived moment [which] did not last long. Before long, new post-correctional forms of crime control emerged and criminology became immersed in applied questions once again ...' (Garland 2000, pp. 13–14).

The inception of 'Critical Criminology' was in the late 1960s. Variously named 'positivism' or 'establishment criminology' was individualistic in focus, technicist in outlook and minimalist in theorising. Its aim was the social engineering of the 'maladjusted' individual into the ranks of the value consensual society. In bio-medical gerontology, viewpoints stating that older people have traits of bodily and mental decline similarly shared the ideas of criminological positivism in claiming the prevalance of pathologies to explain human behaviour (Wahidin and Powell 2004). Despite the discipline of criminology having a rich imagination, the experiences of older people are excluded from the kaleidoscopic vision of the criminological gaze. What can criminology learn from gerontological theories, perspectives grounded in understanding ageing? Firstly, we want to take to task the very notion of 'ageing' and its exclusion in mainstream criminology.

Problematising ageing

Until recently the criminological imagination regarded age as less important than 'race', class and gender and, where age was discussed, focused on the question of youth. People in later life were uncritically constructed as victims of crime, the analysis steeped in a biomedical discourse. In this construction 'old age' tends to be represented as static, portrayed as having negative connotations of physical and psychological decline coupled with social and spatial withdrawal (Bytheway 1995). These ageist ideologies around old age and the meaning of old age both affect and are reflected within criminology, particularly in relation to the construct of victimhood and old age.

Furthermore, there has long been a tendency in matters of ageing and old age to reduce the social experience of ageing to its biological dimension from which is derived a set of normative 'stages'. Accordingly, being 'old', for example, would primarily be an individualised experience of adaptation to inevitable physical and mental decline to the preparation for death.

Estes and Binney (1989) have used the expression 'bio-medicalisation of ageing' which has two closely related narratives: one, the social construction of ageing as a medical problem; two, ageist practices and social policies growing out of thinking of ageing as a medical problem. They suggest that:

> Equating old age with illness has encouraged society to think about ageing as pathological or abnormal. The undesirability of conditions labelled as sickness or illness transfers to those who have these conditions, shaping the attitudes of the persons themselves and those of others towards them. Sick role expectations may result in such behaviour as social withdrawal, reduction in activity, increased dependency and the loss of effectiveness and personal control – all of which may result in the social control of the elderly through medical definition, management and treatment. (Estes and Binney 1989, p. 588)

Every society uses age categories to divide this ongoing process into stages or segments of life. These life stages are socially constructed rather than inevitable. Ageing, too, is a socially produced category. At any point of the life span, age simultaneously denotes a set of social constructs, defined by the norms specific to a given society at a specific point in history. Thus, a specific period of life: infancy, childhood, adolescence, adulthood, middle age or old age is influenced by the social categories and structural entities of a given society. Therefore, ageing is not to be considered the mere product of biological-psychological function, but rather a consequence of socio-cultural factors and subsequent life-chances. Indeed, society has a number of culturally and socially defined notions of what Thomas R. Cole (1992) calls the 'stages of life'. Historically, the stages of life were presented as a religious discourse, which formed the basis for the cultural expectations about behaviour and appearance across the life-course. The life-stage model is still used in taken for granted popular discourse in society which impinges on how our lives are structured, albeit by bio-medical discourses of 'decline'.

In Western societies, an individual's 'age' is counted on a chronological or numerical foundation, beginning from birth to the current point of age, or when an individual has died. Chronological ageing is a habit individuals engage in: 'birthdays' and 'wedding anniversaries' for example. Counting age can be seen as a social construction because it is a practice underpinned by the development of industrial capitalism (Phillipson 1998). Hence, what is critical about ageing is how a society uses the sequence of time to socially construct people into 'categories'. As a classificatory tool, age is important in three ways. First, like sex, age is an ascribed status or characteristic, which is based on attributes over which we have little or no control. Secondly, unlike sex, a specific age is always transitional – constantly moving from one age to another although like sex it is regulated by societal expectations of age-appropriate behaviour. Achieving 'age-appropriate' transitions in accordance with these expectations is rewarded, whereas deviance is punished. Thirdly, although in every society some age groups are more powerful than others, the unique aspect of ageing as a social process is that everyone can expect to occupy all the various positions throughout life on the basis of his or her age.

Older people as perpetrators of crime rather than as victims of crime have been neglected in criminological discourse despite important research about the relationship between crime and ethnicity, class, and gender. The academic study of corporate crime in relation to older people is scarce (Phillipson 1998) and is as unreported as are actual corporate malpractices against older people. For example, in recent years, we have seen the effect of failures in private pension schemes on the lives of older people: Powell and Wahidin (2004) cite a report by the Office of Fair Trading (1997) which found that billions of pounds had been lost by pensioners in private pension schemes invested in corporations. The British Financial Services Authority (1999) estimated up to £11 billion was stolen by private pension corporations which is almost three times the original estimate (Powell and Wahidin 2004). 'The number of victims could be as high as 2.4 million' (*Guardian* 13 March 1998, p. 13 quoted in Powell and Wahidin 2004, p. 52). Coupled with this, came the discovery after the death of Robert Maxwell that he had extracted by stealth £400 million from his companies' pension schemes (Powell and Wahidin 2004, pp. 55-58). Discussions of the mis-selling of pensions are replete with attributions of blame. The questions that have to be addressed are why corporate crime against the aged is scarcely policed and rarely punished, and how this failure contributes to facilitating this type of crime against older people in particular and 'ageing populations' in general?

Theorising ageing studies – age, gender, identity and surveillance

'Old age is seen as shameful, like head lice in children and venereal disease in their older siblings (Stott 1981, p. 3).'

One of the major problems in 'criminology' in recent years is that the study of ageing has not been developed. Theoretical developments in Critical Criminology pertaining to older people have lagged well behind other social and human science disciplines. George (1995) argues that one of the reasons for this invisibility is that gerontological research is seen as 'theoretically sterile'. In other words, why would anyone want to research experiences of older people and crime? Secondly, the neglect of later life issues within criminology arises from the fact that the study of youth, and particularly young offenders, unleashes the voyeur. In contrast, the study of old age and crime, as Pollak (1941) astutely observed approximately 60 years ago, evokes a different reaction:

> Old criminals offer an ugly picture and it seems as if even scientists do not like to look at it for any considerable amount of time ... On the other hand, if the thesis of the interrelationship between age and crime is to hold, an investigation of all its implications has to yield results, and with the tendency of our population to increase in the higher age brackets, a special study of criminality of the aged is required. (Pollock 1941, p. 212)

Notwithstanding this, the emergence of the social theories of age and ageing can be located in the early post-war years with the governmental concern about the consequences of demographic change and the shortage of younger people in work in the USA and the UK (Biggs and Powell 2001). In the post-war years, social gerontology emerged as a multi-disciplinary field of study which attempted to respond to the social, health, and economic policy implications and projections of population change (Phillipson 1998). The wide disciplinary subject matter of social gerontology was shaped by significant external forces: first, by state intervention to achieve specific outcomes in health and social policy for older people; secondly, by a socio-political and economic environment which viewed an ageing population as an emerging 'social problem' for western society (Phillipson 1998). The important point to note is that theories often mirror the norms and values of their creators and their social times, reflecting culturally dominant views of what should be the appropriate way to analyse social phenomena (Turner 1989). Critical gerontology explains adult ageing and how the assumptions contained within theory and policy influence our understanding of the position of older people in society.

Many of the gerontological texts provide a historical understanding of the development of the gerontological field from the first demographic studies conducted in the mid-1940s to the most recent *genre*, that until now have omitted gender issues (Arber and Ginn 1995; Bernard and Meade 1993; Ginn and Arber 1995). Throughout the gerontological literature of the last decade it is emphasised that the voices and needs of older people have to be integrated into policy, and that such policy must not be steeped in the stereotypes of ageing, but must acknowledge and assess diversity and difference.

Birren and Bengston argue that the study of ageing, or gerontology as it is called, is 'data rich and theory poor' (1988, p. 2). They further state that the study of ageing has lacked a strong theoretical core and has tended to ignore until recently an understanding of ageing identity, the body, cultural representations of ageing to name a few, which are central features of an emerging post-modern paradigm in gerontological theory. While a significant amount of data have been generated over the years (around issues such as health and social needs in old age), there has been a lack of theoretical discussion of the meaning and place of ageing within the structure of society.

The role of theory in gerontology and its growth as a discipline coincides with the post-war years. There has been a growth in public awareness and interest in ageing issues: from 'Grey Power movements' to the ageing population, the crisis over pensions, and the funding of the welfare state (Phillipson 1998). Nevertheless, the lack of theoretical integration in British gerontology has been a cause of some anxiety over the last 20 years (Biggs 1999). Fennell, Phillipson and Evers comment:

> Much more characteristic of British research is the lack of attention to theory of any kind. This failing has been a feature of the social gerontological tradition. (Fennell, Phillipson and Evers 1993, p. 42)

The pressures on older people in the work place combined with the rapid growth in early retirement have resulted in a significant shift in the way ageing is experienced and perceived (Achenbaum 1978). Gubrium and Wallace (1990) seek to promote the development of gerontological theory by posing the question 'who theorises age?' Their focus suggests that it is not only professional social gerontologists who theorise age: we all are involved in constructing the 'other' in relation to ourselves. Critical gerontology is concerned with '… a collection of questions, problems and analyses that have been excluded by established [mainstream gerontology]' (Fennell, Phillipson and Evers 1993, p. 13; see Katz 1997). These vary from questions about the role of the state in the management of old age (Phillipson 1982, 1998; Phillipson and Walker 1986; Townsend 1962, 1981; Walker 1987) to issues about the purpose of growing old within the context of a post modern life course (Featherstone 1991). Critical gerontology seeks to problematise the construction of ageing and to identify the conditions experienced by elders in society (Phillipson 1998). We now turn our attention to gerontological approaches which provide some evocative conceptual tools for criminologists to ponder: political economy of ageing; gender and ageing; ageing and postmodernism and ageing and surveillance.

Ageing and social class: political economy of ageing

The political economy of old age emerged as a critical theory on both sides of the Atlantic. Political economy drew from Marxian insights in analysing capitalist society and how old age was socially constructed to foster the needs of the economy (Estes 1979). This critical branch of Marxist gerontology grew as a direct response to the hegemonic dominance of structural functionalism in the form of disengagement theory, the bio-medical paradigm, and world economic crises of the 1970s. As Phillipson (1998) points out, in the UK huge sums of social expenditure were allocated to older people. Consequently, not only were older people viewed in medical terms, but also in resource terms by governments. This brought a new perception to attitudes to age and ageing. As Phillipson states:

> Older people came to be viewed as a burden on western economies, with demographic change … seen as creating intolerable pressures on public expenditure. (Phillipson 1998, p. 17)

Hence, the major focus is an interpretation of the relationship between ageing and the economic structure. In the USA, political economic theory was pioneered via the work of Estes (1979), and

Estes, Swan and Gerard (1982). Similarly, in the UK, the work of Walker (1981) and Phillipson (1982), added a critical sociological dimension to understanding age and ageing in advanced capitalist societies. For Estes (1979), political economy challenges the ideology of older people as belonging to a homogenous group unaffected by dominant structures in society. Instead it focuses upon an analysis of the state in contemporary societal formations. Estes examines how the state decides and dictates who is allocated resources, who is not and why. This in turn has direct implications for retirement, pensions and the health and social care needs of the older population (Powell and Wahidin 2004). As Phillipson (1982) points out, the retirement experience is linked to the timing of economic reduction of wages, and this enforced withdrawal from work has put many older people in the UK in a financially insecure position. Hence, the state can make and break the 'minds and hearts of its populace' (Biggs and Powell 2001). Phillipson (1982; 1986) considers how capitalism helps to socially construct the social marginality of older people in key areas such as welfare delivery. The important argument Phillipson (1998) makes is that inequalities in the distribution of resources should be understood in relation to the distribution of power within society, rather than in terms of individual variation. Similarly, in the USA, Estes, Swann and Gerard (1982) claim that the state is using its power to transfer responsibility for welfare provision from the state onto individuals.

Age and gender

Feminist theorising is one of the most significant areas of theoretical development in approaches to ageing (Arber and Ginn 1995; Ginn and Arber 1995). There are two important issues: first, power imbalances shape theoretical construction; second, a group's place within the social structure influences the theoretical attention they are afforded. Hence, because older women tend to occupy a position of lower class status, especially in terms of economic status, than men of all ages and younger women, they are given less theoretical attention (Arber and Ginn 1995). According to Acker (1988 cited in Arber and Ginn 1995, p. 27) in all known societies the relations of distribution and production are influenced by gender and thus take on a gendered meaning. Gender relations of distribution in capitalist society are historically rooted and are transformed as the means of production change. Similarly, age relations are linked to the capitalist mode of production and relations of distribution. 'Wages' take on a specific meaning depending on age. For example, teenagers work for less money than adults, who in turn work for less money than middle-aged adults. Further, young children rely on personal relations with family figures such as parents. Many older people rely on resources distributed by the state.

Older women are viewed as unworthy of respect or consideration (Arber and Ginn 1995). They claim there is a double standard of ageing arising from the sets of conventional expectations as to age-pertinent attitudes and roles for each sex which apply in patriarchal society. These are defined by Itzin (1986) as a male and a female 'chronology', socially defined and sanctioned so that deviance from prescribed roles is met with disapproval. Male chronology, and identity is constructed around employment and the public sphere, but a woman's age status is defined in terms of events in the reproductive cycle.

It is perhaps emblematic of contemporary western society that ageing marginalises the experiences of women through an inter-connected oppression of gender and ageing. The reason for this as Arber and Ginn (1995) claim, is that patriarchal society exercises power through the chronologies of employment and reproduction, and through the sexualised promotion of a 'youthful' appearance in women.

The point of a feminist analysis in gerontology is to point to the experiences and identities of *older* women. In relation to the study of crime, the exclusion of older women by feminist writers such as Heidensohn (1985) and Carlen and Worrall (1987) has led to an exclusive focus on younger women's experiences of criminal justice. However research on older people in the criminal justice system is very slowly being addressed by a handful of writers such as Judith Phillips (1996), Helen Codd (1998), and Azrini Wahidin (2004).

An examination of sex ratios as age increases highlights the feminisation of later life (see Office of Population Census and Surveys 2005). The imbalance in the numbers of older men and women has a number of consequences, particularly in terms of marital status and living arrangements. Due to increased longevity, and the tendency for men to marry women younger than themselves, women are more likely to experience widowhood. Fewer women than men remarry following widowhood or divorce and consequently more older women than older men live alone. At present, half of women aged 65 years and over and a fifth of older men live alone. In addition, given the predominance of women among the 'very old', this group of women is more likely to live with others and in institutional settings (Arber and Ginn 1995). Therefore, it has been argued that the older female population remains vulnerable to certain types of crime, especially domestic violence (Pain 1997) and elder abuse. Accordingly, if the domestic victimisation of older people is understood in a power relations framework, patriarchy is (at least) a joint suspect with ageism. Parallels have been drawn between ageism and sexism elsewhere, as feminist modes of inquiry, analysis and theorisation provide useful lessons for the conceptualisation of age (Arber and Ginn 1995; Laws 1995). Ageism involves not only a different set of cultural stereotypes of older women (mostly more negative than those of older men), but a different set of relations between older women and the social and economic system.

As Pain (1997, p. 6) points out:

> Theorising age parallels the theorising of gender to some extent. Age as well as gender structures *what* behaviours become criminal, and when certain behaviours become defined as criminal ... Importantly, a high proportion of elder abuse victims are female, and offenders are usually male. (Pain 1997)

Notwithstanding this, while feminist inquiry is useful for understanding the victimisation of older people, there is a danger in assuming that age is much 'the same type of thing' as gender. Uncritical application of one body of knowledge/theory onto another never works out well, and there are problems with simplistic parallels between elder abuse, domestic violence, and child abuse.

Elder abuse in formal or institutional care is the most likely of all to involve a female abuser, as carers as well as clients are overwhelmingly female. Aitken and Griffin comment that this is 'a scenario which defies gender stereotypes and is therefore addressed through the pathologising of the individual — a move commonly used in relation to women who are regarded as transgressing gendered boundaries — or not addressed at all' (Aitken and Griffin 1996, p. 11). Their own work in Northamptonshire supports the existence of a male-dominated pattern of abuse in informal care (within the home), finding that abusers are most often male, more often sons than husbands.

Ageing in a postmodern world

In the 1990s, there has been a vast interest in postmodern perspectives of age and ageing identity, underpinned by discourses of 'better lifestyles' and resulting from the increased use of bio-technologies to facilitate the longevity of human experiences (Featherstone and Hepworth 1993). The intellectual roots of 'postmodern gerontology' derive from Jaber F. Gubrium's (1975) discovery of Alzheimer's disease in the USA and the establishment of boundaries between 'normal' and pathological ageing: old age is seen as a 'mask' which conceals the essential identity of the person beneath. The view of the ageing process as a mask/disguise concealing the essentially youthful self beneath is one which appears to be a popular argument (Featherstone and Hepworth 1993).

There are two underlying issues for Featherstone and Hepworth (1993) which should be understood as the basis for understanding postmodern gerontology. Firstly, the mask metaphor alerts social gerontologists to the possibility that a tension exists between the external appearance of the body, functional capacities, and the internal or subjective sense of experience of personal identity which is likely to become prominent as we age.

Secondly, older people are usually 'fixed' to roles without resources which does not do justice to the richness of their individual experiences and multiple facets of their personalities. Idealistically, Featherstone and Hepworth (1993), argue that a postmodern perspective would deconstruct such realities and age should be viewed as fluid with possibilities not constrained by medical model discourses of declines.

The point of this analysis is not to accept fixed discourses of ageing as represented by victimisation or that older people are a homogenous group. There is an ontologically flexible narrative to the diversity and richness of older people's lives that transcends limited bio-medical and common sense assumptions of the problems faced by persons in later life.

Ageing and the fifth utility – surveillance

For older people, especially within carceral institutions, life is organised around the operational needs of the total institution (Wahidin and Powell 2004), and all movement is under surveillance. Similar to residential homes, on admission they experience distress and depression not only from the transition away from the familiarities of home, but because of being positioned in a state of dependency (*ibid*). At the same time, the voices of professionals become louder and older people's voices are rendered silent in the landscape of power/knowledge and the politics of social relations. To exemplify this, Clough (1988), completed a study of abuse at a residential care home in England. He found that many staff in his study neglected older residents by failing to bathe residents, and by providing insufficient blankets which led to pneumonia. Vousden (1987 cited in Hadley and Clough 1995) claimed that professional surveillance practices destroyed the positive identity of many older people in such a repressive residential regime:

> It is self evident that when elderly, often confused residents are made to eat their own faeces, are left unattended, are physically man-handled or are forced to pay money to care staff and even helped to die, there is something seriously wrong. (Vousden 1987 quoted in Hadley and Clough 1995, p. 63)

Hence, the power/knowledge twist of professional 'carers' was detrimental to policy statements concerning 'choice' and 'quality of life' in residential care. Such care action was a powerful and a repressive mechanism used to indent and strip the identities of residents – and yet this has been seen as a social welfare issue rather than an issue of criminal justice.

It is the risky, unfixed character of modern life that underlies our accelerating concern with control and crime control in particular. It is not just crime that has changed: society has changed as well, and this transformation has reshaped criminological theory, social policy, and the cultural meaning of crime and criminality as well as ageing.

Conclusion

The aim of this chapter has been to connect ageing studies to criminology and to argue that criminologists studying the relationship between crime and later life have to turn to gerontological literature as a place to begin. Criminologists' tendency to ignore the area has left them vulnerable to accusations of replicating ageist discourse (see also Lister and Wall, and Phillips (this book). New roles are emerging for older people in the developed West around work, family, leisure, and criminal activity, among others, so challenging the expectations and roles of older people in society. Critical gerontology can inform criminology from an age-aware perspective bringing a more complex understanding to the experiences of crime and later life.

Those gerontological theories cited have been at the forefront of understanding old age in US, UK, and Australasian academies. Taken together, these theoretical currents have been influential in providing gerontology with a rich social dimension. Such social theories have been used also to analyse pressing social issues such as elder abuse, the gendered nature of age, the politics of power relations between older people, the state/civil society relation, and community care. The purpose of this chapter has been to amalgamate the key ideas of social theories of age in order to stress the importance of ageing to understanding age, crime, and society. No longer can criminologists ignore the importance of gerontological theory in the study of old age and crime. The absence of older offenders in the criminological imagination mirrors where the study of female offenders in criminology was 40 years ago. The lack of research in this area is an implicit form of ageism that implies that the problems of this group can be disregarded, or that ageing criminals are simply not worth discussing. By neglecting crime and later-life as a legitimate area of research we are indirectly replicating ageism and reproducing the hierarchy of power that excludes and invalidates the experiences of an ageing population.

References

Achenbauum, W.A. (1978) 'Old Age and Modernisation' *The Gerontologist*, 18: 307–12.

Aitken, L. and Griffin, G. (1996) *Gender Issues in Elder Abuse*. London: Sage.

Arber, S. and Ginn, J. (1995) *Connecting Gender and Ageing: A Sociological Approach*. Buckingham: Open University Press.

Birren, J. and Bengston, V. (1988) 'Towards a Critical Gerontology: The role of the Humanities in Theories of Ageing' in J. Birren and V. Bengston (eds) *Emerging Theories of Aging: Psychological and Social Perspectives in Time, Self and Society*. Berlin: Springer Press.

Bernard, M. and Meade, K. (1993) *Women Come of Age: Perspectives on the Lives of Older Women*. London: Edward Arnold.

Biggs, S. (1999) *The Mature Imagination*. Buckingham: Open University Press.

Biggs, S. and Powell, J.L. (1999) 'Surveillance and Elder Abuse: The Rationalities and Technologies of Community Care', *Journal of Contemporary Health*, 4 (1): 43–9.

Biggs, S. and Powell, J.L. (2001) 'A Foucauldian Analysis of Old Age and the Power of Social Welfare', *Journal of Aging & Social Policy*, 12 (2): 93–111.

Bond, J., Coleman, P. and Peace, S. (eds) (1993b) *Ageing in Society – An Introduction to Social Gerontology*: London: Sage.

Bytheway, W. (1995) *Ageism*, Buckingham: Open University Press.

Carlen, P. and Worrall, A. (1987) *Gender, Crime and Justice*. Buckingham: Open University.

Clough, R. (1988) *Practice, Politics and Power in Social Service Departments*. Aldershot: Gower.

Cole, T. (1992) *Voices and Visions: Towards a Critical Gerontology*, New York: Springer Press.

Codd, H. (1998) 'Older Women, Criminal Justice and Women's Studies', *Women's Studies International Forum*, 21 (2): 183–92.

Cohen, S. (1973) *Folk Devils and Moral Panics*. Oxford: Martin Robertson.

Curtis, S. (1999) *Children Who Break the Law*. London: Waterside Press.

Estes, C. (1979) *The Ageing Enterprise*. San Francisco, CA: Jossey-Bass.

Estes, C., Swan, J. and Gerand, L. (1982) 'Dominant and Competing Paradigms in Gerontology: Towards a Political Economy of Ageing', *Ageing and Society*, 12: 151–64.

Estes, C. and Binney, E.A. (1989) 'The Bio-medicalisation of Ageing: Dangers and dilemmas', *The Gerontologist*, 29 (5): 587–96.

Featherstone, M. (1991) *Consumer Culture and Postmodernism*. London: Sage.

Featherstone, M. and Hepworth, M. (1993) 'Images in Ageing' in J. Bond, P. Coleman and S. Peace (eds), *Ageing in Society*. London: Sage.

Fennell, G., Phillipson, C. and Evers, H. (1993) *The Sociology of Old Age*. Buckingham: Open University Press.

Garland, D. (2000) *The Contemporary Culture of Crime Control*. New York: Sage.

Garland, D. (2002) 'Of Crimes and Criminals: The Development of Criminology in Britain', in M. Maguire, R. Morgan and R. Reimer (eds), *The Oxford Handbook of Criminology*, 3rd edn, pp. 7–50. Oxford: Oxford University Press.

George, L. (1995) 'The Last Half-Century of Ageing Research – and Thoughts for the Future', *Journal of Gerontology: Social Sciences*, 50 (B)1: 1–3.

Ginn, J. and Arber, S. (1995) *Connecting Gender and Ageing – A Sociological Approach*, Buckingham: Open University Press.

Gubrium, J. (1975) *Living and Dying in Murray Manor*. New York: Basic Books.

Gubrium, J. and Wallace, B. (1990) 'Who Theorises Age?', *Ageing and Society*, 10 (2): 131–50.

Hadley, R. and Clough, R. (1995) *Care in Chaos*. London: Cassell.

Heidensohn, F. (1985) *Women and Crime*. Basingstoke, Macmillan.

Hillyard, P., Sim, J., Tombs, S. and Whyte, D. (2004) 'Leaving a "Stain Upon the Silence": Contemporary Criminology and the Politics of Dissent', *British Journal of Criminology*, 4 (3).

Hirschi, T. and Gottfredson, M. (1983) 'Age and the Explanation of Crime', *American Journal of Sociology*, 89: 552–84.

Hood, R. (2004) 'Hermann Mannheim and Max Grünhut – Criminological Pioneers in London and Oxford', *British Journal of Criminology*, 4 (44): 469–95.

Itzin, C. (1986) 'Ageism Awareness Training: A Model for Group Work' in C. Phillipson, M. Bernard and P. Strange (eds) *Dependency and Interdependency in Old Age: Theoretical Perspective and Policy Alternatives.* London: Croom Helm.

Katz, S. (1997) *Disciplining Old Age: The Formation of Gerontological Knowledge.* Charlottesville, VA: UPV.

Laws, G. (1995) 'Embodiment and Emplacement: Identities, Representation and Landscape in Sun City Retirement Communities', *International Journal of Aging & Human Development*, 40 (4): 253–80.

Pain, R.H. (1997) '"Old Age" and Ageism in Urban Research: The Case of Fear of Crime', *International Journal of Urban and Regional Research*, 21 (1): 16–35.

Pearson, G. (1983) *Hooligan: A History of Respectable Fears.* Basingstoke: Macmillan.

Phillips, J. (1996) 'Crime and older offenders', *Practice*, 8 (1): 43–55.

Phillipson, C. (1982) *Capitalism and the Construction of Old Age.* Basingstoke: Macmillan.

Phillipson, C. (1998) *Reconstructing Old Age – New Agendas in Social Theory and Practice.* London: Sage.

Phillipson, C. and Walker, A. (eds) *Ageing and Social Policy: A Critical Assessment.* Aldershot: Gower.

Pollak, O. (1941) 'The Criminality of Old Age', *Journal of Criminal Psychotheraphy*, 3: 213–35.

Powell, J.L. (2001) 'Theorising Gerontology: The Case of Old Age, Professional Power and Social Policy in the United Kingdom', *Journal of Aging & Identity*, 6 (3): 117–35.

Powell, J.L. and Wahidin, A. (2004) 'Corporate Crime, Aging and Pensions in Great Britain', *Journal of Societal and Social Policy*, 3 (1): 37–55.

Radzinowicz, L. (1988) *The Cambridge Institute of Criminology: Its Background and Scope.* London: HMSO.

Radzinowicz, L. (1999) *Adventures in Criminology.* London: Routledge.

Stott, M. (1981) *Ageing for Beginners.* Oxford: Blackwell.

Townsend, P. (1962) *The Last Refuge – A Survey of Residential Institutions and Homes for the Aged in England and Wales.* London: Routledge and Kegan Paul.

Townsend, P. (1981) 'The Structured Dependency of the Elderly: Creation of Social Policy in the Twentieth Century', *Ageing and Society*, 1: 5–28.

Turner, B. (1989) 'Ageing, Status Politics and Sociological Theory' in *The British Journal of Sociology*, 40 (4): 589–605.

Wahidin, A. (2004) *Older Women in the Criminal Justice System: Running Out of Time.* London: Jessica Kingsley.

Wahidin, A. (2005) 'Older Offenders, Crime and the Criminal Justice System', in C. Hale, K. Hayward, A. Wahidin and E. Wincup (eds) *Criminology*. Oxford: Oxford University Press.

Wahidin, A. and Powell, J.L. (2004) 'Ageing and Institutional Abuse: A Foucauldian Understanding', *International Journal of Sociology and Social Policy*, 24 (12): 45–66.

Walker, A. (1981) 'Towards a Political Economy of Old Age', *Ageing and Society*, 1: 73–94.

Walker, A. (1987) 'The Social Construction of Dependency in Old Age' in M. Loney (ed.) *The State or the Market?* London: Sage.

Chapter 3

Crime, abuse and social harm: towards an integrated approach

Mike Brogden and Preeti Nijhar

Introduction

Searching for a common lexicon

One major problem directly confronts criminologists researching the victimisation of older people. This can be summarised as follows: a justice approach holds that such victimisation is a crime and legal remedies are appropriate. Welfare approaches, suggest that individual needs are paramount and that the resolution must prioritise the well-being of the victim. Attempts to ameliorate and resolve the experiences of victimisation by older people have been bedevilled by an assumption of direct opposition between the language and concepts of criminologists as opposed to those of practitioners. Justice versus welfare ideologies have frequently been posed as antithetical. This chapter argues for a new approach through the concept of *zemiology* or *social harm* as a means of reconciling the apparently irreconcilable.

Successively, the chapter considers the obstacles to a harmonisation of approaches – the disparate range of forms of victimisation, and the traditional criminological impediments to such research. It argues that there is a false dichotomy between justice and welfare approaches, one which ignores the common elements. Using the vehicle of the fear of crime debate, the chapter argues that a *social harm* approach allows a reconciliation of the apparent opposites in synthesising justice and welfare concerns.

The diffuse nature of victimisation

Let us consider five cases of the victimisation of older people – from Edwardian England; from the career of Harold Shipman; from experiences in a British elderly care institution; from the annals of corporate Britain; and finally, from a major case of pension fraud.

In his socialist novel of early twentieth century England, Robert Tressell (see Tressell 2004) satirises social class attitudes to life and death proceedings by the local bourgeoisie of a south coast council chamber. Tressell's liberal spokesman demanded higher wages for the council's workforce because of the lack of provision for them in their later life. In response, to the guffaws of the rest of the Chamber, Councillor White responded that there was no real problem because the lifespan of working class people was some 20 years less than that of the middle class. Fortunately, they died earlier at little cost in their later life to the rest of the 'community'. An increase in wages to permit savings was therefore unnecessary.

The Shipman case is well known. Dr Shipman, in the course of some 30 years as a GP, killed deliberately at least some 250 people, all but a very few of pensionable age. Nearly all were women. As the worst recorded serial killer in modern British history, he apparently chose victims who could be deemed as marginal to the mainstream of Manchester society. His motivations will always be obscure, but he seems to have been generally motivated by a desire to eliminate people, who were 'trouble' to his practice, awkward ones whom he regarded as making too many demands on his professional time.

Thirdly, there are many recent controversial cases in Britain such as in the recorded 'early' deaths at Greenwich Hospital in 1991 (BBC *News 24*, 1999). Elderly patients were dying because of an unspoken policy of 'involuntary euthanasia' designed to ease pressure on the NHS. Police investigated 60 cases of pensioners who died allegedly after being deprived of food and water by hospital staff. A senior consultant claimed that the severe pressure on beds might have led to a tendency to limit care where the outcome was doubtful and that people who started to resist early discharge were seen as an encumbrance.

Fourthly, there is the case of the asset-strippers, Alchemy Limited. Alchemy reportedly terrified old age pensioners by threatening to evict them from care homes in south-west London. It wanted to close Holybourne House in Roehampton, one of three homes it owned in the area, because it was not sufficiently profitable. The site had more value than profits from care. Yet Alchemy had promised to provide residence and care for life when it took over the homes. Alchemy only agreed to transfer residents to its other homes because Wandsworth Council threatened to take it to court. Joyce Steen, daughter of the oldest resident at Holybourne House, Nellie Day, 98, says, 'These people just put money before people. Financial gain is their aim, and hang the people'. (See: www.socialistworker.co.uk/1689/sw168906.htm)

A final illustration is the experience of the *Daily Mirror* pensioners under the rule of the late Robert Maxwell. Maxwell legally transferred their pension savings to save his own investments and *illegally* failed to return them. In consequence, some 50,000 thousand *Mirror* pensioners lost the bulk of their retirement provision (Spalek 2001).

The five illustrations represent several distinct types of the extreme victimisation of older people. They cover intentionally a gamut of different experiences, seeking to demonstrate that the terms 'crime' and 'abuse' are unsatisfactory if one is to reconcile the dichotomy between criminologists researching offences against older people and social workers involved in studies of elder abuse.

Tressell's fictionalised example would rarely be regarded as abuse or crime – there was a 'natural' attrition in the lives of working class people in Edwardian Britain due to their conditions of work and lifestyle. Orthodox criminology – the conflation of administrative and realist criminologies – regarded the matter as beyond its terms of reference. Legally, early deaths as a consequence of an involuntary lifestyle have promoted only marginal contributions from criminology – regulatory offences under health and safety legislation normally fall outside the criminological mainstream. Stratification and gender factors may have particular effects on early death, but while these may be of sociological concern, they are topics that would not appear on current criminological syllabuses.

The Shipman case is treated with some kind of popular puzzlement as the bizarre actions of a particular individual, despite the common elements of victims' age, marginality, and gender. Serial killers are the stuff of daytime TV documentaries. They may no longer feature in popular culture to the same extent as in the Victorian penny dreadfuls. However, the criminological evidence on serial killing has little to say. Concepts such as 'psychotic' leave clear that killings on the horrendous scale such as that of Shipman are beyond the criminological imagination. Criminological contributions to the explanation of the most serious serial murders in British experience are noticeably remarkable only by their absence. As criminology has nothing of value to say about serial killings, the Shipman murders would fall by default from criminological analysis.

In the Greenwich Hospital case, few commentators apart from the ageing enterprises, used the term abuse. Despite an initial police investigation, conceptions of crime rarely appeared in public comment. Involuntary assisted deaths – involving omission rather than commission – attract no criminological research funding. Despite their prevalence, the most common form of homicide in Western society is left only to the speculation of journalists and even then, arouses little of the prurient interest that would characterise the deaths from similar causes of a different age group such as in cases of child death from neglect. Braithwaite (1993), in his pioneering study of the regulation of care homes has not set a precedent which criminologists have followed. In the practice of asset strippers, Alchemy, after their previous thwarted attempt to dismember Rover car production, at best no crime appears to have been committed and only some of the inhabitants of the homes regarded it as a form of abuse. 'Profit before (old) people' is a practice of little current criminological interest. The killings of older people by sins of omission rather of commission are rarely the subject of criminological enquiry (Brogden 2001). Finally, Spalek's study of the *Mirror* pensioner case is analysed as a form of corporate crime. No other criminologist has recognised the financial consequences of such crimes against older people's savings for their post-labour years.

We have deliberately chosen to illustrate this argument, as above, through some of the most serious forms of crime against older people, in order to emphasise the need for a common approach. The cases are selected not because of their relatively extreme character – indeed, Shipman apart, they are regular occurrences. Rather it is because such forms of victimisation are at different poles of a continuum of *social harm* that happens to older people. They are, in a sense, ideal types of the experiences of older people. They allow us to focus on the starker features of harmful experience. Homicide is at one end of a legality-abuse continuum and emotional abuse and neglect of older people in the household and in care are at the other. They are different only in the extremity of experience of the former, and in the way different victimisation experiences have become the property of different agencies encapsulated within different epistemological paradigms. Examining such cases through a criminological lens allows us to raise critical questions about the failure of criminologists to be interested in, to develop theories, to conduct empirical research, and to offer policy guidance with regard to older people as victims.

The failure of criminology

This chapter is concerned with the need to develop a common lexicon and discourse which might enable criminologists and social workers to engage in an intellectual debate. There are several key problems that contribute to that criminological malaise in investigating the victimisation of older people – a socially constructed criminal law definition of 'offence'; the artificial opposition between welfare and justice paradigms; the private space/public space dichotomy; the development of a realist victimology which has arbitrarily ignored older people and primarily gendered status; the heterogeneity of the older groups; and the structural location of older people.

- *Legality*: formally, criminology operates within a legal framework. The previous alliance with the sociology of deviance seems now largely to have been forgotten as administrative criminology and policy requirements increasingly direct criminological research to focus simply on breaches of the criminal law. In at least two of the cases cited above, the victimisation of older people falls outside that legal paradigm;

- *Opposing paradigms:* the victim experiences of older people have long been colonised by a welfare/treatment paradigm with social workers, psychiatric, and medical specialists as the gatekeeping personnel (Brogden and Nijhar 2000). In particular, professionalism, especially within the medical occupations, has ensured 'Keep Out' signs for alternative approaches;

- *Private space:* the latent inheritance of sociological functionalism and of a golden age myth has long constructed the experience of older people as legitimately secluded behind household windows and the foyers of care institutions. To this sociological remnant has increasingly been added the profit motive, as private companies control access, transparency of external scrutiny being regarded as a threat to their profits;

- *Homogeneity:* young people, males and females, and ethnic groups are readily recognisable as social categories. The same clarity does not apply to older people due to a variety of factors – varying years of chronological retirement, the differential affects of disability when conflated within an ageist caricature, and differences between the 'young–old' and the liminal;

- *Gender:* both the earlier and the more critical victimology have concentrated on the female experience, especially with regard to sexual attacks in public space and with regard to such experiences in the household. Victimology in particular, largely prompted by a feminist agenda, contrarily had the effect of sidelining older people in the particular instance of fear of crime studies (often disparaging their victim experiences as being misplaced);

- *Structural location:* in a socially exclusive society, older people are often regarded as consumers not producers, and as marginal to political and social processes. Only a minority of them constitute an influential consuming market.

The false dichotomy: justice and welfare

The primary reason that criminologists in recent years have not ventured into the context of the victimisation of older people relates to the tradition of a false opposition between the two dominant paradigms in criminology. Pedagogy in criminology has commonly resorted to the heuristic device of presenting contrasting criminal justice and welfare paradigms. Such an often contrived opposition provides accessible teaching materials and techniques. The paradigms appear to reflect radically different schools of thought, of discourse, of practitioners, of approaches and of results – especially when located in the classical and positivist origins of criminology.

Those contrasting paradigms are starkly represented in Brogden and Nijhar (2000), amongst others (see Table 3.1 below).

These models, ideal types, represent often diametrically opposed paradigms. Drawing upon different historical, sociological, and

Table 3.1

Paradigms	Criminal justice	Welfare/abuse
Focus	Offender	Victim
Primary concern	Legal offence	Victim needs
Instruments	Legal powers	Diagnosis
Personnel	Police/courts	Social workers/medical staff
Resolution	Legal order	Rehabilitation/cure

Source: Brogden and Nijhar 2000.

philosophical schools of thought, classical and positivist, they have represented in social science, the Scylla and Charybdis of intellectual debate – and more pragmatically, effective teaching practices. The latter in particular are important because generations of criminology students have been encouraged to develop an anti-positivist critique (if not pro-classical theory) and hence a disparagement of practices such as the focus on 'pathological' abuse and treatment by social workers and associated practitioners. But useful as a teaching device, they often provide caricatures of practice.

In order to develop an approach, one that allows criminal justice academic and abuse scholars to work together in comprehending and seeking to alleviate older people's experiences of victimisation outlined at the outset of this chapter, we need to find some way of reconciling these apparent oppositions. Critical criminology with all its blemishes, offers one way forward (Hillyard *et al.* 2004).

The common elements of crime and abuse against older people

What then has criminology to offer in way of explanation of the cases listed at the outset of this chapter? What have they in common? Criminology like other social sciences has been bedevilled with the creation of new concepts to explain the self-evident. But there is a problem. If criminology has to combine with other disciplines to elucidate the epistemological problems of research into the victim and criminal experiences of older people, a common vocabulary is necessary. We have to start from the recognition of the generally accepted features, from grounded theory, of the key features of such victimisation. This is not part of an obsessive search for a definition, but rather heuristically intended as a device for progressing towards a more congruent relationship in studies of the victimisation of older people.

It is now generally acknowledged that such experiences include the following:

- the presence of a victim;

- the victim is regarded by his/her position not of a fixed chronological age, but socially constructed by others as different through an ageing process;

- the victimisation must range from the physical (direct force, sexual assaults and so on) emotional, financial loss, neglect/omission of necessary acts, and self-neglect;

- the existence of an offender/abuser (in the case of self-neglect, an authoritative agency);

- the harm conducted may consist of measurable activities, but it must also include qualitative social recognition of emotional and psychological harm being incurred by the victim;

- the law is an inadequate guide to such harm: rather the key guides are social mores and ethical standards;

- the occurrence of the activity in private space – from household to institution;

- the assumption of a 'trust' relationship between victim and perpetrator.

Critical victimology has long discarded the myth that some potential victims have 'attracted' crime – (what was called by critics, 'victim-blaming'). But current research is much more contrary over the argument that some groups are more likely than others to be a victim (especially in a designated location such as in a 'closed' location, in a care or nursing institution, or a status of 'socially excluded'). Any person, once socially constructed as older, can become a victim. While clearly some groups are more likely to be victims than others of a particular form of harm, there is no such thing as a 'natural' victim of elder victimisation.

Social construction offers more guidance. Where being older is coupled with other socially structured stigmas – being disabled, marginal through lack of involvement or employment, isolated and dependent – it is more likely to attract a perception of abuse, in particular where age is related to victimisation. Conversely, where such stigmas are not present – such as older people in a gated citadel for the wealthy – there may be the reverse effect. In the latter case, older people being seen as part of a consuming rather than of a producing market may enable a positive label to be attached, and consequent social perception of victimisation to be less. Further, unlike the earlier labelling theory to which it owes its criminological origins, constructionism embodies an assumption of differential power relations, mainly structurally conceived. Chronological reliance on age categories in criminology has hindered this approach

– although recently challenged by studies of older prisoners. Indeed chronological age is itself a social construction based primarily on the valuation given to labour power and the productive value of the person's labour.

Using age simply as an analytical category to provide a framework for analysis is also unhelpful (see, for example, the work on prisons in this book). Further, medicalising age – the connotation of age and disability – relates to a conflation of different discourses. Self-evidently, there is no necessary relation between disability and chronological age although the previous reification of elder abuse has helped conflate the two. Traditionally, age in itself has tended to be viewed as an empirical category – essentially a biological phenomenon, something to be treated by doctors, and to be understood through physiological changes and concomitant physiological decline that are seen as inevitably accompanying old age – which has kept it off the criminological agenda (Pain 1999). When coupled with a notion of dependency, it enhances the failure to recognise the so-called dependent as often an active agent. In this chapter, ageism is regarded as a social construct, culturally portrayed, but crucially embedded in specific power relations – often but not always structurally based in material factors (Pain 1999). But social constructionism often inherits from labelling theory a view of the victim as passive, rather than as active. This is not intrinsic to the theory, and we reject it.

The private space concept may at first be misleading, appearing to connect elder victimisation to 'crimes of the household' and by implication to the whole range of studies relating to the various forms of domestic abuse. In this context, private space is determined by the existence of a doorkeeper whose motivation may be either familial, commercial, or bureaucratic. Family members may discourage, directly or indirectly, analyses of harm to intimates. But so also do private corporations in the major industry of private care. Some professionals also hinder for a range of reasons the development of enquiries in bureaucratic organisations. Describing elder victimisation in this way allows the use of household abuse insights where appropriate, but also permits, for example, recognition of structural factors allowing engagement with other bodies of theory such as the sociology of the professions, organisational theory, and corporate crime approaches.

The 'trust' factor is perhaps overplayed. Many older people and for that matter, their carers, are thrust into a situation in which obligations may be assumed by outsiders, but not necessarily by the participants. Again, we lack contributions from the sociology of the professions in terms of the degree of control exercised: over the spatial territory in which the victimisation occurs, over the discourse used to define the problems, over access to the nature of 'secret' knowledge in the construction of the harm conducted, and over the power to influence subsequent decisions. There has been a minimal attempt to research this problem of the relationship between professional carer and client, a curious situation given the wealth of earlier studies of professionalism.

The sources of social harm: the example of the fear of crime

By drawing on several sources, concepts of 'social harm' (or what we shall call 'zemiology') are being developed by a stream of critical criminology. The latter locates the source of such social harm within the larger social and economic inequalities of society and urges criminologists to re-focus their analyses at that level. In this context, social harm as a concept is being utilised as much as a device to reconceptualise the focus of criminology generally as it is to further a particular epistemological discourse. Social harm furnishes a tool which allows devotees of the orthodox welfare and justice paradigms to be seen not as competitors in opposition but rather as potential collaborators.

To elucidate this argument, we draw on the 'fear of crime' debate. The contribution of administrative criminology to understanding older people's concerns with crime against older people, argue succinctly that the problem was not crime *per se*, but rather that the simple factor of 'fear' was the problem. Older people were the least likely to be victims of criminal behaviour, but the most likely to be fearful of it. This kept them in effect imprisoned with a narrowly constrained lifestyle. That fear had been reinforced by both unscrupulous private security operators who commercially wished to create a market for their product, as well as media and policing campaigns that focused on the apparent vulnerability of the elderly. The problem for policy therefore was, in effect, to dispel this fear by revealing the 'truth' about the minimal probability of such victimisation.

However that approach contained two major faults – one empirical and the other methodological. The empirical problem is now self-evident. Because much older victimisation occurs behind closed doors – in private space, like forms of domestic violence – it was rarely recorded and not susceptible to inclusion in either the recorded criminal statistics or to a lesser extent in the new orthodoxy of the victim (crime) surveys. There were other empirical flaws. Several studies from the late 1980s onwards suggested that in relation to fear of personal crime and fear of property crime, older adults do not have higher levels of fear (for example, Lagrange and Ferraro 1989 onwards). To this empirical critique was added a contribution from gender studies – such as Pain's (1998) argument, that older women may have hidden fears of actual past harm, independently of recent victimisation in private space, memories which continue not just into later age, but also commute from the private to the public domain.

The second problem was methodological, and its recognition a key contribution to the re-conceptualisation of abuse and criminal victimisation as social harm. The technical problem was high non-response rate amongst elderly poor to victim surveys – fear of someone arriving at the door with a clipboard – undermined the representativeness of many earlier victim studies. Additionally victim studies of older people frequently confuse two quite different concepts in their category discourse: 'fear of crime' and 'worry about crime'. Commonly the two were treated as synonyms. Fear of crime was commonly used as an alternative to worrying about crime and *vice versa*. However, the two are not identical concepts as several studies have now shown. Fearing crime is much more personal, often based on direct experience, past or present. Worrying about crime is a second order matter. Considered separately, older people often have no greater fear of crime than do other social groups. But they do worry about it – though often only in the same way that they are concerned with a constellation of social harms such as problems of finance, of pensions, and of social security, ill-health, social isolation, disability, and so on. Fear of crime cannot be treated in isolation. It is a quality of life issue which has linkages with the wider political, social and cultural anxieties of individuals. Focusing on it directly through the instrument of the crime surveys often distracts attention from other key issues. However, one value of victimisation surveys is that they have the capacity to shift the focus away from what concerns a state agency to what may be the priorities of the general public. While they remain crime-focused, the more recent surveys (see Gadd *et al.* 2002), using a more qualitative methodology, recognise other forms of victimisation and harm concern than crime *per se*.

Elevating crime as 'the' social harm

But what has happened in practice, because of the prominence of victim and crime surveys in measuring social harm experiences, is that crime has been elevated into undue prominence, the *sine qua non* for action. In effect, crime has been elevated, socially constructed as a first order problem, with other forms of social harm relegated to a second division. There are several implications of this development.

Firstly, it has reinforced the dichotomy between welfare and justice paradigms. Crime is the *raison d'etre* of the criminal justice system. It has come to represent the major way other social ills are constructed under a law-and-order mandate. Secondly, constructing, reifying crime as *the* problem coincides with particular developments in policing, in particular the development of community-oriented policing (COP) and the new system of community wardens. These increase the police's professional mandate to intervene in non-justice matters of which crime is regarded as a symptom (Brogden and Nijhar 2005), especially in the major variant of COP, the 'broken windows' or zero-tolerance approach. Where crime is explained to the problem-solving police officer as a consequence of underlying factors ranging from dilapidated housing to unemployment to lack of leisure facilities for 'unruly youth', the police come to construct those types of potential social harm as police and justice work, in effect as justice problems. The police have come to 'own' a whole range of harms outside their legal orbit (see Public Reassurance and Quality and Life Study 2003/4).

Resources devoted to the more general forms of social problems are increasingly regarded simply as inputs into crime as the major type of social harm. Policing expands, in resources and in social authority (but not expertise), at a time of relative contraction of social services, from housing to social work, committed to dealing with a range of social harms that affect older people. However, when open-ended questions are used in victim surveys, the crime (the formal police *raison d'être*) often does not appear in the top five concerns of older people (Ditton and Farrell 2000). Crime artificially displaces the wider constellation of social harms.

Thirdly, historical generic terms – nuisances, public order, street detritus, and so on – that impinge on the welfare of older people are deconstructed and then reified as a crime problem. Technologies developed to deal with social harms such as personal alarms over health risks for older persons are now incorporated into a crime alarm measure. Fourthly, '... by attempting to set an objective legalistic definition of crime independent of the subjective definitions of the various sub-groups within society, victimisation research commonly trivialises that which is important and makes important that which is trivial' (see: www.malcomread.co.uk/JockYoung). 'Nuisances' become defined as the problem rather than say, housing conditions.

Where inter-agency partners develop under a community safety umbrella (contracts with the local community under the umbrella of proximity policing in Western Europe), the lead partner who dominates the 'cooperation' is invariably the state policing agency. The police call the shots, determine the location of malaise expenditure, and reconstruct community problems as crime problems in which tautologically, the police become the key role players. For example, high unemployment and problems of social security are increasingly reconstructed as causes of crime. Far from the inter-agency partners being enabled, as intended, to recognise and to resolve the range of social harms which affects a community, they are reconstituted into explaining and responding to the crime problem.

Where social groups are encouraged by external agencies to contribute to the resolutions of local social problems, the dominant structures that appear with state support are 'consultative' bodies such as Community Police Forums and Neighbourhood Watch Schemes (in the former case, often seeking to usurp through a 'democratic' relationship with the police, the legitimate powers of locally elected officials). The fear of crime debate illustrates how concerns with generic social harms (dilapidated housing, youthful recreation, and blocked access routes) are redefined as being the property of a justice agency.

Reconciling justice and abuse paradigms: zemiology and social harm

Zemiology is the holistic study of the social, psychological, physical, and financial harmful consequences of social phenomena. It has recently become the dominant motif of critical or idealist criminology's attempt to analyse and combat social and structural infractions.

Historically, before the reification of criminal law in Western Europe, there was little division in judicial decision-making between behaviour that might constitute (in present-day criminal law discourse) an 'offence' and that constituted as deviance from the dominant social mores. In his satirical play, '*The Rise and Fall of the City Mahagony*', Bertolt Brecht's (1930) main character Jim Mahoney, who propagates anarchy as the means to human happiness, is sentenced to minor punishment because of several (legal) offences, but then is sentenced to death because of his (non-legal) offence of indigence. The state regarded the non-criminal offence of social harm as of greater magnitude. Early academic jurists explored the notion that social harm should be the primary criterion for the development of the criminal law (retaining it within the purlieu of administrative criminology), the product of an uneven contest between unequals, a criminal law that reflects entrenched interests and constrains criminologists simply to act as technicians within that given framework (see Feinberg 1987). Social norms based on the principle of social equality should be the basis of criminological investigation.

The concept of social harm however did have some influence during the enlightenment as part of the process of construction of modern criminal law (Wasik 1998). It features markedly in Beccaria's principles for the foundation of law. The role of the victim in criminal legislation will also be that of the subject of social harm. In Germany, the concept has been developed as a notion of the 'common good' (*Rechtgut*) – destruction of, or damage to, a common good constitutes social harm. The victim is the subject of the common good. However, legal process and especially criminal law have been remarkably reticent about developing the concept of social harm in recent years. In criminology (in its administrative mode), it represents probably the key distinction from victimology, and one signifier of the latter as a sub-discipline within social science.

The concept of social harm contains key ingredients:

- a recognition that criminology must operate beyond a legally restrictive mandate;
- that instead its primary aims should be to discover how social order is produced and how harmful deviance restrained;
- that it should not operate with a notion of legal subjects, but with a conception of the social subject;
- that it should restore the foci of the sociology of deviance of the 1960s and 1970s;
- that it should recognise that the source of harmful acts is the extent and quality of differential power relations.

Firstly, we need critically to deconstruct the subject matter of criminology away from a sole reliance on those injurious acts defined as such by the criminal law – theft, criminal violence and so on – in order to establish that a vast range of harms – ageism, emotional abuse, medical negligence, bureaucratic misdemeanours and so on should also be within the remit of criminology (Muncie 2000). Realist and administrative criminology are trapped within a legal definition of 'crime' – essentially a technical matter. Social harm takes from the abolitionists the view that if our concern with crime is driven by fears for social stability, personal and collective safety, and social justice, then we are well advised to look beyond 'crime' to discover where the most dangerous threats to persons and property lie.

Secondly, the key problematic for criminology then becomes not crime or criminal behaviour but social order and how that order is produced and struggled over (Shearing 1989), and how social justice is achieved. Social order is problematic in society, where there exist more or less diverse forms of inequality. What kind of actions of victimisation disrupt that social harmony and how do social scientists investigate the conditions under which such disruptive forms of power relations can be constrained? Criminology and abuse, under the social harm rubric, represent one part of that struggle.

Thirdly, current criminology operates with the boundaries of notions of legal subjects, essentially an artificial construct. The clichés of the 'man on the Clapham Omnibus', the legal citizen, implying that people are social and legal equals, are a non-sequitur. As critical legal studies contributions demonstrate for legal citizens in the criminal justice process, equality before the law actually conceals essential inequalities of condition. Laws which treat *all* people as equals conceal inherent inequalities (as recognised for example, in the desirable recent courtroom developments with regard to child and female victims of sexual attacks which have recently moved away from that premise). One of the problems with much human rights work is that it aims for a notion of equal treatment for all under the law, failing to appreciate that inequality (i.e. positive discrimination) is necessary in many cases where the subjects are manifestly socially unequal (see Brogden and Nijhar 2000). Social contracts necessitate a relation between equals. Legal contracts are often between unequals. The power differential in the 'trust'/dependency contract between the older person and the care professional, medical practitioner, or carer, embodies varying degrees of social inequality.

Fourthly, the notion of social harm involves a conception of the 'collective' as opposed to the individual. Not merely does harm involve two parties in an interactional process, but it also requires a notion of social justice. In effect, an injury to one is an injury to all. The negligence accorded to one elderly person in a nursing ward is not just a harm to that individual, it also infringes that social justice principle by allowing a breach against one supposedly marginal member. Further, negligence is rarely a one-off practice, it becomes routinised and others are also subject to it, until it institutionalises the practice.

Finally, the concept of social harm takes from Foucault (with all the problems now recognised in the contributions from that diverse body of theory) the importance of the different foci of power relations in the construction of harmful behaviour. Power is not just exercised by physical force, or through the conduct of the law: it also operates through control over knowledge and especially in this case, of medical knowledge. 'What is crime' rests crucially on the power to define and the power to police certain 'transgressions', which in an unequal society results in little attention to other actions, such as those committed by superordinates as opposed to subordinates:

> ... social justice perspective demands that the issues of social harm, human rights and societal justice become a focus of the study of criminal justice. The social justice perspective allows for the examination of policy issues as diverse as genocide, institutionalised racism, organised crime, and environmental destruction that are generally ignored in the study of criminal justice administration in addition to traditional criminal justice issues. (US National Association of Social Work, Statement of Principle, 1999)

Towards a common lexicon

Apart from the arguments discussed above, there are many problems with developing a common discourse which allows practitioners to collaborate with academic criminologists. This is not just a problem of converting oppositional approaches to the victimisation of older people into a common understanding. As we note above, discourse is not just neutral, it also operates as a powerful structure in its own right. Discourse, the power to define, and the power to explain and to resolve, is a key part of larger structures of the construction of deviance. Developing an appropriate lexicon is part of the further struggle to reconstruct the older victims of social harm as active rather than passive in their own construction of well-being.

The impediments to a common language and concepts are obvious. For example, how does one 'punish' someone who has not broken the criminal law? Secondly, many of the abuse categories are non-quantifiable. Thirdly, if the criminal law (and for that matter, much of human rights legislation) is no longer the final arbiter of appropriate and inappropriate behaviour what is the source of the social mores that would guide common research and practice? One way forward lies in a series of papers by Braithwaite (for example, 2001) in which that criminologist seeks to develop alternative guides to those of law and organisation, to govern conduct in nursing homes. More generally, the earlier sociology of deviance transiently committed not just criminology and (unevenly) the various 'caring' professions into an alliance. Criminologists in particular need to reappraise their own history. Further, there are particular developments in practice. For example, while restorative justice approaches have many failings (you cannot reinvent the informal problem-solving structures of pre-industrial societies) there are common developments. Examples are those procedures which allow a potential reconstruction of criminology and practitioner approaches towards common objectives and understanding. There are glimmers of hope in combining efforts to deal with victimisation experiences of older people under the rubric of social harm.

References

Braithwaite, J. (2001) 'Regulating Nursing Homes: The Challenge of Regulating Care for Older People in Australia', *British Medical Journal*, Aug 25, 323 (7310): 443–46.

Brogden, M.E. and Nijhar, S.K. (2000) *Crime, Abuse and the Elderly*. Cullompton: Willan.

Brogden, M.E. (2001) *Geronticide: Killing the Elderly*, London: Jessica Kingsley.

Brogden, M.E., and Nijhar, S.K. (2005) *Community Policing: National and International Models and Approaches*. Cullompton: Willan.

Ditton, J. and Farrell, S. (2000) *Fear of Crime*. Aldershot: Ashgate.

Feinberg, J. (1987), *Harm to Others*. Oxford: Oxford University Press.

Gadd, D., Farrall, S., Dallimore, D. and Lombard, N. (2002) *Domestic Abuse against Men in Scotland*. Glasgow: Scottish Executive Central Research Unit.

Hill, R. and Robertson, R. (2003) 'What Sort of Future for Critical Criminology?', *Crime, Law and Social Change*, 39 (1): 91.

Hillyard, P., Pantazis, C. and Tombs, S. (eds) (2004) *Beyond Criminology: Taking Harm Seriously*. London: Pluto Press.

Lagrange, R.L. and Ferraro, F. (1989) 'Assessing Age and Gender Differences in Perceived Risk and Fear of Crime,' *Criminology*, 27 (4): 697–720.

Muncie, J. (2000) 'Decriminalising Criminology' in G. Mair and R. Tarling (eds) *Selected Proceedings*, British Criminology Conference, 3.

Pain, R. (1997) 'Constructing the Older Victim of Crime', *International Journal of Urban and Regional Research*, 21: 1.

Pain, R. (1999) 'Theorising Age in Criminology' in M. Brogden (ed.) *Selected Proceedings*, British Criminology Conference, Belfast, 2.

Shearing, C.D. (1989) 'Decriminalising Criminology', *Canadian Journal of Criminology*, 31 (2): 169–78.

Spalek, B. (2001) 'White Collar Crime Victims and the Issue of Trust' in R. Tarling (ed.) *Selected Proceedings*, British Criminology Conference, Leicester, 4.

Tressell, R. (ed.) (2004) *The Ragged Trousered Philanthropists*. London: Penguin Modern Classics.

Wasik, M. (1998) 'Crime, Seriousness and the Offender–Victim Relationship in Sentencing' in A. Ashworth and M. Wasik (eds) *Fundamentals of Sentencing Theory*. Oxford: Oxford University Press.

Chapter 4

Crime and older people: the research agenda

Judith Phillips

Introduction

The link between age and crime has long been established – offending was seen as purely a 'youth' phenomenon while the fear of crime belonged to the realm of older people. Such stereotypes still hold in popular perceptions of criminology. Additionally, older people are viewed as of significant standing in the community as judges, magistrates, boards of visitors, probation officers and panel members. In the last 15 years however the focus on age and crime has broadened and changed to incorporate older people as offenders (for example, as a consequence of elder abuse) and perpetrators of serious crime rather than just as victims or dispensers of punishment through the courts.

This chapter gives an overview of the current state of research in the broad area of crime and older people, focusing primarily on older offenders and in particular those in prison. Significant amounts of research on the broad spectrum of elders, crime and the criminal justice system exist in the USA (Aday 2003; for a summary see Rothman, Dunlop and Entzel 2000); however the focus of this chapter is on research findings within the UK. The chapter begins with a brief analysis of why this issue is timely and significant; it then argues that to evaluate our state of knowledge and highlight the current gaps in our research we need to integrate a criminological with a critical gerontological perspective. By adopting an ageing and lifecourse approach we can unravel the key issues for a research agenda; understand how the processes of age and crime are related, and develop appropriate policy and practice responses. Finally the chapter maps out a research agenda for theory development, policy and practice.

A timely issue

There are a number of reasons why this issue has been raised on both criminological and gerontological research agendas. The demographic profile of the UK, with an increasing ageing population, provides the potential for increasing numbers of people committing crime in later life and with increasing longevity for many younger offenders to be surviving into later life. With an increasing lifer population resulting in a doubling of prisoners serving life sentences in the last ten years and (Howse 2003), stiffer prison sentences, together with the increasing incidence, awareness and detection of elder abuse, the issue of age has gained attention on the criminological agenda.

Older people were previously a hidden, invisible population in the criminal justice system and in social policy and practice. Crime used to be thought of as a youth phenomenon which people grew out of; consequently prison is designed around the able-bodied young male. Such an emphasis has 'marginalised the dimension of ageing'. When crime was committed by older people in the community it was often, and still is, a matter for social services to police rather than criminal agencies. A care and welfare rather than a justice and punishment approach pervaded (Taylor and Parrot 1988; Thomas and Wall 1993).

On the gerontological agenda, despite a considerable history of literature and research on older people in institutions (Townsend 1962; Peace et al. 1997) and on the family life of old age (Townsend 1956; Phillipson et al. 2001) there has been a neglect of older people in prison institutions or caught up in domestic violence in the private sphere of home (McCreadie 1996). When crime has arisen on the agenda it is the fear of crime that has received most attention and characterised older people as victims, powerless and vulnerable (Midwinter 1990; Help the Aged 2002a). Fear of victimisation among older people has in some quarters been seen as a greater problem than crime itself (Williams 1999) with gender, location and environment and past experience of crime and abuse being more significant than age in producing a fear of crime (Help the Aged 2002b).

Only in the last two decades in the UK have we moved from seeing older people as just fearful of crime to an increasing recognition of older people as victims of crime in the private domain through elder abuse (by carers, for example) and the public domain (by strangers) and secondly, older people as offenders emerging as a significant issue not only for the prison and probation service and the criminal justice system, but for health and social care agencies. The lack of consideration and increasing health and social care needs of older people caught in the criminal justice system has raised this as a crucial issue for gerontologists and criminologists.

On the policy and political agenda the issue is timely. Political sensitivities revolve around whether release on licence of older but 'high profile' offenders is possible, as notorious prisoners grow older; Myra Hindley provided probably the most famous example. Similarly there have been discussions about healthcare and death and dying issues (promoted in the media by the health of Ronnie Biggs). The question of bringing war criminals/sex offenders to trial many years after the event has also raised the issue of older people, frailty and criminal justice.

Policy responses however have been reactionary. One of the few policy responses to the issue of older offenders has been to consider segregation for older offenders by establishing an older offenders' wing at Kingston prison; a reaction to concerns about prisoners' mobility caught the attention of the press and media (*Guardian*, 30 January 2001) and promoted its attention to a 'geriatric crime wave'.

However legislation in other areas will have an impact on crime and ageing in different settings – the Human Rights Act 1998 and the Disability Discrimination Act 1995 impinge on the situation of older people and crime. Significantly the National Service Framework for Older People (Department of Health 2001) which sets out standards to be followed in terms of incontinence service, strategies for combating ageism and liaison between prison healthcare staff and health and social care workers in the community has not been evaluated in respect to its application to prisons and may be difficult to implement.

The issue is also timely in that numbers and profiles of older people in the criminal justice system and the extent of crime are being better recorded and we are able to get a much clearer picture.

We know more than we did a decade ago about the risk factors of abuse, situations in which abuse is likely to develop and the characteristics of abusers (Biggs, Phillipson and Kingston 1995). Increasing research on the incidence and definition of elder abuse and better ways of recording domestic crime are raising the profile of elder abuse in policy and practice.

The current research agenda in relation to older offenders reflects a number of the above areas – the demographics of old age crime; explanations of crime; and latterly the health and social care needs of older offenders. The scoping study carried out by the Centre for Policy on Ageing and Prison Reform Trust (Howse 2003) provides a comprehensive account of the background of growing old in prison. We know that the proportion of older prisoners is growing in the prison population with an increase from 1 to 2.3 per cent of prisoners under sentence between 1990 and 2000 – it almost trebled in a decade (Table 4.1); making this the fastest growing sector of the prison population. Three quarters of older offenders have been convicted of violent or sexual offences; most are men. Yet the size of the increase in women's incarceration is also significant with a two and a half times increase in 10 years since 1992 (HMCIP 2004). Around 44 per cent of women are either foreign nationals or from ethnic minority backgrounds (HMCIP 2004). Minority ethnic groups are also hugely over represented in the prison population of older offenders in general (Howse 2003).

There has been some research on explanations of crime, but because of small numbers in the UK most of this work has been done in the US. Issues related to dependency, economic conditions (council tax refusal for example) and cultural changes such as changes in customs of respecting elders, have all been put forward as triggers for crime in old age.

Table 4.1 Growth of the Older Prisoner Population

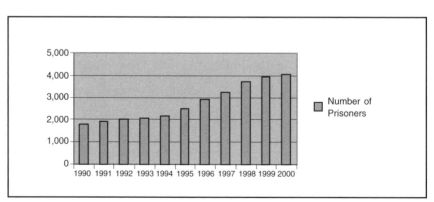

Source: Howse 2003.

Health and social care needs

There is an increasing number of studies in this area (Fazel *et al.* 2001; Tarbuck 2001; HMCIP 2004). Physical decline and vulnerability are to be feared in prison where a premium is put on physical strength (Howse 2003). The psychological impact of growing old, as well as the possibility of living with a disabling condition in an unsuitable environment in the criminal justice system is therefore a major consideration. In one scoping study 80 per cent of older prisoners reported longstanding illness or disability. Thirty per cent have a diagnosis of depression (Howse 2003). Clear evidence exists of the links between crime and depression – whether it is fear of crime or the psychiatric prevalence among offenders (Office of National Statistics 1998).

There is now evidence that older prisoners' physical health is much worse compared to older people in the community (Tarbuck 2001). This disparity was compounded in the past by the lack of access to generalist NHS health care. We know from Azrini Wahidin's study of older women offenders that women's health needs are different from those of men – gynaecological problems and osteoporosis are significant issues for older women (Wahidin 2003). The neglect of health care is a 'grey area' as increasing incidents of neglect and abuse could be highlighted in the courts with reference to the Human Rights Act 1998.

One of the key issues here is that older offenders are being forced into a dependency which need not exist with access to proper health and social care. The vulnerabilities often associated with old age are exacerbated by lack of facilities in prison and lack of access to proper social care assessment as well as health assessment.

Social care needs

With increasing emphasis on health care there has been little consideration of the social care needs of older people in the criminal justice system. Social support cannot be underestimated as people grow older. The importance of social networks and social support is crucial in old age – in the realm of the fear of crime as well as for older offenders. We know that carers who abuse are often isolated; in relation to older sex offenders, network links with family and grandchildren can be severed and the consequences severe (Phillips 1996), although in relation to prison literature of other older offenders we know little about this. What we do know is that long term prisoners often have unrealistic and static conceptions of what their family relationships should be about (Jamieson and Grounds 2002). Support as prisoners grow older can also have an effect inside too. Lack of social stimulation through work in prison can lead to social death and exacerbate social care needs as offenders age (Jamieson and Grounds 2002). In a report by the Chief Inspector of Prisons in 2004 ('No Problems, Old and Quiet: Older Prisoners in England and Wales') health and social problems experienced by older offenders were highlighted, with inadequate responses by the prison service, bordering on abuse. Many older prisoners had problems with depression, incontinence, personal hygiene and mobility, exacerbated by the prison environment and lack of sensitivity to ageing issues by prison officers. Many felt unsafe as a consequence.

The above are all areas which have led to this issue coming onto the agenda in policy, practice, criminological and gerontological arenas. What can gerontology offer to the study of crime and older people? What can a critical gerontological perspective bring to this area? Taking this framework, a research agenda will be proposed as a way forward for an integrative approach.

Gerontological frameworks for understanding and investigating crime and older people

Wider theories of ageing

Gerontological theory can underpin research in this area. Disengagement theory and theories of productive ageing (forced disengagement) can apply. Theories of family violence and social learning theory are also useful in explaining crime in later life, yet these apply to any age group. Disengagement theory, where older people disengage from their functional roles in society and bio-psychological changes impact on individuals has been used in some research (Feinberg 1984) yet this, like many other theories, views ageing in a negative light. More recently the theory of 'healthy' or 'productive' ageing provides a more positive view with older people living longer, healthier and functional lives. In terms of criminal behaviour the likely explanation is that 'those who commit crimes in later life are affected by social, psychological and physiological resources' (Flynn 2000, p. 78). Crime in later life is viewed as a product of the varying effects of bio-psycho-social changes impacting on individuals as they reach a different stage in the life course. Theories incorporating all these aspects need to be considered.

One of the most important theoretical debates is the social constructivist debate on crime and older people. How crime and older people are socially constructed is crucial to add to our understanding. The argument stresses that older people are marginalised by society and are thrown into dependency and discriminated against through social forces and inequalities and not through biological processes. The criminal justice system, health and social care agencies may just reinforce this dependency. A critical perspective emerges from a social constructivist position and can underpin many of the gerontological issues below.

Definition, numbers and diversity

Much of the debate on older offenders is over how to define 'old'. Some studies define 'old' as aged 60+ (to compare with community samples of older people of pensionable age) or 70 (when health needs may increase), an arbitrary distinction in community as well as institutional studies. Within the prison system someone aged 30 can be viewed as 'old' by younger prisoners and staff. Several studies adopt a 50+ definition (Phillips 1996; Wahidin 2001). This definition is also based on the assumption that conditions associated with age are accelerated in prison and condensed in time periods so someone aged 50 is like someone aged 60 in the community. However, the categorisation is not adequately defined or explained and different studies use different age categories. Subjective age is often different again.

Consequently, ageing may be a better, more inclusive and non-stigmatising term. The focus on *ageing* is important in the struggle to define what is 'old'. By looking at ageing it engages younger prisoners who may need to think long term as lifers or their trajectory in their life of crime. This is a useful term because there are commonalities between young and older offenders – a life in flux, mentally, physically and biologically in transition from adolescence to adulthood or through coping with physical decline in old age; self-concepts and traits are similar – feelings of insecurity, inadequacy, lower tolerance of life, worries about the future and immediate survival, lack of work, time which is unstructured (Wolk 1963; Feinberg 1984). There is a need to think of ageing issues rather than a set age. In respect to the fear of crime, age itself is less important than other variables such as gender, past experience of abuse and violence and geographic location (Chadee and Ditton 2004).

Ageing can span 50 years – with very different groups within this age range; just as with research in the general population we have to be cautious in our definitions and assumptions of what should be badged under this term. This has particular significance for cross cultural and cross national research on this issue.

The diversity of older people is reflected in the different area of crime. Taking older offenders, for example – the profile of older prisoners is different from older people in the community; the experiences of 'career criminals' who have offended throughout their lives will be very different from the first time offender and different still from the lifer who has 'aged in place' – in prison. Such diversity therefore needs to be acknowledged in how we approach this topic. Not all older prisoners will be dependent and some younger offenders will suffer conditions and diseases associated with ageing.

Ageism

Consequently, the images of older people and crime are paternalistic: as vulnerable victims; the confused shoplifter, their behaviour seen as 'part of normal ageing' or jokingly referred to as old lags or 'mad or sad' (Midwinter 1990; Codd 1998). Thus, they have traditionally been treated more leniently by police than younger offenders.

Research is challenging these myths and notions of ageing criminals and notions of powerlessness, particularly as age spans all crime – sex offending, fraud and drug trafficking. Researchers have found that competence rather than irrationality characterises the actions of offenders and victims and a rights and justice approach should therefore be followed (Brogden and Nijhar 2000).

Gender

A further distinction needs to be made in terms of gender. The lack of a gender dimension in research is only partly justified by the low numbers of older women in the criminal justice system. Taking the older prison population as stated earlier they are predominantly men, sex offenders. Yet the high number of male sex offenders should not dominate and mask gender and age patterns (Bramhall 2004). The arena is ripe for a feminist analysis, beginning to emerge in the work of Helen Codd (1998) and Azrini Wahidin (2004). Older women tend to be imprisoned for fraud and drug offences; several are foreign nationals raising the issue of triple jeopardy as these women face racism as well as ageism and stigma. Not only is the nature of the crime an important distinction, but the experiences of men and women through the courts and how they are viewed within prisons is crucial. Fear of crime can also be distinguished in gender terms with women fearing burglary and men mugging in public places. In terms of elder abuse, there is research to show that there are gender-specific differences in the form and type of abuse which occur, women being more prone to neglect while men are more likely to physically abuse (Biggs, Phillipson and Kingston 1995). Helen Codd looks at how the media views ageing women offenders – castigating them as 'sad, bad or mad'; the powerful manipulative older woman; the good or bad carer or giving women a humorous portrayal (Codd 1998). However research needs to take women's offending seriously at whatever age.

The 'gero-graphy' of crime

Over the last 30 years there have been discussions about the influence of environment on crime, both in terms of its design and layout and accessibility of buildings and in the way space is controlled, used and observed (Herbert 1979). Until recently, little work looked at older people's views of space and place and the hazards of their environment in this respect.

Scharf, Phillipson and Smith (2002) illustrate the significance of environment, indicating that older people who live in deprived neighbourhoods are more vulnerable to crime than those living in other neighbourhoods. Of people participating in the survey 40 per cent had been victims of one or more types of crime in the 2 years prior to the interview. While crime surveys repeatedly show that older people are relatively unlikely to be victims of crime their study showed otherwise, particularly for ethnic minorities. Vulnerability to crime is linked to poverty and social inequality as many studies over the years have suggested (Social Exclusion Unit 2002). This is important to factor in to the current social exclusion agenda.

People's perceptions of place and time were also affected by their experience of crime. In relation to the fear of crime, time and space play important roles – feelings of insecurity about going out at night, particularly among women. Lower levels of satisfaction were reported with their neighbourhood among those reported as victims of crime. Neighbourhood satisfaction is also linked to older people's sense of identity. Dissatisfaction with a place can translate into a loss of identity and reduced quality of life for older people

No research however exists on how environment and space constrain or provide opportunities for older offenders to commit crimes or hide detection.

The dimensions of space, place and crime also raise a further issue of 'ageing in place' – particularly for lifers in prison. The debates on ageing in place have focused around people living in the community; the debate is yet to be extended to long-term institutions. There is very little in the literature on 'ageing in place' over long periods of time in residential and nursing institutions and we have little comparative data between institutions in the community and prisons. With lifer sentences increasing, this aspect will take on significance. Environmental disadvantage and limited physical activity is significant in knock-on effects of poor health and chronic disability (Marquart *et al.* 2000).

We know little of the experience of ageing to late old age in prison, the meaning of prison as 'home' or the uncertainties of how one's last days will be spent.

The physical environment of the prison – whether it is an old Victorian institution or modern purpose-built setting will influence how people experience later life in terms of their mobility and health; whether its location is local to contacts or distant (which a specialist prison for older offenders would be) away from family and friends will influence the psychology of how people perceive their environment. Again research does not exist in this area, partly due to the small numbers of older offenders in each prison.

Time

Time is another important concept within this framework. Ageing is synonymous with the passing of time. Azrini Wahidin (2001; 2004) in the first study of older women in prison in the UK looked at the significance of time for older women in prison. The meaning and use of time within prison was pivotal to their identities. Marking time inside however is very different from outside. Time inside becomes indefinite for some – empty:

> Time has stood still in that everything goes on and on in the same repetitive way. It is as if the nineteen years could have been fitted in one year. MM, age 53, 20 years in prison. (Wahidin 2001, p. 106)

In her study women stated their frustration in having to mark time until release; time which was mediated by rules and routines which can act as further punishment. 'Time is constructed to discipline and bring about the social death of the outside self through temporal and sensory deprivation' (Wahidin 2001, p. 118). The women in the study however found ways of surviving time and such strategies are important for research in this area. How older women cope with the stress of incarceration; what strategies they employ and how they view discontinuities with families, friends and life outside is crucial in a policy and practice agenda around resettlement

A study looking at ex-Republican prisoners serving long sentences found that many found it difficult to find purpose in the future and face irrevocable losses of time and life history (Jamieson and Grounds 2002).

Lifecourse

Related to time is the issue of lifecourse and life review. Lifelong confinement; recidivist or recalled or first timer will all have different experiences in relation to adaptation, coping mechanisms and adjustment to life in and out will vary depending on the group and individual life experiences.

Some in the criminal justice system will have spent their lives in crime. In Taylor and Parrot's 1988 study they found that older prisoners were just as likely as younger ones to have had previous convictions. The Centre for Policy on Ageing/Prison Reform Trust study found that 50 per cent of older offenders had previous convictions (Howse 2003).

The importance of lifestyles over the lifecourse will also have an impact. US studies found that many of the health problems of prisoners are from a lifetime of abuse – through smoking, drug taking and not necessarily a result of imprisonment – the onset of disabling conditions in prison will have major implications (Marquart *et al.* 2000).

In the realms of elder abuse, research shows us that complexities in relationships earlier in life have an impact on relationships in older age. Abuse as a child may be directed the other way in adulthood, although there is decreasing evidence to support the cycle of violence theory. Bridget Penhale (1995) notes the similarities between elder and child abuse transmission of violence across generations; the focus on attempts to control behaviour; and reluctance of society to admit family violence exists. Additionally, the imbalance of power and deprivation of rights can be attributed to the two arenas. Further, research looking at ambivalent and conflict relationships highlights the difficulties in providing care where previous abuse has taken place or for sex offenders (Phillips *et al.* 2003).

Life review and meaning of life

Taking stock of life and its achievements and disappointments may be a significant factor for older people. Thomas Cole stresses the need to recognise the importance of developing a new sense of meanings and purposes in the later half of life (Cole 1992). Telling a life story is essential to personhood in later life extending self control and expression in people's lives (Bornat 1994). The way that the situation is perceived by individuals involved and how they explain their circumstances is crucial. How do older people in the criminal justice system see themselves – as victims, offenders or as both? How do such people shape their identity and contribute to their quality of life?

Identity

Increasingly research is linking this to the issue of identity. The gerontological literature recognises that identities are available to people and are not simply as given – reconstruction of identity is possible; there are a number of ways of growing old beyond that of the myth of decline. To what extent can people involved in the criminal justice system take control of their identity? Estes, Biggs and Phillipson (2000) argue that older adults require elements of continuity and stability of identity as well as options for change. What factors restrict identity for those constrained by their socially constructed environment – in the community or in prison? As Wahidin found for older women prisoners:

'Most of us are walking around with masks on. The real people underneath, you seldom get to see' (Wahidin 2001, p. 183).

She examined how the gender assumptions and stereotypes of the lifecourse played out in a prison environment. Women were caught in both gendered and ageist expectations; they struggle to preserve a sense of self in an environment which attempts to reinvent the self.

A research agenda

Having mapped out what a critical gerontological perspective could add to this arena, the question is what research agenda needs to be highlighted? Time, gender, ageism, geography and lifecourse approaches all underpin the following three areas where we have little or no research. By adopting such a framework we can highlight the key issues for a research agenda; understand the processes involved in ageing and crime as well as develop appropriate policy and practice responses. The next section highlights three areas – transitions in and out of crime; listening to the voices of older offenders; policy and practice issues.

Transitions in and out of crime and the justice system

Earlier studies (Taylor and Parrot 1988; Thomas and Wall 1993) looked at how older people have been treated by police and the courts as offenders, yet there has been little work on what happens after prison, or while on probation (i.e. what social support and resettlement needs do they have? Who gets released and on what grounds if they are terminally ill for example?) What peer support exists outside? There is little research on older people as long- term victims although some work quoted earlier demonstrates the lasting adjustments people make as a result of crime – we need to know what makes older people resilient? What family and social relationships continue, particularly for the high number of sex offenders? What is the level and content of the provision of care and what is the role of formal agencies in resettlement? Who pays for their care if needing nursing or residential provision?

From limited research we know that inequality, homelessness, institutionalisation and a lack of role outside prison can perpetuate and encourage dependency, deny autonomy and can lead to recidivism. Prison-made inmates are destitute, homeless and dependent on the state as they have little entitlement while inside. Restoring to offenders some level of control and responsibility during their time in prison would at least give them some direction in life, yet few behavioural programmes are geared to the needs of older people. Ex-prisoners also have families who may find coping with life in their communities difficult (although most are not married). We need further research to see the wider impact of crime. Ware's study (2001) of offenders 50+ leaving prison, found that many experienced severe depression, hopelessness and despair. We also need more knowledge on the health and social care needs of older offenders across their sentence – with longer life expectancy and longer sentences, monitoring will be important for management decision making. Taking a longitudinal and lifecourse perspective in research will be crucial.

Voices of older offenders

In our research methods there is a need to be sensitive to the voices of older offenders and to take a narrative, biographical approach. Lifecourse approaches above have become more available in research

65

(Phillips 1996; Wahidin 2001; Frazer 2002; Jamieson and Grounds 2002), yet further insights are required to understand what it means to age as a victim or offender. Qualitative longitudinal approaches are crucial to an ageing and lifecourse perspective; in order to understand crime in later life we need biographies of crime.

Policy and practice issues

Research is also needed on the policy agenda. Two major questions to be discussed are:

1. *Should older people be treated as a separate group in the penal system?*

   There are arguments for and against this, yet little research has been carried out to inform policy and practice. There is evidence to suggest that prisoners don't want to be separate on the basis of age as they play a role within the mainstream prison population. Travel to and for family can significantly sever relationships if they are segregated into specialist provision. From the prison perspective older people provide stability in prison populations and hence this is good for the prison population. There are also issues around timing – at what point should someone be moved? This could be detrimental to their health needs and can be seen as a form of abuse. On the other hand, an age integrated approach, which currently operates has led to older prisoners' fear of abuse by younger prisoners and the lack of consideration to their health and social needs. More recent calls have been for a national strategy for assessing and providing for older prisoners' needs following evidence of neglect in the system (HMCIP Report 2004) and in coming to a decision on this issue.

2. *What policy perspectives should be followed – a welfare or justice approach? Needs or rights approach?*

   The criminal justice approach has only recently challenged the welfare approach. Brogden and Nijhar (2000) suggest that by focusing on a needs approach older people have been castigated as dependent, and incompetent; they are natural victims and attract crime. They advocate that a rights approach should be adopted – with legal and moral rights to health care and assessment by social workers for their social care needs. However, the question exists as to whether equivalent health and social care can be provided in prison following access to an assessment as it might be in the community?

Finally this leads to a consideration of a clear need to develop a research into practice agenda establishing:

1 A partnership at the interface between health and social care is crucial if there is to be an interdisciplinary approach and a single assessment to be used within prison. This may be hard to achieve, but research on the function of Primary Care Trusts in this respect will be necessary.

2 How to assess risk? Risk assessment of frail older people is a specialist job. Issues such as autonomy versus the protection of self and others as well as disability and mobility issues are crucial to add to the assessment of risk. Research-based approaches to assessment can assist in this task.

3 How can a positive ageing agenda be applied in practice in this arena of crime and older people?

4 Ageism and triple jeopardy can lead to suspicion; rejection, feelings of no hope, and hostility after release. A focus on the level of support prior to and following release and resettlement should be the subject of a programme of research, including family ties, employment prospects etc.

5 More appropriate rehabilitation and resettlement practices need evaluation.

6 Good practice examples and better statistics are still in short supply and need expansion and wider demonstration. This may involve investigating international projects and those spanning all age groups, for example, restorative justice – applying approaches used with younger offenders to ageing populations.

7 A national strategy for older prisoners incorporating research on the above issue is a crucial step forward.

Conclusion

A lack of knowledge and conceptual frameworks surrounds crime and older people. Consequently policy has been localised and responsive. This chapter argues that we need to take an ageing and lifecourse approach to these issues to unravel the key issues for a research agenda in the twenty-first century. There are a number of policy and practice debates which need to take place before we embark on a strategy of segregating older offenders, looking at crime and old age as separate from crime and the general population and considering age as the key variable in research. Many of the issues affecting older people will affect younger members of society. There is a need for more empirical research incorporating an integrated gerontological and criminological perspective if we are to be able to make sound policy and practice decisions such as these.

References

Aday, R.H. (2003) *Ageing Prisoners: Crisis in American Corrections.* Westport, CT: Praeger Publishers.

Biggs, S. Phillipson, C. and Kingston, P. (1995) *Elder Abuse in Perspective.* Buckingham: Open University Press.

Bornat, J. (ed.) (1984) *Reminiscence Reviewed.* Buckingham: Open University Press.

Bramhall, G. (2004) 'Older Offenders and Community Penalties', Paper given at the *Ageing, Crime and Society* Conference, Royal Statistical Society, London: March.

Brogden, M. and Nijhar, P. (2000) *Crime, Abuse and the Elderly.* Cullompton: Willan Publishing.

Chadee, D. and Ditton, J. (forthcoming) 'Are Older People Most Afraid of Crime? Revisiting Ferraro and La Grange in Trinidad', *British Journal of Criminology* ND.

Codd, H. (1998) 'Older Women, Criminal Justice and Women's Studies' in *Women's Studies International Forum,* 21 (2): 183–92.

Cole, T. (1992) *The Journey of Life: A Cultural History of Aging in America.* Cambridge: Cambridge University Press.

Department of Health (2001) *National Service Framework for Older People.* London: HMSO.

Estes, C. Biggs, S and Phillipson, C. (2003) *Social Theory, Social Policy and Ageing: A Critical Introduction.* Buckingham: Open University Press.

Fazel, S., Hope, T., O'Donnell, I. and Jacoby, R. (2001) 'Hidden Psychiatric Morbidity in Elderly Prisoners', *British Journal of Psychiatry,* 179: 535–39.

Feinberg, G. (1984) 'A Profile of the Elderly Shoplifter' in E. Newman, D. Newman and N. Gerwritz (eds) *Elderly Criminals.* Oelgeschlager, pp. 46–8. Cambridge: Gunn and Hain.

Flynn, E. (2000) 'Elders as Perpetrators' in M. Rothman, B. Dunlop and P. Entzel (eds) *Elders, Crime and the Criminal Justice System,* pp. 43–80. New York: Springer.

Frazer, L. (2002) *Ageing Inside: A Study of Older Prisoners in England and Wales: Prevalence, Profile and Policy.* Unpublished MSc in Policy Research, University of Bristol.

Help the Aged (2002a) *Older People and Fear of Crime.* London: Help the Aged.

Help the Aged (2002b) *Tackling Older People's Fear of Crime.* London: Help the Aged.

Herbert, D. (1979) 'Urban Crime: A Geographical Perspective' in D. Herbert and D. Smith (eds) *Social Problems and the City*, pp. 117–138. Oxford: Oxford University Press.

Her Majesty's Chief Inspector of Prisons (2004) *No Problems, Old and Quiet: Older Prisoners in England and Wales,* A Thematic Report. London: The Home Office.

Howse, K. (2003) *Growing Old in Prison: A Scoping Study on Older Prisoners.* London: Centre for Policy on Ageing and Prison Reform Trust.

Jamieson, R. and Grounds, A. (2002) *No Sense of an Ending: The Effects of Long-term Imprisonment amongst Republican Prisoners and their Families.* Monaghan, Republic of Ireland: SEESYU Press.

Marquart, J., Merianos, D. and Doucet, G. (2000) 'The Health Related Concerns of Older Prisoners: Implications for Policy', *Ageing and Society*, 20: 79–96.

McCreadie, C. (1996) *Elder Abuse: Update on Research.* London: King's College.

Midwinter, E. (1990) *The Old Order: Crime and Older People.* London: Centre for Policy on Ageing.

Office of National Statistics (1998) *Psychiatric Morbidity among Prisoners.* London: HMSO.

Peace, S., Kellaher, L. and Willcocks, D. (1997) *Re-evaluating Residential Care.* Buckingham: Open University Press.

Penhale, B. (1995) 'Similarities, Differences and Synthesis' in P. Kingston and B. Penhale (eds) *Family Violence and the Caring Professions*, pp. 245–61. Basingstoke: Macmillan.

Phillips, J. (1996) 'Crime and Older Offenders', *Practice* 8 (1): 43–55.

Phillips, J. Ray, M. and Ogg, J. (2003) *Ambivalence and Conflict in Ageing Families: European Perspectives*, Retraite et Societe, No. 38: 80–108 L'Europe du grand age: entre families et institutions, Caissse Nationale D'assurance Vieillesse, Paris.

Phillipson, C. Bernard, M. Phillips, J. and Ogg, J. (2001) *The Family and Community Life of Older People.* London: Routledge.

Rothman, M., Dunlop, B. and Entzel, P. (2000) *Elders, Crime and The Criminal Justice System – Myth, Perceptions, and Reality in the 21st Century.* New York: Springer.

Scharf, T., Phillipson, C., Smith, A. and Kingston, P. (2002) *Growing Older in Socially Deprived Areas: Social Exclusion in Later Life.* London: Help the Aged.

Social Exclusion Unit (2002) *Reducing Re-offending by Ex-prisoners*. London: Social Exclusion Unit.

Tarbuck, A. (2001) 'Health of Elderly Prisoners', *Age and Ageing*, 30: 369–70.

Taylor, P. and Parrot, J. (1988) 'Elderly Offenders', *British Journal of Psychiatry*, 152: 340–46.

The *Guardian* 30 January 2001, 'Old Timers' in *G2*.

Thomas, T. and Wall, G. (1993) 'Investigating Older People who Commit Crime', *Elders: Journal of Care and Practice*, 2: 53–60.

Townsend, P. (1956) *The Family Life of Older People*. London: Routledge and Kegan Paul.

Townsend, P. (1962) *The Last Refuge*. London: Routledge and Kegan Paul.

Wahidin, A. (2001) *Life in the Shadows: A Qualitative Study of Older Women in Prison*. Unpublished PhD thesis, Keele University.

Wahidin, A. (2003) 'Women, Old Age and The Prison System' in *Criminal Justice Matters*, Autumn, 53: 38–40.

Wahidin, A. (2004) *Older Women in the Criminal Justice System: Running Out of Time*. London: Jessica Kingsley.

Ware, S. (2001) 'Alone, Elderly and still Banged Up', *The Howard League Magazine*, 19 (2): 8.

Williams, B. (1999) *Working with Victims of Crime: Policies, Politics and Practice*. London: Jessica Kingsley.

Wolk, A. (1963) 'The Geriatric Delinquent' in *Journal of American Geriatrics Society*, 11 (7): 653–9.

Chapter 5

'As if I just didn't exist' – elder abuse and neglect in nursing homes

Thomas Görgen

Introduction

The chapter reports results from a multi-method study on elder abuse and neglect in German nursing homes. Its focus is on qualitative interviews in a sample of eight facilities. Interviews provide evidence on the phenomenology of elder abuse and neglect in residential care. The chapter covers physical abuse, psychological abuse and verbal aggression, neglect, inappropriate uses of mechanical and chemical restraints and paternalistic and infantilising behaviour. Data from a questionnaire study among nursing home staff and from an analysis of public prosecutor files complement the results of the interview study. The text discusses the relative contributions of different data types and the importance of using multiple perspectives in the study of elder abuse and neglect in residential care.

During the last decade, elder abuse and neglect in nursing homes have become topics of media reports and political debate in Germany. TV documentaries bear titles like: 'Nursing home nightmare' or 'You'd better not grow old'. Reports about deficient care around some local protective services have been established and manifestos have been issued (cf. Aktion gegen Gewalt in der Pflege 1999). To a considerable degree, this discussion dates back to the implementation of mandatory long-term care insurance in Germany in 1995/96. One major deficiency of the law upon which this insurance is founded is its emphasis upon physical handicap and frailty and its underestimation of resources needed to care for the demented elderly (Klie 1998).

Since 'abuse' has strong sexual overtones in German, the term 'violence' is more common. The German discussion on 'violence against the elderly' is characterised by a broad concept of 'violence' which includes neglect and non-physical forms of maltreatment. However, discourse focuses largely upon one specific type of 'violence in elder-care', i.e. neglect caused by structural deficiencies, especially by staff shortage (Görgen 2003b).

Victimisation of elderly people in general and elder abuse in long-term care in particular are topics for which large-scale standardised victim surveys are of limited value. This approach must be supplemented (or replaced) by the use of multiple other data sources (cf. Pillemer 1988). A German study on elder abuse and neglect in nursing homes (Görgen 2003a; 2004) combined qualitative interviews in nursing homes, a questionnaire survey among nursing home staff, and an analysis of cases of elder abuse and neglect known to criminal courts and state survey agencies (see Table 5.1 for sample characteristics and sizes).

An interview study on abuse and neglect in residential long-term care

Two hundred and fifty-one semi-structured interviews were conducted in eight nursing homes in the Federal State of Hesse in central Germany. Homes were randomly chosen from a comprehensive registry of long-term care institutions. In the course of the sampling process, 14 nursing homes were contacted, 6 of which refused to participate. Interviews were conducted with nursing home owners and administrators, a multitude of sub-groups of staff working in the fields of care and social work, residents, their family members, friends and legal guardians, doctors, clergy, and state survey agencies (Table 5.2). Residents, staff and management were interviewed on-site. The average length of the interviews was about one hour. They were transcribed and analysed through a complex process combining computer-assisted content-analysis and structured discussions of each interview by the research team.

For each interview, a summary judgement of the respective nursing home was calculated. Table 5.3 shows that these overall judgements were generally favourable. The most positive views were expressed by nursing home managers on the one hand and residents on the other.

Table 5.1 Methodological Approaches in the Study on Elder Abuse and Neglect in Residential Care

No.	Methodological approach	Sample size
1	In-depth interviews in nursing homes; multiple sub-samples	251 interviews in eight nursing homes
2	Questionnaire survey among nurses working in residential long-term care	361 nurses
3	Analysis of public prosecutor files of cases of elder abuse in nursing homes/expert survey among state survey agencies; standardised data from on-site checks	35 files/188 on-site checks

Source: Görgen 2003a; 2004.

Table 5.2 Sub-samples of Interview Study

(251 interviews in eight nursing homes, Germany, 1999/2000)

Sub-sample	N	%
Residents	63	25.1
Management	17	6.8
Nursing staff	81	32.3
Other staff (e.g. social workers)	15	6.0
Volunteers	9	3.6
Residents´ family members and friends	17	6.8
'External experts' (clergy, doctors, legal guardians)	42	16.7
State survey agencies	7	2.8

Source: Görgen 2003a; 2004.

There are, of course, negative evaluations by residents, like an 81-year old man saying 'I must live a life that does not suit me, a non-life. It's a non-life in here. No violin, no accordion, nothing erotic'. A closer look reveals that residents' positive judgements do not exclusively reflect satisfaction, but also attitudes of modesty and denial of one's own needs. As a 91-year-old female resident put it, 'I wouldn't say anything

Table 5.3 Interview Study: Summary Judgements of Nursing Homes by Sub-samples of Interviewees

(251 interviews in eight nursing homes, Germany, 1999/2000; five-point scale from 1 = 'very positive' to 5 = 'very negative'; ratings based on interview transcripts)

Sample	N	M	SD	% Negative judgements	% Positive judgements
Residents	63	1.89	1.02	11.1	85.7
Management	17	1.88	0.70	0.0	82.4
Nursing staff	81	2.28	1.06	19.8	65.4
Other staff (e.g. social workers, volunteers)	24	2.04	0.91	8.3	75.0
Residents' family members and friends	17	2.06	0.97	11.8	76.5
'External experts' (clergy, doctors, legal guardians)	42	1.93	0.97	7.1	78.6
State survey agencies	7	2.43	0.79	14.3	71.4

N = Number
M = Mean
SD = Standard deviation
Source: Görgen 2003a; 2004.

bad about other people [i.e. the nursing staff]. I don't do such things'. A 77-year-old woman stated, 'I can't complain […] I have to be glad that such places exist, [so] that I can stay in here'. If residents regard any criticism as morally reprehensible, if their overall satisfaction is founded upon the perceived lack of alternatives, their opportunities to exercise consumer sovereignty are limited. Such attitudes may be especially characteristic of the present older generation. The inability of severely demented patients 'to evaluate quality information or to act rationally given such information' (Eika 2003, p. 7) is a stable feature that will inevitably continue to impede consumer sovereignty (and has led to the factual exclusion of dementia patients' voices from the interview sample). Individual barriers combine with structural features of health care systems in which nursing home residents are recipients of services rather than customers who decide how to invest their financial resources. Weak consumer sovereignty has been cited as implying low quality-effective demand and substandard quality in long-term care (Eika 2003; Meyer 2001). However, usefulness and adequacy of measures to enhance consumer sovereignty in long-term care are disputed (Williams 1994).

Predominantly positive judgements of life and work in a specific nursing home do not mean absence of deficiencies. Table 5.4 presents data from interviews with nurses on different types of resident abuse and neglect. Questions were not restricted to standardised reference periods. More than two thirds of the nurses reported they had behaved abusively or neglectfully at least once or had observed such behaviour. Most interviewees described rather less severe incidents. Paternalism and infantilisation, psycho-social neglect and psychological abuse and verbal aggression were reported more frequently than physical abuse, neglectful care or the inappropriate use of restraints.

The similarity of prevalence rates for self-reported and observed behaviours is partly due to the fact that the interview time was sometimes too short to ask extensively about observed incidents when subjects elaborated on their own behaviour.

Table 5.4 Interview Study: Behaviour Reported by Nursing staff (As Actor/ As Observer)

(Life-time prevalence; 81 interviews in nursing homes, Germany, 1999/2000)

Behaviour	Subject as Actor		Subject as Observer	
	N	%	N	%
1. Physical abuse	16	19.8	17	21.0
2. Psychological abuse/verbal aggression	30	37.0	46	56.8
3. Inappropriate use of mechanical restraints	12	14.8	9	11.1
4. Inappropriate use of chemical restraints	10	12.3	17	21.0
5. Neglectful care	22	27.2	32	39.5
6. Psychosocial neglect	29	35.8	29	35.8
7. Paternalism/infantilisation	46	56.8	38	46.9
At least one of behaviours 1 to 7	**57**	**70.4**	**63**	**77.8**

Source: Görgen 2003a; 2004.

Physical abuse of nursing home residents

There were only a small number of straightforward reports from victims and relatively few self-reported incidents of physical violence from nursing staff. The latter fall into one of three categories: (1) non-intentional infliction of pain; (2) use of coercion during nursing activities to enforce residents' compliance; and (3) impulsive reactions to aggressive behaviour from residents. Most cases reported by nurses were of low to moderate severity and put little blame and guilt on the actor. The picture changes if reports from observers are included. For example:

- A female nursing home director describes the case of a male registered nurse on a night watch. He was about to finish his shift when he had to wash a demented female resident who had soiled herself and her bed. He cut the old lady's fingernails with toenail scissors in a very rough manner and hurt her severely. He was dismissed summarily.

- A male nursing home director mentions an attack of a male head nurse against a mentally ill resident: 'The [male] resident approached the nurse, and he inadequately tried to keep him at arm's length by kicking him – an excess reaction. As he was a senior staff member we had to say "no, that's intolerable".'

- The 81-year-old husband of a demented resident reports an incident witnessed by people from an office building opposite the nursing home. These employees called the police when they saw how a nurse beat the interviewee's wife. The victim's husband said: 'I do believe that she hit her. But my wife had soiled herself and had grabbed her faeces with her hands. It was a kind of reflex movement, but they [the witnesses] interpreted it in a different manner.'

- A 51-year-old nursing aide reports: 'There was a time, when residents [living on her ward] frequently had haematoma in the morning.' She suspected a nurse on the night shift of abusing demented residents who behaved aggressively. She did not communicate her suspicions to anyone. 'I had a suspicion, but, you know, suspecting and proving [are two different things]...'.

These examples indicate how differently witnesses react to cases of physical violence. The nurses in the study mainly described cases in which they failed to intervene in cases of abuse. Although incidents demanded management to take measures against the offender, it was apparent that some managers adopted a wait-and-see stance. There was no linear relationship between the severity of the incident and celerity and severity of intervention.

In a number of the most severe cases, nurses on night duty were named as offenders or suspects. Night shifts are generally characterised by a skeleton staff. This can mean that they are over-stretched and unable to cope with the level of work. Abuses are hard to detect if physical violence is directed against residents who suffer from dementia or are otherwise unable to communicate and if acts are committed in ways that leave little or no unmistakable physical traces.

In several severe cases of physical maltreatment, nurses' behaviour seemed to be triggered by residents' faecal incontinence. At least in some nursing homes and wards, faecal incontinence appears to be a constant topic among nurses. Some nurses lack professional skills and knowledge and react to incontinence in an emotionally upset manner as if soiling resulted from intentional behaviour. A female occupational therapist put it this way: 'They speak about it [faecal incontinence] with a great deal of aggression, with anger. They do not talk about it in a matter of fact way. Sometimes it happens when the nurse has just put on new sheets – and the nurse reacts as if it was directed at her.'

Psychological abuse/verbal aggression

The interviews contain numerous reports from actors, victims and witnesses about non-physical incidents of abuse by nurses. Impolite and verbally aggressive behaviour is much more common than physical abuse. A 33-year-old male nurse said: 'I've often heard yelling, I've never seen slapping.' A 55-year-old clergyman phrased his impressions of nurse–resident-interactions this way: 'There is a certain level of snottiness.'

Interviews with nurses reveal tendencies to normalise and neutralise verbally aggressive behaviour. Three main lines of reasoning are discernable:

• Verbal aggression is an excusable 'only human' reaction to work stress (a 39-year-old nursing aide: 'Sometimes, I raise my voice. It simply has to get out. After all, I'm only human.')

• Verbally aggressive behaviour performed with the intent to control or to shape residents' behaviour is regarded as legitimate and indispensable to maintain a reasonable degree of order within the institution. A male nurse states: [some residents are] 'quite stubborn. I must get a bit louder, otherwise it doesn't work'.

• Some nurses expressed the view that their conduct is justified by residents' previous aggressive behaviour. A 59-year-old ward nurse said: 'When this resident yells at me, "You're a lesbian! A pig!", and so on, it may happen that I yell back at her. Otherwise, she won't understand what she has done to me.'

In many cases, norms by which nurses judge nurse–resident-interactions differ from norms in extra-mural interactions between service suppliers and clients. They are similar to norms governing interactions between parents and children or within hierarchically structured institutions. Some institutions appear to be at least ambiguous in the standards of conduct they convey to staff. A 17-year-old female volunteer said: 'Residents don't have the right to yell at us. If they do, we may yell back. That's what the nursing home told us.'

Besides verbal aggression, interviewees report other behaviour that violates residents' dignity and sense of shame. Some of this behaviour emerges from a lack of sensibility and empathy. For example, a female nursing director reports that when she started her job as director, it was common for nurses to leave doors open while washing or toileting residents. Other incidents of humiliating behaviour include putting on diapers to save time and against a competent person's declared will, or refusing to help an old woman to put on a bra, saying that 'it's useless, it's hanging, it's flabby'.

Like physical abuse, incidents of verbal aggression are sometimes prompted by faecal and urinary incontinence and by nurses' feelings of disgust. Residents' non-compliance is a further risk factor. In a couple of cases residents complained about nurses expecting and demanding more functional autonomy than they actually possessed and reacting impatiently to apparent 'non-compliance'. A 92-year-old female resident speaks about a nurse yelling at her: 'Because she thinks, I could do more myself. … But I can't. My fingers are all stiff.' A young female volunteer says about a colleague: 'When a resident asked her to help her straighten up her underwear she started yelling, "Yesterday you did it on your own, so you can do it on your own today as well!".'

Other behaviour aims directly at humiliating and hurting residents. A nursing home director reports how a demented woman was victimised by a group of nurses: 'I heard hooting and applause. When I reached the first floor, there were four or five nurses surrounding a demented resident who was naked, and they cheered her on to dance naked in the hall. I stopped this ... Those who were remorseful got away with a meeting with the director. But we had to fire two who remained unapologetic about what they did, arguing that "it wasn't all that bad" and "the woman seemed to enjoy it"'. In this case, the nurses' collective behaviour was intended to degrade the care recipient. To justify it, the offenders used arguments which further insulted and denigrated the victim.

Neglect

There are few reports of specific incidents of neglect, but a lot of statements about the consequences of staff shortage in especially critical time periods (i.e. weekends, nightshifts, school holidays, times when many nurses report sick). Under conditions of time pressure and inadequate staffing, nursing is reduced to basic and indispensable activities at the expense of holistic care and psychosocial support.

As far as neglectful care is concerned, deficiencies are reported mainly in the fields of personal hygiene (bathing, washing, shaving, nail care, toileting, clothing), pressure sore prevention and patient positioning, mobilisation and activation. An employee of a state survey agency speaks of 'makeshift care' especially on weekends. A young female volunteer reports that personal hygiene is sometimes 'reduced to a cat's lick'. More severe incidents of neglect include residents lying in their excrement for hours or the intentional use of cheaper but less absorbent diapers at night: 'Some colleagues use only thin diapers in the evening ... In the morning, sometimes people were wet to the bone' (a 33-year-old male nurse).

Such deficiencies not only present health risks, but affect people's self-esteem and sense of dignity. As a 30-year-old legal guardian put it: 'They still notice such things ... It hurts their dignity ... When I said to staff, "Isn't it a bit filthy, that jacket?" or "Hasn't she been wearing that jacket for 5 or 6 weeks?", they answered "Well, she'll soil her clothes again, anyway".'

Time pressure impedes strengthening residents' resources and preserving their functional capacities and autonomy (an occupational therapist: 'He might be able to wash himself. But nurses do not have the time to wait until he has finished'). Nurses sometimes intentionally use strategies to reduce residents' demand for care: 'If someone rings the bell one hundred times a day, it may happen that one forgets to put the bell within that person's reach' (a nursing home director).

In most nursing homes there appears to be permanent neglect in the psycho-social field. Many residents complain about this and nurses report it as unavoidable under present staffing conditions. Some interview excerpts illustrate how residents suffer from a lack of meaningful communication and personal closeness. An 81-year-old woman describes her everyday interactions as follows: 'They [nurses] rush in. "Good morning!" They wash me, and that was it – for the whole day!' Another 81-year-old says: 'Haven't spoken to anyone for a couple of days. As if I just didn't exist.' An 86-year-old female resident describes the change she experienced after the institution she lived in moved to a new building: 'The old house, it was primitive, very primitive. But I felt at ease there … It was private. It wasn't like this one. It was a completely different relationship. People had time to talk to you … It was primitive, but … it was all so close.'

Risk of neglect is especially high for those who cannot speak out for themselves, i.e. the most severely handicapped and demented residents. Contrary to physical violence, neglect is often not seen as something for which the nurse is individually responsible and can be blamed: rather it appears as a structural problem ('You can't blame it on the nurse. It's a political problem' – as an employee of a state survey agency stated).

Inappropriate use of restraints

A rather complex picture emerged concerning the use of mechanical and chemical restraints (i.e. devices used to inhibit free movement or to control behaviour). As far as standard mechanical devices like belts, bed rails or 'geri-chairs' are concerned, there was a high degree of rule consciousness and compliance with rules among nurses. According to nurses, managers, and external experts, permanent or repeated use of mechanical restraints without a court order has become rare in the course of the last decade. Reform of German guardianship law in 1992 with its emphasis on principles of self-determination and rights preservation appears to have actually strengthened the residents' position.

On the other hand, there are a number of more subtle functional equivalents to the aforementioned mechanical restraints. Two examples may illustrate this.

- A 67-year-old female resident reported that staff tried to stop her from leaving the building: '"If you do that again', she said, "we'll lock you up in your room".' In this case, freedom of movement is not restricted by physical barriers or devices. Instead, compliance is enforced by a threat to confine this resident to her room.

- There were reports of nurses restricting residents' freedom by arranging furniture in ways that impeded freedom of movement. 'To keep her seated, we surrounded her chair with tables', a nursing aide said; the daughter of a resident reported that she found her mother 'sandwiched in so that she could not run away'.

Other cases include staff deliberately not helping residents to get out of bed or to rise from their chair. Often, nurses do not regard such techniques of restraining a person's freedom as subject to approval by a court. Although in most cases they are applied with the intent to protect residents from hazards (falls, traffic accidents, etc.), lack of external control makes them 'insidious forms of restraint' (Bennett, Kingston and Penhale 1997, p. 88).

Few nurses are aware of the functional and legal similarities between the use of sedatives and of mechanical restraints to control a person's behaviour. In German law, both are regarded as measures equivalent to coercive institutional placement (German Civil Code, Art. 1896 No. 4). Typically, staff members refer to medical prescriptions to explain and justify the application of sedatives. However, interviews show that psychoactive medication is not only used for medical reasons, but also to control residents' behaviour. Sedatives are given to residents who behave aggressively, to those who want to leave the nursing home, who are loud, who resist care, or who harass nurses sexually. The nurses' actual influence is extensive. In many cases their reports to doctors are at the starting point of prescriptions of psycho-active medication. As a 55-year-old general practitioner put it: 'You depend upon what nurses tell you. You can't be there 24 hours …Even the best neurologist can be duped if the information isn't correct.' A 43-year-old registered nurse confirms this view: 'He [the doctor] relies upon what nurses tell him. What else should he do?' Especially if medication is not prescribed scheduled but on an as-needed basis, staff have so much influence concerning amount and timing of medication.

With regard to the inappropriate use of sedatives there are multiple opportunities for committing offences and for protecting oneself from detection and prosecution. As far as motivational aspects are concerned, there are cases of inappropriate restraint use in which restraints are imposed for the purposes of discipline or convenience (cf. Parmelee and Lawton 1990). The interviews show that management puts an emphasis upon autonomy and we found that 'frontline nurses' are often strongly biased towards security.

Paternalistic and infantilising behaviour

The interviews contain numerous examples of paternalistic and infantilising behaviour and attitudes towards the residents. The residents and those suffering from dementia in particular were compared to children whose behaviour had to be controlled and restricted. For example, a 40-year-old aide said: 'Sometimes you have to talk to them like … in kindergarten'. Another nursing aide put it this way: 'Rules may not always be pleasant for the individual … But it starts in kindergarten: children must learn that they are not the only ones. And here, it's the same.'

In some interviews, residents' dependence appears as a prerequisite of work attractiveness as nurses speak about the emotional importance of being needed. A 54-year-old aide said: 'I need someone I can mother. I just need that … Children and old people are almost equal.' Another (60-year old) aide spoke about her choice of the nursing profession: 'I don't have children. … So, I could give all my love to the elderly. They are my children.'

Reports of authoritarian behaviour towards residents demonstrate power differences between nurses and residents and the perceived need to discipline and control the latter. A 59-year-old aide stated that some residents were 'spoiled' and needed 'clear boundaries'. Another example is a 51-year-old nurse who describes how she sent a resident who had insulted her to her room.

Nurses also describe acts of 'benevolent coercion', that is, using physical force or deception in the perceived interest of the resident. Such views and behaviour are mainly characteristic of less qualified staff. Some nursing aides, when speaking about their work, refer to experiences they had when raising their own children, thus deriving professional norms of conduct from the private sphere.

A questionnaire study among nurses in residential eldercare

Three hundred and sixty one nursing home employees participated in a questionnaire survey that was conducted at 27 nursing homes in a metropolitan area in central Germany. The response rate amounted to 36 per cent. As the survey was conducted in German, the highly multi-national composition of nursing home staff was an obstacle to a higher rate. Eighty-one per cent of the sample were female and the mean age of the respondents was 41 years. Sixty-three per cent of the subjects were qualified nurses, the remainder were mainly people with only a short professional training as nursing aides.

Drawing on the *Conflict Tactics Scales* (Straus 1979) and the instrument used by Pillemer and Moore (1989), the questionnaire listed 46 acts and omissions which might be regarded as abusive or neglectful if directed against residents. Of the total sample 71.5 per cent reported at least one incident during the last twelve months (Table 5.5). Non-physical abuse and neglectful care were reported by more than 50 per cent. Prevalence rates of self-reported psycho-social neglect, inappropriate use of mechanical restraints and physical abuse were between 24 per cent and 30 per cent.

A figure of 71.2 per cent reported having witnessed at least one incident performed by a colleague during the previous 12 months. Again, verbally aggressive behaviour and neglectful care was the most common form of abuse. Thirty-five per cent said they had witnessed incidents of physical abuse of residents by staff members. Similarly to the interviews, the number of nurses reporting any type of observed abuse or neglect was almost identical to the number of subjects reporting such behaviour as their own. But for any specific type of abuse or neglect, the prevalence of observed behaviour is larger than that of self-reports.

Most reports of physical violence referred to actions that were performed in the course of nursing activities (e.g. intentionally touching a resident in a rough manner, holding a resident's nose to force him to open his mouth). Very few nurses reported severe forms of physical maltreatment like beating a resident or intentionally bathing him or her in too hot water. Between 2 and 4 per cent indicated they had intentionally pinched, pushed or shoved a resident.

Contrary to what had been expected, the overall ratio of residents to nurses on subjects' wards was uncorrelated to the total number of self-reported offences or to any of the offence categories (like physical abuse or neglectful care). However, *the correlation between the ratio of residents to registered nurses and self-reported incidents was significant* ($r = .22$, $p<.01$). This picture was even more clear cut for observed incidents for which the *correlation with the ratio of residents to registered nurses* was ($.35$, $p<.001$); again, the number of observed incidents was uncorrelated to the overall ratio of residents to nurses. With regard

Table 5.5 Victimisation of Residents by Nurses During Previous 12 Months

(Survey among nursing home staff comprising 361 participants, Germany, 2001)

Behaviour	Self-reported		Observed	
	Yes	%	Yes	%
1. Physical abuse	85	23.5	126	34.9
2. Psychological abuse/verbal aggression	194	53.7	223	61.8
3. Inappropriate use of mechanical restraints	102	28.3	142	39.3
4. Inappropriate use of chemical restraints	20	5.5	45	12.5
5. Neglectful care	194	53.7	215	59.6
6. Psychosocial neglect	107	29.6	123	34.1
7. Sexual abuse/sexual harassment	0	–	4	1.1
At least one of types 1 to 7	**258**	**71.5**	**257**	**71.2**

Source: Görgen 2003a; 2004.

to abuse prevention, a high percentage of qualified nurses may be a more effective way to reduce residents' risk of victimisation than merely increasing the number of nursing staff at a given ward.

Self-reported abuse and neglect correlates significantly with ratios of residents with special impairments (suffering from dementia or incontinence or being wheelchair-bound) to registered nurses (r between .26 and .27, p<.01). Nurses who report high numbers of abusive and neglectful acts and omissions show little satisfaction with their job (r = -.18, p<.01) and with their superiors (r = -.22, p<.01); in particular, they report frequent conflicts with the head nurse (r = -26, p<.001). The number of self-reported offences tends to be larger when nurses report many physically aggressive acts from residents (r = .40, p<.001). Nurses who report many incidents show stronger symptoms of emotional exhaustion (r = .32, p<.001). They tend to use alcohol (r = .40, p<.001) and medical drugs (r = .28, p<.001) as means of coping with stress.

An analysis of public prosecutor files on cases of institutional elder abuse and neglect

Thirty five public prosecutor files on cases of elder abuse and neglect in nursing homes were analysed, most of them originating in the years 1998 to 2000. Analysis of this sample shows two prototypical cases.

The first refers to neglect and insufficient medical treatment. Usually, incidents are reported to police by relatives of severely ill or already deceased residents. They typically sue for bodily injury, negligent homicide, or maltreatment of wards (German Penal Code, Art. 225). The typical victim is over 80 years old, suffers from multiple diseases, and has severe decubitus ulcers. These ulcers finally cause relatives to demand criminal prosecution. Typically, cases are filed against nursing home managers and executive nursing staff, sometimes also against physicians. Usually, these cases end with a dismissal of criminal proceedings (according to Art. 153, 153a and 170 II of the German Procedural Code). Police, public prosecutors and judges are confronted with multiple problems. For example, the causal connections between nurses' behaviour and victim's bodily harm or even death often cannot be proven with sufficient certainty. Individual responsibility for an omission and culpability within complex institutional structures are hard to determine. In some cases, police are informed weeks or even months after the incident was first detected by relatives. The evidence often consists mainly of relatives' testimonies.

The second type refers to cases of physical maltreatment and sexual abuse by nursing home staff or managers. Typically, either the victim or a colleague of the offender informs the police or public prosecutors. In most cases, the offender is convicted. Cases of elder abuse in nursing homes in general and of neglect in particular present serious problems for police investigations especially if one or more of the following conditions are present:

1. the victim is dead, demented or otherwise unable to communicate;
2. there are no competent third party eyewitnesses;
3. there is a large delay between the offence and its first report to police;
4. indicators of abuse and neglect are insufficient or at best ambiguous;
5. documentation of nursing activities is inadequate;
6. responsibility for an omission is hard to determine within complex institutional hierarchies.

The chances of conviction are small and in some cases, the police seemed to accept without further investigation the managers' or nurses' statements that a resident could not be questioned because of his/her physical or mental health status. Furthermore, many cases of neglect mainly reflect structural problems of residential care – especially insufficient staffing.

Methodological implications

The study of institutional elder abuse confronts researchers with a multitude of methodological problems. While standardised victimisation surveys are often regarded as the best method to determine prevalence and incidence of crime and problem behaviour, they are of little use if applied to subjects who are unable to report and evaluate things reliably or even to read a questionnaire or to hear or understand interview questions. Nurses can be asked about possible incidents of abuse or neglect committed by themselves or by colleagues, but not everyone will be motivated to respond comprehensively and frankly. Institutional data on abuse and neglect are always limited to incidents and deficiencies that are known to the respective agencies.

In a field where validity of every single method is severely limited, methodological triangulation (cf. Flick 1992) in the sense of researchers applying multiple research techniques to the same topic can be an appropriate strategy. In the present study, an approach combining quantitative and qualitative data, a multitude of perspectives and data on detected and undetected cases has contributed to a more comprehensive picture of abuse and neglect in long-term care.

- In-depth interviews in nursing homes permit detailed analysis of violent episodes. Residents can be included in the sample. On the other hand, such interviews are time-consuming and costly and only small samples can be studied.

- A questionnaire survey among nursing home staff yields prevalence and incidence data on abuse and neglect, including data on offences not known to the police or the courts. It is economical and guarantees a high degree of anonymity and confidentiality. However, this approach is neither adequate for the study of rare and severe types of abuse, nor does it provide detailed descriptions of abuse episodes.

- A document analysis of public prosecutor files yields a multitude of data on single cases of elder abuse and neglect as well as on the process of criminal prosecution. Information on relevant incidents is limited to those (mostly severe) cases that are known to police or courts. Thus, the method does not produce a comprehensive picture of abuse and neglect.

The limited usefulness of standardised victimisation surveys in elder abuse studies is particularly visible in residential long-term care. However, this restriction is not confined to institutional settings. Practical viability of victim surveys is related to frequency and severity of the offences under study. This approach is most suitable for widespread types of crime involving individual victims.

Further, standardised victimisation surveys presuppose that people are able (and willing) to report their experiences as victims in the required format. Of course, high age does not preclude this ability. But in the developmental phase which gerontologists call the fourth age (Baltes and Smith 2003), many changes take place that affect people's victimisation risks, their ability to demand criminal prosecution, and the probability that victims will be part of the sample of a large-scale victim survey. These changes concern perception, motor co-ordination, speed of reaction, physical strength, health status in general and chronic diseases, physical disabilities and mental health, in particular. Dementia affects the patients' capacity to recognise that they are being (or have been) victimised. It can affect their ability to testify in court and to participate in victim surveys. This means, the perpetrators of abuse will probably not be prosecuted and the victims are placed outside the reach of survey research.

Most of our current knowledge on victimisation of elderly people is part of a victimology of the third age not the fourth. Proceeding to a more comprehensive picture of the most vulnerable segments of the elderly population requires methodological pluralism far beyond standardised victimisation surveys.

Conclusion

The research reported in this chapter shows the usefulness of combining different methods and data sources when studying elder abuse and neglect in residential settings. Though there is no evidence that physical violence against care recipients is common in German institutions of long-term care, severe incidents obviously happen. Night shifts appear as especially critical periods and violence is sometimes triggered by residents' faecal incontinence. Whereas there is widespread normative consensus among nurses concerning the unacceptability of physical abuse, verbally aggressive behaviour towards residents is often regarded as justified (mainly to enforce residents' compliance) or at least as excusable (when under stress or in reaction to aggressive behaviour by residents). The study shows that nurses are generally well aware of the legal requirements of using mechanical restraints. As far as the use of sedatives to control residents' behaviour is concerned, nurses tend to stress physicians' responsibility and to underestimate their own influence concerning medical prescriptions. Psycho-social neglect appears to be common in long-term care institutions. Interviews reveal many instances of infantilising behaviour, which is especially characteristic of less qualified staff. Data from a survey among nursing home staff point to the importance of staff qualification for abuse prevention and at connections between dysfunctional strategies of coping with work stress (especially consumption of alcohol) and self-reported abuse and neglect.

With regard to abuse and neglect of nursing home residents, police investigators, criminal prosecutors and researchers all face serious barriers These barriers are even higher when residents suffer from dementia which at the same time renders them extremely vulnerable to many forms of victimisation.

References

Aktion gegen Gewalt in der Pflege (1999) *Für eine menschenwürdige Pflege: Memorandum der Aktion gegen Gewalt in der Pflege (In Support of Nursing Care Which Respects Human Dignity: Memoir of Action Against Violence in Nursing Care)*. Bonn, Germany: AGP.

Baltes, P.B. and Smith, J. (2003) 'New Frontiers in the Future of Ageing: From Successful Ageing of the Young Old to the Dilemmas of the Fourth Age', *Gerontology*, 49 (2): 123–35.

Bennett, G., Kingston, P. and Penhale, B. (1997) *Dimensions of Elder Abuse: Perspectives for the Practitioner*. Basingstoke: Macmillan.

Eika, K.H. (2003) *Low Quality-effective Demand* (Memorandum 36/2003). Oslo: University of Oslo – Department of Economics.

Flick, U. (1992) 'Triangulation Revisited: Strategy of Validation or Alternative?', *Journal for the Theory of Social Behaviour*, 22: 169–97.

Görgen, T. (2003a) 'Befunde zweier empirischer Forschungsprojekte zur Opferwerdung älterer Menschen' (*Results From Two Empirical Studies on Elderly Victimisation*), in R. Egg and E. Minthe (eds) *Opfer von Straftaten:*

kriminologische, rechtliche und praktische Aspekte, pp. 179–93. Wiesbaden: Kriminologische Zentralstelle.

Görgen, T. (2003b) 'Gewalt gegen ältere Menschen – Anmerkungen zur konzeptuellen Fassung eines neuen Forschungs- und Praxisfeldes' (Violence Against Elderly People – Annotations on Conceptual Framings of a New Area of Research and Practice) in E. Kube, H. Schneider and J. Stock (eds) *Kriminologische Spuren in Hessen: Freundesgabe für Arthur Kreuzer zum 65.Geburtstag,* pp. 139–48. Frankfurt/M: Verlag für Polizeiwissenschaft.

Görgen, T. (2004) 'A Multimethod Study on Elder Abuse and Neglect in Nursing Homes', *Journal of Adult Protection,* 6 (3): 15–25.

Klie, T. (1998) 'Pflege im sozialen Wandel. Wirkungen der Pflegeversicherung auf die Situation Pflegebedürftiger' (Care in Social Transformation: Effects of Long-term Care Insurance Upon the Situation of Care Recipients), *Zeitschrift für Gerontologie und Geriatrie,* 31: 387–91.

Meyer, D. (2001) 'The German Charitable Welfare System: A Criticism From the Viewpoint of Ordnungspolitik', *Annals of Public and Cooperative Economics,* 72 (1): 103–33.

Parmelee, P.A. and Lawton, M.P. (1990) 'The Design of Special Environments for the Aged', in J.E. Birren and K.W. Schaie (eds) *Handbook of Psychology of Ageing,* (3rd edn), pp. 464–88. San Diego, CA: Academic Press.

Pillemer K.A. (1988) 'Combining Qualitative and Quantitative Data in the Study of Elder Abuse' in S. Reinharz and G.D. Rowles (eds) *Qualitative Gerontology,* pp. 257–73. New York, NY: Springer.

Pillemer, K.A. and Moore, D.W. (1989) 'Abuse of Patients in Nursing Homes: Findings From a Survey of Staff', *Gerontologist,* 29: 314–20.

Straus, M.A. (1979) 'Measuring Intra-family Conflict and Violence: The Conflict Tactics (CT) Scales', *Journal of Marriage and the Family,* 41: 75–88.

Williams, B. (1994) 'Patient Satisfaction: A Valid Concept?', *Social Science and Medicine,* 38 (4): 509–16.

Chapter 6

The realities of elder abuse

Gary Fitzgerald

Introduction

This chapter considers the position of vulnerable older people who are abused within the UK, and the legislative and policy approaches taken to protect them. Neglect and mistreatment of older people in the UK are not rare events, but have not received much attention, either from the public or statutory agencies. Despite growing concerns there has been no prevalence study to quantify the extent or impact of elder abuse and the only source of information is the helpline operated by 'Action on Elder Abuse'. Within the UK, nations are at different stages in developing protective measures. England and Wales have encouraged multi-agency strategies targeted toward all vulnerable adults, while Scotland and Northern Ireland have yet to initiate legislative processes. Generally, abused older people are predominantly women over the age of 70 years old, living alone at home, although there is a disproportionate level of abuse within care homes. Abusers tend to be male, either paid staff or family members, but are rarely the 'hands on' family carer. The most prevalent abuses are psychological, financial and physical (Fitzgerald 2004). Moreovoer, there is a low expectation of standards of care, human rights and the status of older people within the UK and this contributes to elder abuse. All of society is affected by this, including Governments who are pragmatic toward protective legislation; providers who routinely fail to deliver quality care; and older people who accept poor standards without complaint. This chapter draws from the work of the charity, Action on Elder Abuse, which has operated across the four nations of the UK since 1993, and in particular the data obtained through the Elder Abuse Response Helpline.

Within the UK elder abuse is addressed through national policies that are generic in nature and which seek to address the protection of all vulnerable adults in a universal sense, regardless of the specific manifestation of their vulnerability, e.g. age, disability, or mental health. While England and Wales have been at the forefront of these developments, both Scotland and Northern Ireland are also formulating strategies and policies that mirror the 'vulnerable adult' approach. This is significantly different from most other countries, where elder abuse is a clearly defined and a uniquely addressed issue at national level, and it remains too early to evaluate whether or not this will prove to be an effective method of challenging and reducing the abuse of older people.

However, reports to the Action on Elder Abuse (AEA) helpline suggest that, at local government level, protective strategies are evolving which increasingly take into consideration those attitudes and approaches that are ageist and discriminatory and which consequently contribute to the abuse of older people. In doing so they consider the age of the victim as the context in which abuse occurs rather than the cause of the abuse itself. It is therefore possible that this more generic approach will have the additional advantage of addressing the wider societal abuse which is inherent within UK health and social care services and which operates to the disadvantage of older people. Such policy-related abuse invariably dictates that an adult with a primary long-term need (e.g. a learning disability) is re-categorised as 'old' at 65 years of age and consequently is likely to lose a range of support services which were previously provided. They are then perceived as the victims of 'elder abuse' rather than victims of 'adult abuse', although it is unlikely that this re-classification either improves or worsens their experience at the hands of the abuser.

The uniqueness of elder abuse

However, in considering the uniqueness of elder abuse itself, there are several issues that need to be considered. The first is to recognise that many abuses could also be considered crimes (e.g. theft, assault, neglect, rape, breach of the Human Rights Act 1998) and by defining them as something different there is a real danger of lessening the impact or importance of the acts themselves, and thereby lessening the consequent importance of the victim in comparison with younger age groups. UK societies do not readily view the assault of a 90-year-old in the same way as an assault upon a 30-year-old and this creates the implication that such abuses might be tolerable, i.e. it almost suggests an unspoken permission to abuse or to engage in 'poor practices'. Partly this is about perceptions of ageing, but it is also about *why* the older person is assaulted or abused, i.e. the motivation of the abuser and the societal environment in which the abuse occurs.

Regardless of age, each person is entitled to the protection of basic human rights. Help the Aged argues that 'the necessary safeguarding of human rights, particularly those protected under Articles 2 (the right to life), 3 (to protection from inhuman and degrading treatment), and 8 (the right to respect for private and family life) must be secured by the actions of the State if they cannot be protected by individual redress. The argument is that the State has a positive duty to protect vulnerable people where there is the potential that they will be unable to take such actions for themselves.

An obvious example of this approach may be found within the domestic violence (DV) arena where it is currently possible to prosecute a case without the active participation of the victim. This strategy was developed in direct response to the recognition that the unique vulnerability and circumstances of 'DV' victims could on occasions make it impossible for them to take proactive action to ensure their own protection. Consequently the State intervenes and overrides the apparent wishes of the victim or, more accurately, takes action in recognition of the underlying coercive nature of the abusive relationship and thereby ensures the victim's protection.

However, it is questionable as to whether the 'criminal' nature of some abusive situations involving older people is recognised in the same way. Indeed there would be merit in considering the extent to which criminal acts committed against older people are actually viewed as crimes in reality, and how many abusers are prosecuted. Calls to the AEA helpline regularly demonstrate the 'double-think' that can occur in such situations, with older people's legal rights dismissed in a manner that would be unacceptable and unlikely if they were 20 or 30 years younger. At times the illegality of the act becomes eclipsed by the unwillingness of those around the older person to accept the reality of what has occurred; it is a deniability that works to the advantage of the abuser and the disadvantage of the older person. But in avoiding or ignoring the issue of criminality, there is a real danger of colluding in the discrimination against the older person, and in so doing leaving them outside of ordinary civil and human rights. This danger of collusion exists whether or not that failure to act is a consequence of a genuine desire to protect the victim from further distress or from other similarly laudable motivations. In short, while many protective concepts and approaches within social policy are obviously or potentially applicable to elder abuse there are differences in societal attitudes with regard to older people which discourage their application.

To elaborate upon this point further we need to reconsider the DV example cited previously. The State had no difficulty in recognising that there were circumstances in which an adult with the mental capacity to make informed decisions nevertheless could not protect themselves and became effectively trapped into an abusive relationship. As a result, action can now be taken that may override the apparent wishes of such a victim, but which is nevertheless in their best interests. By legislating in this manner the State took on a role that could have been perceived as interfering in the private family life of citizens and of acting in the capacity of a 'granny State'. But such arguments were not entertained and instead a social/political position was established that recognised the duty of care which should exist between the State and its vulnerable citizens.

And yet, in legislative terms, it remains possible to neglect an adult (who has mental capacity) to a point near to death without committing a crime – because there remains a reluctance to legally define the circumstances in which one adult can be assumed to have taken direct responsibility for the care and well-being of another. It is this 'double-think' that has its roots in the perceptions held about older people in particular and other vulnerable adults in general.

There are many derogatory stereotypes to describe old age: 'senile', 'crumbly', 'wrinkly', 'gaga', 'old git', and 'geriatric'. But as Norman (cited in Glendenning 1997, p. 64) argued, 'we don't call a sick child a paediatric, or a woman having a hysterectomy, an obstetric'. The words used about old age are invariably infantilising: such as 'old folk', 'old girls' and 'second childhood'. And it is this derogatory approach to the individual older person that can translate into a socially constructed view that older people are a burden on society. As Phillipson argues, ageing has been seen as an increasing problem since the birth of the welfare state, epitomised by enforced retirement, 'elderly medicines', the loss of 'self' into a homogenous group of the 'elderly', and a growing dependency which 'increases the burden on the hard working, non-elderly population' (Phillipson 1988, p. 56). However, by 'constructing' older people as both dependent and a burden, it is implied that society has developed a feeling that all people over 65 years old need care. And the implication of nurturing such a dependent (and growing) population is that older people are made much more vulnerable through disempowerment, stereotyping and, ultimately, a denial of their basic human rights. Hence, the challenge is to go beyond individual prejudices and recognise that dependency is often enforced, and that we should consequently seek to work in a way which empowers people to take control over their own future and not to 'infantilise them'.

Understanding the nature of abuse

In that context we need to consider what we actually mean by abuse. For example, can a grandchild who punches an 80-year-old, disabled grandparent be placed in the same category as the care worker who forgets to knock on a resident's door before entering, or who provides direct personal care to an older person without any social interaction? Clearly, the first scenario is grounded in the idea of 'intent to inflict harm', and the concepts of abuse or assault fit relatively easily, while the second is perhaps less clear, as it is less likely that the care worker *intended* to inflict harm. It is this second category that is often described as 'poor practice'.

However, there is an issue here about power and dependency. If the resident fails to complain, that does not mean abuse did not occur. There is need to look at how the poor practice is experienced by the recipient (in this case the resident), in order to understand whether the practice is abusive. Would the resident choose to be treated in that way if they were able-bodied and could have a greater say in the intervention that is occurring? If the answer is negative, then the practices employed are probably abusive, and in effect could also constitute an assault or intimidation, as in the earlier example.

In attempting to understand abuse most organisations use the five standard categories (physical, sexual, financial, psychological and neglect), but the over-arching definitions also invariably include an understanding of institutional abuse and an awareness of institutional racism. These terms can be seen from the perspective of institutions which employ regimes that are essentially abusive in their construction, as well as environments that are systematically abusive in their practices, including ageism and ingrained racism. This was graphically illustrated by the conditions within Nye Bevan Lodge, a local authority home in Southwark, South London, where:

elderly, often confused residents were made to eat their own faeces, left unattended, physically manhandled, forced to pay money to care staff and even helped to die. (Vousden 1987, p. 18–19)

However, by switching perspectives and regarding a scenario primarily from a client-centred viewpoint it is possible immediately to reinforce the importance of that individual, instead of simply relying on preconceived notions of 'norms' for older people. In short, perhaps Biggs, Phillipson and Kingston's (1995) brief sentence conveys most poignantly what needs to be considered:

Beginning to see elders as objects rather than human is the foundation on which a continuum of petty slights and abuses builds into active mistreatment. (Biggs *et al.* 1995, p. 15)

The citizenship of victims

As adult protection is evolving there is a growing awareness of the need to place independent living and the protection of older people within a wider citizenship framework. By doing so the objectives of abuse prevention, adult protection and community or residential support become part of the broader intentions of community planning (including social inclusion, crime and disorder, regeneration, neighbourhood renewal and supporting people etc). Such a switch in policy focus seeks to underpin the wider and, albeit implicit, intentions of *No Secrets*.[1] Rather than regarding vulnerable older people as primarily clients and patients needing protection, citizenship seeks to reinforce the mutual obligations (between individual and society) inherent in social inclusion policies and suggests that 'joined up' governance at local, national and UK levels is the most effective way to confront elder abuse.

In addition, however, regulation is also beginning to be re-evaluated, as it becomes increasingly apparent that the external inspection of care and health provision cannot by itself deliver the cultural changes that are necessary to eliminate poor practices. Consequently, there is a move toward reframing minimum standards of care provision to include not only effective engagement with providers themselves, but also the degree to which patients, residents, and clients exercise control over their own lives. In part, this is a response to the complexities of the social care market, but it is also a consequence of the growing realisation that the scale of elder abuse may be greater than first envisaged.

Prevalence of abuse

There has been only one study on the community prevalence of elder abuse in the UK and there has been no research whatsoever into abuse within institutions in this country. In the community-based study a routine social survey was used to overcome some of the difficulties encountered with research methodology – the Office of Population Censuses and Surveys (OPCS) Omnibus survey.[2] This was a representative sampling survey that took place in 100 different sites throughout Britain during May 1992, involving 2,130 adults (593 aged over 60 years old and 1,366 people who were in regular close contact with an older person). The survey excluded older people in institutions and those who were too ill or disabled to participate. This is an important limitation, as it excluded some older people who may have been at greater risk of abuse, and certainly at greater risk of harm from any given abuse.

Three categories of abuse were surveyed – physical, oral, and financial. Oral abuse (which is categorised by AEA within psychological abuse) was measured by asking whether a close family member or relative had recently frightened them by shouting, insulting them or speaking roughly to them. Physical abuse was measured by asking whether any close family member had pushed, slapped, shoved or been physically rough with them in any other way. The questions about financial abuse asked whether any close family member had taken money or property from them without their consent.

Of the 593 people aged 60 or more who were surveyed, 5 per cent reported having been orally abused, 2 per cent reported physical abuse and 2 per cent financial abuse. The study did not identify the extent of multiple abuses and did not identify the timeframe involved in these abuses. It also included questions to 1,366 people who were in regular close contact with an older person, using the same abuse criteria. This indicated higher rates of oral abuse (9 per cent), but a lower rate for physical abuse (0.6 per cent) There has not been a replication of this study.

While some of the research difficulties were overcome by this approach it was nevertheless limited in scope. It remains however the only indicator of the potential scale of elder abuse within the

UK, and is mirrored by research in other countries, e.g. Finland 5 per cent, Australia 4.6 per cent, America 3.2 per cent, Canada 4 per cent (Department of Health 2001). In the UK, if these percentages were to be applied to the older population living in their own homes, they would indicate that some 5 per cent of older people were being subjected to oral abuse by family members, equating to 500,000 people. However, the limited nature of the study suggests the need for caution in drawing such conclusions.

At the time of writing a national funding charity, Comic Relief, is commissioning a two-year UK wide prevalence study into elder abuse, reporting in March 2007. The Department of Health in London is partially funding the study, which will additionally consider the barriers to reporting that may be experienced by older people. This will be a crucial piece of research and it is anticipated that it will have major social and political implications for the adult protection agenda. However, in the interim, the information collected through the AEA helpline remains the primary indicator of the nature of elder abuse within the UK.

Definitions of abuse

The AEA helpline has been in operation since 1997 and uses a definition of abuse that is very specific and is focused upon a breach of trust. This is important because it identifies those abuses where it would be reasonable for the older person to have trusted the abuser (e.g. relatives, staff who are employed to perform tasks on their behalf etc.). As such it excludes abuse perpetrated by strangers (e.g. distraction burglary or mugging):

> A single or repeated act or lack of appropriate action occurring within any relationship where there is an expectation of trust which causes harm or distress to an older person. (1997: iv)

The definition differs from that used within *No Secrets* in that it does not restrict attention to just those older people who 'are or may be in need of community care services' or who 'cannot take care of themselves' or 'protect (themselves) from significant harm or exploitation'. By its nature the *No Secrets* definition is based on a health/social care model, i.e. it assumes that a vulnerable person must be in need of external support, and it ignores the emotional impact of an abusive relationship. This consequently excludes a range of abuses that are psychological in nature, but which may not be readily definable as 'significant harm or exploitation'. It is in that context that elder abuse should be considered, to collectively challenge the societal attitudes reflected by Holstein in 1996:

> For those who work with abused and neglected older adults the likelihood of achieving an ideal solution is slim. While the public may be appalled at newspaper descriptions of elder mistreatment, that dismay rarely translates into political action. Despite outrage, few understand the roots of the problems that lead to elder abuse and neglect, and therefore few assume responsibility for activities designed to address these deeper causes. It is unlikely that this picture will change in the immediate future. (Holstein 1996, p. 83)

In considering the data from the AEA helpline it is important to remember that it can only give an indication of the nature of abuse from the perspective of those able (either mentally or physically) and willing to use a telephone. Abuse often occurs in closed environments, e.g. in institutions such as care homes or behind the 'closed door' of people's own homes and in these settings victims may not have the means or opportunity to access a helpline. Some callers to the service are in such settings, but have temporarily found privacy in which to call, or have left that setting permanently and are able to speak freely. Nevertheless there may be significant numbers of victims who could not access the helpline even if they knew about it.

In addition, AEA also maintains a press cuttings service and posts examples of reported abuse onto the charity's website. On average there are 35 examples of abuse identified per month through this process, almost invariably being reported in local newspapers. It is only in the last two years that the national media have begun to take an interest in elder abuse, but this remains at a lesser level than the attention given to the abuse of children. This approach is a reflection of wider societal attitudes, where there is a general acceptance that older people will receive poorer services and a less significant response to their needs than other groups within society.

The realities of elder abuse

The vast majority of those who were reported to the AEA helpline as suffering abuse were women (67 per cent), with 22 per cent of men identified as victims. In a smaller percentage of cases (11 per cent) both men and women were facing abuse at the same time, and more than half of these (50 per cent) were in some form of institutional support, primarily care homes. The fact that more women than men were identified as suffering abuse is likely to be a reflection of the reality that women live longer than men and are consequently more likely to be living alone. However, it is their circumstances that make them vulnerable in such situations, not their gender. The majority of men of all ages in the UK live with a partner, but vastly larger numbers of women, particularly over the age of 80, live on their own.

More than three quarters of abuse (78 per cent) was perpetrated on people who were over the age of 70 years old, with 16 per cent of that abuse affecting people over the age of 90 years old. For both genders however the period between 80 and 89 years of age was the time of most vulnerability to abuse. Men however were less likely to report being abused.

> Because of their adherence to social expectations, it is likely that many men do not disclose the abuse they suffer; therefore, the real prevalence is likely to be much higher than is acknowledged either by victims or by the services. (Pritchard 2001, p. 79)

The type of abuse most frequently reported to the helpline was psychological (34 per cent), followed by financial abuse (20 per cent) and physical abuse (19 per cent). Neglect was identified in 12 per cent of cases. The total number of incidents of abuse reported between April 1997 and December 2003 was 10,528, with 44 per cent of callers reporting more than one type of abuse occurring at any one time. In 37 per cent of situations two abuses were occurring simultaneously.

When looking at abuse in more detail it was apparent that some may be influenced by the gender of the victim. For example, men appeared more likely to face financial abuse or neglect than did women. But women were more likely to face physical or psychological abuse. However, the only category that showed an increase in reporting was that of sexual abuse (3 per cent) – compared with the analysis in February 2000 which identified only 1.9 per cent – and there were no obvious explanations for the increase. It may be the result of a wider awareness of the nature of elder abuse, leading to increased reporting, or it may be the result of the introduction of Adult Protection policies within each local authority area (again leading to increased awareness), or it may be the result of other factors. Some concerns have been expressed by practitioners that there could be an actual increase in abuse itself, caused by serial abusers moving from childcare environments (where there is increased vigilance and controls) to adult care environments that are less regulated. While there is no statistical evidence to support this concern it is worth noting that such abuse can be perpetrated, not for sexual gratification, but to satisfy the urge to control and dominate:

> Sexual offenders are attracted by the vulnerability and availability of their potential victims and those who suffer from physical and mental impairment may be especially at risk. (Ogg and Bennett 1992, pp. 998–99)

Consequently it is important to note that sexual violence affects older women as well as those who are younger.

Neglect and a 'duty of care'

Neglect was formally recognised as a category of abuse in *No Longer Afraid* (DoH 1993) and reiterated within *No Secrets*, reflecting the requirements of the Human Rights Act 1998. However, there is little evidence that criminal prosecutions have been readily forthcoming, even where the level of neglect by care staff has been extreme. For example, one of the most common indicators of neglect that comes to the attention of AEA relates to the incidence of pressure sores. 'Also called pressure ulcers (death of skin and underlying tissues from the effect of pressure, friction and shear) these are a quality indicator and the development of pressure sores implies neglect' (O'Dea 1999, p. 192). The magnitude of this condition is illuminating '... with approximately 10 per cent of hospital inpatients developing pressure ulcers' (O'Dea 1999, pp. 193–94). However, a consistent theme emerging from adult protection work is the apparent failure by investigators to consider pressure sores with the degree of seriousness that the above statement implies and victims may often die as a consequence, with death certificates indicating septicemia or pneumonia as the cause of death.

There also appears to be a lack of general knowledge relating to the circumstances in which a member of the public can be considered to have assumed a 'duty of care' under case law and consequently charged for any failings in that regard. Although this option has been available for 30 years it has not been used, perhaps because the law deals more readily with acts of commission rather than omission. In the case law in question (see Regina *v* Stone and Dobinson [1977] 2 All ER 341), however, it was recognised that a crime was capable of commission *by omission*, where duty of care had been assumed. In that case a couple had assumed the care of a relative who died in appalling circumstances, severely emaciated and with infected bedsores and other problems. Both defendants were convicted of negligent manslaughter.

Financial abuse

> Financial abuse occurs in 10 to 15 per cent of cases involving registered enduring powers of attorney, and more often with unregistered powers. Expressed as a percentage this may seem to be a relatively minor problem, but 10,000 powers will be registered with the Court of Protection this year alone and frauds involving six figure sums are by no means unprecedented. (Lush 1999)

Of all calls to the helpline regarding financial abuse, the misuse of unregistered powers of attorney continues to be one of the greatest concerns expressed. The ease with which abusers are apparently able to convince older people that an unregistered Power of Attorney has conveyed a level of financial control – and other controls – to the abuser is worrying. This is particularly so given that it is impossible to quantify how many of these unregistered documents are actually in the community. A predominant theme that emerges is the expectation of a relative that they will inherit the bulk of an older person's estate, and the consequent desire to preserve as much of that estate as possible can result in the older person living in squalor.

Reporting abuse

However, where relatives or older people contact the helpline it is usually because they are unhappy about something that is happening or has happened to someone else and they are unable to obtain change or redress through the immediate options available to them. In some cases this is because they are unaware of their rights (e.g. the existence of complaints processes or regulatory bodies), and in other cases it is because they have failed to obtain a response that is acceptable to them. This is equally true for the category of friends/ neighbours (11 per cent) who contact the helpline.

The next highest group of callers to the helpline are paid workers (19 per cent) who contact it because they have seen something, or been told to do something, that concerns them, or because they are investigating a complaint/abuse referral and are seeking advice on options or legislation. Often where workers are seeking to report an abuse that they have witnessed they are doing so with varying levels of anxiety and fear of the consequences for themselves.

Despite the existence of the Public Interest Disclosure Act 1998 it is not the experience of AEA that this has created a culture in which social and health care employees feel able to disclose abuse. Indeed, it continues to be suggested that disclosure can lead to loss of employment, and, in some cases, people have reported that they felt it necessary to leave the area completely and live elsewhere. In some situations these pressures may be through deliberate intent by the employer. In other cases however it may result from the whistleblower feeling unable to continue in that employment, particularly where there is a feeling that the employer did not act with sufficient resolve.

In gender terms there are more men reported as individual abusers (41 per cent) than women (25 per cent). Overwhelmingly male abusers are family members (64 per cent). But, while this is equally true for women (51 per cent), there is also a significant proportion (33 per cent) of women identified as paid staff and, in that context, it is particularly worth noting that, in a third of all circumstances (33 per cent), the abuse is perpetrated by more than one person in collusion.

Although 23 per cent of this 'collusive' abuse is perpetrated by family members a staggering 62 per cent is by paid staff, i.e. abusive practices that are institutional and passed from one worker to another. This actually gives a two-fold message, the first being a negative one about the quality of formal care. But the second message is that this form of abuse can be addressed by culture change and training. It has the potential to be prevented.

Challenging abuse

To address elder abuse therefore it is necessary to consider a wide variety of factors, ranging through societal attitudes, the extent of environments in which it occurs, and the multitude of people potentially involved. This suggests that successful intervention strategies must start from the perspective that prevention is always better than intervention, because the reality of protective work is very often about reducing the *potential* for abuse rather than stopping the act itself. Clearly, it is not possible to control what occurs behind every door or regulate every relationship so the focus needs to be toward effecting cultural change instead.

In the absence of an immediate intervention strategy therefore it is crucial that practitioners switch toward preventive work rather than concluding that nothing can be done and close the case. While it might not be possible to provide protection to the older person at that precise moment it might be possible to work towards providing protection in six months' time instead, once the victim's confidence has been gained and they have been assisted to recognise and accept the options available to them.

Successful adult protection however requires multi-layered strategies that operate simultaneously and it needs co-ordination between agencies, the sharing of information and a willingness to seek expert advice from others. This invariably involves strong leadership from the top down, co-ordination between practitioners, liaison that keeps the older person at the centre of planning, and empowerment. None of this is complex, but all of it requires resistance to pressures that can be intense – heavy caseloads; budget and time constraints; resource and training difficulties; the temptation to see an older person's refusal of help as an opportunity to close the case, or evict, or ignore.

Poor practice forms the greatest percentage of abuse perpetrated by paid staff, but there are also major opportunities being lost within the judicial arena to address the problem. Consequently, there needs to be a significant investment in training as one guaranteed method of reducing the potential for abuse. This approach has been informed by research in both America and the UK which indicates that training can directly impact upon levels of abuse. In 1988 and 1991, Pillemer (1988) conducted research into abuse within nursing homes and concluded that the quality of care was shown to have been better in homes that could afford to hire staff with better training and where staff–patient ratios were relatively high. Nurses and nursing aides with lower levels of education were likely to have more negative attitudes towards older people (*ibid.*). British research has subsequently confirmed this conclusion (Baillon *et al.* 1996).

Conclusion

In the last five years progress has been made within the UK to highlight and challenge the abuse of older people. However, there remain major barriers to older people gaining access to their legal and civil rights, and these barriers are created partly by societal perceptions and partly by the vulnerability, and hence potential dependence, of the older victims. To overcome these difficulties and move forward we need to enable the provision of training for those people who interact with potential victims, including providers, inspectors, lawyers, judges, police and investigators. Providers need training in how to provide quality care – and increasing numbers of experienced social and health care staff are beginning to question training strategies that rely either on theory, without practical training in caring techniques, or which are not in reality a training process at all, e.g. National Vocational Qualifications, which assess current skills and knowledge, but do not develop new practical skills.

Regulatory inspectors in social and health care need training appropriate to the services they are inspecting, i.e. an inspector of nursing homes should have a good knowledge of nursing practice. But they also need training in understanding what constitutes abuse, what are unacceptable thresholds that warrant enforcement action, how their role should integrate with adult protection policies, and how to focus on outcomes instead of processes. Investigators need training in how to investigate, what options can be considered when seeking solutions, and what legislation can be utilised to progress protection. Police, lawyers and judges need training in understanding the dynamics of elder abuse, how to enable vulnerable people to achieve justice and, perhaps most importantly, how to ensure that ageist assumptions do not negatively affect investigation, prosecution and sentencing. And, finally, abuse training needs to be integrated into the professional programmes for nurses, doctors, including general practitioners, pharmaceutical advisers in Primary Care Trusts etc. Ultimately, it is only when all those who have a role in protecting, supporting and caring for older people also achieve an understanding of the nature and complexities of abuse that we can collectively challenge and begin to seriously affect its root causes.

Notes

1 *Guidance from the Department of Health on the Development of Multi-agency Policies for Adult Protection*: (2001).
2 Social Survey Division. *OPCS Omnibus Survey, May 1992,* June 1996. SN: 3088. Colchester, Essex: UK Data Archive [distributor].

References

Baillon, S., Boyle, A., Neville, P.G. and Scothern, G. (1996) 'Factors That Contribute to Stress in Care Staff in Nursing Homes for the Elderly', *International Journal of Geriatric Psychiatry*, 11: 219–26.

Department of Health (1993) *No Longer Afraid.* London: HMSO.

Department of Health (2001) *Guidance from the Department of Health on the Development of Multi-Agency Policies for Adult Protection. (No Secrets)* London: DoH.

Fitzgerald, G. (2004) *Hidden Voices.* London: Help the Aged.

Glendenning, F. (1997) 'What is elder abuse and neglect?' in P. Decalmer and F. Glendenning (1997) (eds) *The Mistreatment of Elderly People*, pp. 1–34. London: Sage.

Glendenning, F. (1999) *The Abuse of Older People in Institutional Settings – Institutional Abuse.* London: Routledge.

Harding, T. and Gould, J. (2003) *Memorandum on Older People and Human Rights.* London: Help the Aged.

Holstein, M. (1996) 'Multidisciplinary Decision-making: Uniting Differing Professional Perspectives', *Journal of Elder Mistreatment: Ethical Issues, Dilemmas and Decisions.* New York: Haworth Press.

Lush, D. (1999) *Bags of Money, the Financial Abuse of Older People,* Working Paper No. 4. London: Action on Elder Abuse.

McCreadie, C. (1996) *Elder Abuse: Update on Research,* Age Concern Institute of Gerontology. London: King's College.

O'Dea, K. (1999) 'The Prevalence of Pressure Damage in Acute Care Hospital Patients in the UK', *Journal of Wound Care,* 8 (4): 192–94.

O'Loughlin, A. and Duggan J. (1998) *Abuse, Neglect and Mistreatment of Older People: An Exploratory Study.* Dublin: National Council of Ageing and Older People.

Ogg, J. and Bennett, G. (1992) 'Elder abuse in Britain', *British Medical Journal,* 305: 998–9.

Phillipson, C. (1998) *Reconstructing Old Age.* London: Sage.

Pillemer, K.A. (1988) 'Maltreatment of patients in nursing homes', *Journal of Health and Social behaviour,* 29 (3): 227–38.

Pillemer, K.A. and Bachman-Prehn R. (1991) 'Helping and Hurting: Predictors of Maltreatment of Patients in Nursing Homes', *Research on Ageing,* 13 (1): 74–95.

Pritchard, J. (2001) *Male Victims of Elder Abuse*. London: Jessica Kingsley.
Vousden, M. (1987) 'Nye Bevan would turn in his grave', *Nursing Times*, 83: 18–19.

Chapter 7

Deconstructing distraction burglary: an ageist offence?

Stuart Lister and David Wall

This chapter is based upon research conducted in preparation for a Home Office funded evaluation of the Leeds Distraction Burglary Project (see Lister, Wall and Bryan 2004). Although statistically a relatively rare occurrence, distraction burglary has created considerable public concern during recent years because of the predatory way in which older people are specifically targeted as victims and its potentially devastating impact. The premeditated manner by which offenders engage directly with victims in order to deceive them and gain entry to their dwellings distinguishes distraction burglary from more conventional forms of burglary in which offenders typically seek to avoid victim contact by entering dwellings unnoticed (Bennett and Wright 1984; Wright and Decker 1994).

Major concerns about distraction burglary were voiced following the violent death of 82-year-old Leeds pensioner Isabel Gray in 1997 (*Yorkshire Post*, 10 February 2002) and the findings of the subsequent police investigation. The profile of the offence was further raised in 2000, following the formation of the Distraction Burglary Taskforce, a national partnership established by the Home Office which, in its turn, triggered a range of co-ordinated anti-distraction burglary initiatives across an array of agencies. This heightened focus on the offence led to distraction burglary becoming a recorded sub-category of the Home Office's 'burglary dwelling' offence category, in April 2003. For this purpose, it is defined as:

> any crime where a falsehood, trick or distraction is used on
> an occupant of a dwelling to gain, or try to gain, access to the

premises to commit burglary. It includes cases where the offender first enters the premises and subsequently uses distraction burglary methods in order to remain on the premises and/or gain access to other parts of the premises in order to commit burglary. (Home Office 2004)

The formalisation of distraction burglary allows for the easier monitoring of reporting levels. However Thornton *et al.* (2003, p. 51) warned that a narrow definition premised on the use of a trick may fail to capture the variation found within distraction-type victim–offender interactions. Indeed, subsequent research by Lister *et al.* (2004) into variations in the ways that older people are victimised found that not only does 'distraction burglary' frequently overlap with other non-distraction forms of burglary, but it comprises a range of variations within the broader *modus operandi*. Because of this, it will be argued herein that distraction burglary should be understood as a family of offences which incorporates a diverse range of strategies and rationales, each requiring different preventive strategies.

This chapter deconstructs distraction burglary in order to illustrate its many complexities and distinguishing features. Part one discusses what is known about the prevalence of distraction burglary, and explores what is currently known about offenders and their tactics of deceit. Part two identifies the victims and outlines their profiles. The third part situates distraction burglary within a broader debate about age, risk and crime prevention, while questioning some of the implicit assumptions made in discourses surrounding old age and victimisation. We conclude by raising questions about the reification of older people as a coherent unit for the delivery of criminal justice policy.

The prevalence of distraction burglary

Assessing the overall extent of distraction burglary has long been problematic because prior to April 2003 it was not disaggregated from other burglary dwelling offences within official crime statistics. However, statistics collected between 1999 and 2001 from all 43 police forces in England and Wales, showed annual fluctuations of between 15,000 and 19,400 distraction burglaries (Home Office 2002). Analysis of recorded crime data gathered from 41 police forces revealed that overall levels of prevalence remain at a broadly similar level, with

15,000 distraction burglaries being recorded during 2003–2004, albeit two forces failed to participate in the audit (Ruparel 2004, p. 1). Distraction burglary accounts for 4 per cent of all dwelling burglaries in England and Wales, with variance across urban and rural police forces of between 0.4 per cent and 7.7 per cent (Ruparel 2004).

While these figures indicate that distraction burglary is a relatively rare occurrence, many of these offences are likely to remain 'hidden' from official burglary statistics. Steele *et al.* (2001), for instance, identified that police recording inconsistencies sometimes lead to the misclassification of distraction burglaries as fraud or robbery offences, or they are treated as 'non-crime' incidents or merely filed as 'intelligence reports' (*ibid.*, p. 16). Moreover, victims may be less likely to report these offences to the police in comparison to other forms of burglary. The embarrassment that can result from 'being conned' within fraud and deceit offences, and the feelings of self-blame that often follow, may suppress victims' willingness to call the police and engage with the criminal justice system (Home Office 2001). Equally, the social isolation of some distraction burglary victims means there may be an absence of significant others, such as immediate family members, to encourage them to report offences to the police. There is also likely to be a low ratio of 'attempt burglary by distraction' offences reported to the police in comparison to 'attempt burglary by force' offences. Whereas the latter often lead to visible or audible signs of forced entry (e.g. damaged window sills or triggered burglar alarms), the former, we can speculate, are likely to involve little more than a doorstep rebuttal – as such, the occupant may not realise they have just repelled a burglar.

Possibly the most accurate assessment of the extent of distraction burglary is drawn from the findings of the British Crime Survey (BCS), the national household victimisation survey which avoids police reporting and recording shortfalls. The 2002–2003 BCS found an annual 'burglary with entry' rate of 561,000 (Simmons and Dodd 2003). Of these, 4 per cent involved the use of false pretences as the method of entry – in 14 per cent of cases the head of household was aged 60 or over, (Budd 2001) and a further 5 per cent of offenders pushed past the person who opened the door (Home Office 2004). As we shall describe later, some of these latter incidents are initiated as distraction burglaries, suggesting that between 4 and 8 per cent of all burglary dwelling offences with entry might actually be distraction type offences.

Distraction burglars

While there has been a tradition of ethnographic research into the offending routines of residential 'street' burglars (see for example, Shover 1973; Maguire and Bennett 1982; Bennett and Wright 1984; Cromwell *et al.* 1991; Wright and Decker 1994), little research has considered the various tactics that are employed by 'distraction burglars'. The empirical information that does exist is mainly drawn from local police intelligence reports, the victimisation studies of Jones (1987) and Thornton *et al.* (2003; 2004) and the interviews conducted by Steele *et al.* (2001) with convicted offenders.

As Shover (1973) acknowledges, the division of labour necessary to enact a burglary requires offenders to work co-operatively within networks from which they harness skill sets, not just to facilitate offending, but also to ensure the efficient distribution of stolen goods. Research by Steele *et al.* (2001, pp. 55–56) into distraction burglary suggests that its social organisation involves the use of 'tipsters' who identify 'suitable targets' for distraction and then broker information about the victim and their whereabouts to offenders. The same research also indicates the existence of informal tutelage between offenders which reproduces patterns of offending across peer groups and down generations. Indeed, distraction routines display relatively high levels of 'professionalism' in terms of organisation, planning and division of labour - hence, the tendency for distracters to operate in pairs. Typically, a 'distracter' will divert the occupant by enticing him or her outside or into a specific area of the house, while an accomplice 'sneaks in' to the household unobserved in order to steal cash, jewellery and other portable items. During the act of deception, 'distracters' employ a range of techniques of subterfuge which demonstrate the application of sophisticated interpersonal skills. Sometimes they gain entry to a dwelling by impersonating agency officials who have legitimate reason to visit households unannounced and exploiting the householder's fear of losing key domestic utilities. Or else they may exploit the victim's goodwill, usually by requesting their assistance or asking for information. Unsurprisingly therefore, most distraction burglaries have been found to occur on weekdays, during daylight hours (Steele *et al.* 2001).

Although distraction burglaries regularly exhibit high levels of planning and organisation, the degree of sophistication can vary. There is, for example, a cadre of offender who, after establishing that the occupant is alone or too frail to resist, may simply enter the property uninvited, often by barging past the victim (see Jones 1987).

As Wright and Decker (1994) observe, the *modus operandi* of burglars is fluid because the burglary procedure does not always follow a rigid and pre-planned format. Consequently, offenders adapt their behaviour in response to the unfolding situation; therefore a burglary that begins as a 'distraction entry' may subsequently become a 'forced entry' (see Thornton *et al.* 2003, p. 21), or even an 'aggravated burglary' (with violence), particularly if the offenders believe that a large amount of cash is kept in the house. Perhaps in response to the threat of violence, Thornton *et al.* (2004) found that a minority of victims claimed not to be deceived by the offender's bogus guise, but allowed them entry all the same.

The above offence dynamics usually enable offenders to exit the dwelling as they entered, without the occupant realising he or she has been victimised. This also buys time for the offenders, enabling them to leave the area and even the region before the offence is reported to the police. There is almost always a witness to these crimes because at least one of the offenders has face-to-face contact with the victim during the distraction, so it is perhaps unsurprising that offenders are keen to leave the wider vicinity with haste. Many offenders, therefore, regularly commit offences across several police force boundaries, often within a relatively short space of time. A police detective explained the regional context to this pattern of offending:

> And what you find with bogus offenders is they're very clever. They'll hit three forces in the space of an hour, and they tend just to cherry pick. They'll come along the M62 or up the M1, which tend to be the two corridors we get hit on, and they'll just drop off and do crime. They'll pick a point, sort of West Yorkshire, South Yorkshire, Derbyshire, and bang, bang, bang, so they'll have done three crimes in three counties. Or they'll come to Leeds and maybe hit four divisions in the space of a day, so all that is [recorded], is one crime in every division.

Because this risk-avoidance behaviour reduces the likelihood of offenders being identified locally it acts to hinder the effectiveness of police investigations. As a result, the detection rates for distraction burglary are generally lower than those of 'burglary dwelling', fluctuating between 4 and 6 per cent (Home Office 2001, p. 6; see Lister *et al.* 2004). Our research found that offences committed within these 'crime sprees' are not necessarily restricted to distraction burglary, but can include a range of other acquisitive and violent crimes, including robbery, auto-crime and (non-distraction) burglary of dwellings and commercial premises. Therefore, simply to apply the label 'distraction burglar' to this pattern of offending is possibly misleading and potentially constrains the scope for any remedial action.

The tactics of deceit

Our analysis of police burglary records found much diversity in the offending routines and behaviours that fall within the 'constructed' recording category called 'distraction burglary'. Offenders employ a range of guises to gain the confidence of the householder, but also use various distraction tactics and strategies of legitimation to gain entry to the dwellings. Such sophistication illustrates the importance of understanding 'distraction burglary' as a 'family' of deceptions for the purposes of crime prevention campaigns and criminal investigations. These different guises display a range of distinct tactics that fall into three basic sets within which are sub-groupings that illustrate further the complexity of the offence.

The first set of distraction tactics is used by *bogus officials* who employ recognisable symbols and tokens of trust (Lyon 2002; Clarke 2004) – uniforms and/or credentials – that convince victims of the bearer's credibility. This group impersonates workers who have legitimate and regular business calling on households and so do not attract attention to themselves as being 'out of the ordinary'. Once their credibility has been falsely established the householders allow them to enter. They include *bogus utility workers*, such as electricity and gas meter readers, or water board officials; *bogus public servants* such as council officers, police officers, officials from social services, health workers; and o*ther bogus workers*, postal workers or delivery operatives pretending to collect or drop off goods, boy scouts, charity collectors, door-to-door salespeople from 'recognised' outlets, often retail industry household names.

The second group, *bogus domestic contractors*, are workers who are also seen operating regularly in urban neighbourhoods, 'cold calling' on householders and offering 'good deals' on products or services – deals which enable the distraction. They are defined by their highly developed interpersonal skills which are used to present a 'plausible' story, argument or sales pitch to a potential victim in order to distract or deceive them (or both). Colloquially referred to by the police as 'bogey propmen' or 'rogue traders', *bogus domestic contractors* reflect the diversity of domestic services that a householder might reasonably require, including knife sharpeners, gardeners, roofers, drain cleaners, tarmac layers, and window cleaners. They rely less on abstract tokens of trust to gain entry to households, than upon their interpersonal skills to present a convincing sales-pitch (Steele *et al.* 2001). This group also may defraud householders through a variety of deceitful commercial strategies, most commonly over-charging for incomplete work or systematically inflating quotations for services.

The third group, *other types of distracters*, are not bogus officials, workers or contractors, but ordinary members of the public who knock on doors uninvited. They frequently claim to be in need of emergency assistance, often requesting the use the toilet or telephone, a drink of water or information about a fictional friend or relative in the neighbourhood. One common type of deception is the 'Hamster Trick' and its variants, whereby children ask for help recovering their hamster from the householder's garden, distracting the householder's attention from the entrance.

The absence of a 'bogus' guise in these *'other types of distraction'* suggests that these burglaries occur at the less organised end of the offending spectrum and are therefore more likely to be opportunistic in nature, committed by local offenders who exploit their familiarity with a neighbourhood to select suitable targets to victimise. This interpretation is supported by an analysis of incidents recorded on the police database, which indicated that the involvement of younger offenders within distraction burglary is largely restricted to 'other types of distraction'. Of course many younger distraction offenders are unlikely to appear credible when impersonating agency officials who are expected to be older. Similarly, their offending methods may be constrained by unequal access to resources in the form of uniforms, equipment and transport (Mullins and Wright 2003).

Figure 7.1 illustrates the diversity of distractions by showing each offending guise as a percentage of all recorded distraction burglaries occurring in West Yorkshire between September 2000 and November 2003.

In common with the conventional wisdom about distraction burglars impersonating officials and workers, the guise of a bogus utility worker features in a large proportion of offences (32 per cent). Bogus public servants account for just over an eighth of offences (13 per cent), while other bogus workers account for less than a twelfth (8 per cent). Bogus domestic contractors' commit just over a sixth of offences (17 per cent), which appears to indicate a fluidity in *modus operandi* between fraudulent property repairs and distraction burglary

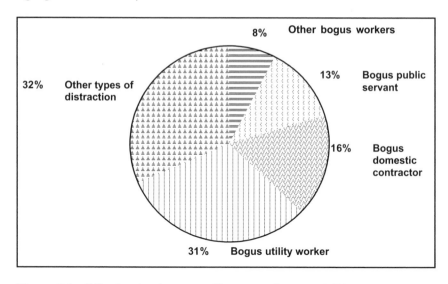

Figure 7.1 Offender (*modus operandi*) entry guises n = 3498
Source: West Yorkshire Police recorded incidents of distraction burglary.

(see Steele *et al.* 2001). Perhaps most surprising is that almost one third of offences were committed by 'other distracters' (32 per cent), who do not operate under the guise of any type of bogus official and – we suggest – are more likely to be locally based and less organised offenders (see also Jones 1987, p. 195). This finding serves to counterbalance media and political, and some academic discourses on distraction burglary which tend to emphasise in isolation the role of highly organised, bogus official type offenders (see for example Home Office 2001). As Christie (1986) has argued, the social construction of the 'ideal victim' evokes notions of the 'ideal offender', who is portrayed as a distant and de-humanised, 'non-person'.[1] However, common narratives which depict 'the distraction burglar' as being 'a dangerous man coming from far away' (*ibid*, p. 26) fit less well with images of local children recounting stories of lost hamsters.

Constructing victims as 'suitable' targets

The analysis of victimisation data by Lister *et al.* (2004) broadly reflects the findings of previous studies (e.g. Steele *et al.* 2001; Thornton *et al.* 2003) by confirming that distraction burglary victims are predominantly elderly, female and white.

Four out of five (82 per cent) of all victims were over the *age* of 70 and over half (57 per cent) were over 80. The average age of victims was 77, indicating that offenders either target people within the 80 years or over group more than any other; or that people in this age group are comparatively less successful at preventing their own victimisation – or both. This finding gives increased weight to the argument that distraction burglars commonly act in a similar manner to domestic burglars in constructing typologies of preferred targets that are based upon a subjective assessment of potential risks and rewards (Cornish and Clarke 1986). In so doing, they associate the ageing process with increasing levels of vulnerability and therefore construct older people as 'suitable targets' (see Steele *et al*. 2001).

Offenders appear to assume that older people are more likely than other age groups to exhibit the following range of behavioural traits: live alone; remain in their homes for long periods during the day; acquiesce to doorstep callers; fail to check visitors' identification badges carefully (if at all); undertake cash transactions at the doorstep; keep cash savings at home; fail to miss stolen items; make poor identification witnesses; fail to report the offence to the police (see Home Office 2001). However, the extent to which these traits are age-specific is very debatable. Whilst some of them may be age-specific because of the structural and economic dependency of many older people, others appear to be informed by culturally prescribed, ageist constructions of older people's attitudes and behaviour.

However, like any age group, older people are a heterogeneous group, possessing different attitudes and outlooks, behavioural characteristics, states of health, social and economic status, life styles and experience. It is intuitive therefore that some people within this socially constructed cohort will display tendencies that make them more susceptible to distraction burglary than others. As such, the level of vulnerability and susceptibility to victimisation among older people is likely to vary significantly. Importantly, however, stereotypical and ageist assumptions appear to inform the offenders' constructions of older people as a generically vulnerable and frail population category, and therefore as 'suitable' targets (see Steele *et al*. 2001). Thus the prevalence of older people within distraction burglary statistics may reflect systematic ageist targeting attitudes by offenders as much as their actual level of personal vulnerability.

The analysis of the *gender* of distraction burglary victims revealed that over two thirds (69 per cent) of victims were female, whereas just under a quarter (25 per cent) were male. These data demonstrate that distraction burglary victims are not only predominantly elderly, but disproportionately female. This gender profile may be attributable to two interrelated factors. First, the demographic fact that women usually outlive men means that older women tend more often to live alone than men (National Statistics 2004, p. 3). This 'knowledge' reinforces offender perceptions of women as the most 'suitable targets', not least because the commission of a distraction burglary is made easier if the householder is the single occupant. In only 6 per cent of incidents were more than one person recorded as 'the victims' at any single crime scene. Importantly, even accounting for some local variations in police recording practices, these data conclusively show that distraction burglary victims are mainly single people living alone (see Home Office 2001, p. 7). Secondly, Steele *et al.* (2001) found that offenders make gendered assumptions about the physical and social vulnerability of elderly women, as well as their overall lack of capability to repel distraction burglars. Finally, the analysis of the *ethnicity* of victims found them to be almost exclusively white Europeans (99 per cent). This reflects the findings of Thornton *et al.* (2003) who described distraction burglary as a 'White-on-White' offence, but also suggested that lower reporting rates among ethnic minority groups generally may partly explain this disproportionately low level of victimisation.

The preceding analysis shows that 'age', 'gender', 'single occupancy' and 'ethnicity' each play a role in structuring the pattern of victimisation. It suggests therefore that some people will be confronted with circumstances of 'quadruple jeopardy', an understanding which at the very least allows some analytical purchase over the distribution of finite crime prevention resources (a point to which we return below).

'Older people' and crime victimisation

The preceding analysis of victimisation situates distraction burglary within a broader debate about the value of segregating older people as a discrete unit of analysis for crime prevention activity (see Mawby 1988; Midwinter; 1990; Pain 2003). Although research findings consistently demonstrate that older people are the age group that is least at risk of becoming victims of burglary (see Chivite-Mathews and Maggs 2002), our analysis shows that they disproportionately experience *distraction* burglary. For this reason alone, it is deserving of crime prevention resources. However, such risk analyses also fail to reflect the impact of specific types of victimisation across the age groups.

The findings of research into the impact of burglary upon older people are ambiguous (see Mawby 2004). On the one hand, Donaldson (2003) found that its impact is relatively serious and that mortality rates can increase as a consequence. On the other hand, Maguire and Kynch (2000) found little evidence to show that burglary had a greater overall impact upon older victims than younger ones. As stated earlier, it is difficult, if not unwise, to generalise about the impact of crimes such as burglary. Incidents of burglary vary in both form and seriousness, from the unnoticed loss of a negligible sum of cash to the violent robbery of a person's entire life savings. Similarly, the emotional, financial and physical impacts of distraction burglary on older people undoubtedly vary because the heterogeneous nature of the cohort – in terms of their wealth, health, life experience and social status – indicates varying capacities to cope with, and recover from, episodes of victimisation.

As found with other externally constructed groupings in society, some older victims will simply put their victimisation down to experience, others will be more deeply affected. However, there are a number of characteristics specific to distraction burglary that can work upon the vulnerabilities associated with ageing to intensify the trauma of victimisation: the lingering memories of personal, sometimes violent, contact with the offender during the commission of the offence; the humiliation of being deceived; the lasting impacts of financial and sentimental loss (Thornton *et al.* 2003); the violation of sentimental attachments to a hitherto 'safe' home environment (Sexsmith 1990). When combined, these characteristics of distraction burglary victimisation can be devastating to the individual, precipitating a downward mental and physiological spiral that, according to a consultant paediatrician interviewed during the course of our research, can lead to the eventual demise of the victim. So, although it can be argued that the prevalence of distraction burglary is still relatively rare when compared to all recorded burglaries, its circumstances, characteristics and consequences demand that it be treated very differently. However, in so doing, it is important to question critically the *linking of age with risk*, notably within crime prevention interventions and criminal justice policy.

Linking age with risk

Although our analysis shows that it is appropriate for distraction burglary reduction initiatives to focus upon older people, the ageing process impacts upon levels of vulnerability gradually. It is, therefore, important to distinguish between 'younger' and 'older' old people. Lister *et al.* (2004) found that people over the age of 65 account for 87 per cent of all distraction burglary victims, which is quite staggering evidence of the link. However, further investigation found that almost three quarters (72 per cent) of the victims were aged 75 and over. Moreover, despite the fact that there were 11 per cent fewer people aged 75 and over in the population of the geographic area from where these data were collected, they were over five-and-a-half times more likely to suffer a distraction burglary than those aged between 65 and 74 (15 per cent of victims).

These findings suggest that when using age as the sole basis for distributing finite resources, distraction burglary reduction initiatives could most usefully target people aged 75 and over and emphasise the need for initiatives to prioritise resources and tailor activities across the 'older' age ranges. The danger is that if all 'older people' are considered to be at equal risk, crime prevention projects may take the easy option and engage predominantly with those 'young' old people who are easier to access because of their relative health and mobility. This may not be the most efficient use of resources because, as described earlier, the 'older' old people who are most at risk from distraction burglary, are also likely to be the hardest to reach. However, general awareness raising campaigns should not exclude those falling outside this age range because it is important to catch people early in order to enable them to internalise crime prevention messages over the longer term (see Thornton and Hatton 2004).

Emphasising 'vulnerability' instead of 'age'

As the link between age and risk comes under scrutiny, then so the coherence of 'older people' as a unit for analysis and, therefore, as a focus for crime prevention policy initiatives and implementation comes into question. As we have emphasised, older people are as heterogeneous and diverse in their personal experiences, attitudes and behaviour as any other age group (Bytheway 1995). While the circumstances of some, especially those living alone, leave them relatively exposed to distraction burglary, the circumstances of others do not (Anderson 1998). As a consequence vulnerability, linked to the ageing process, is a far more reliable predictor of risk than age itself. Confusion between the two must clearly be avoided because although 'old age' overlaps with 'vulnerability', the two are not synonymous.

In assessing 'vulnerability', it is also important not to exclude other fields of enquiry (Pain 2003), as the known profile of distraction burglary victims, described earlier, also varies according to gender, ethnicity and 'single occupancy'. Future research and practice into distraction burglary should explore factors beyond age that might also shape the distribution of victimisation. Gaining this knowledge, especially at a local level, enables the development of more 'intelligence-led' approaches towards allocating crime prevention resources. Indeed, if the targeting of victims by offenders is highly selective then scope exists for the distribution of crime prevention resources to be informed by a similar degree of selectivity. Other relevant factors are likely to be: socio-economic status; location of residence; household and tenure type; domestic living circumstances; physical and mental health capabilities; and everyday lifestyle routines and practices.

Consideration of these other factors brings at least four interrelated benefits to crime prevention policy formation in this area. Firstly, as suggested, it enables crime prevention strategies to be more intelligence-led in the distribution of finite resources. Secondly, it implies that personal circumstance and specific types of behaviour are primary determinants of victimisation, which is important to recognise because behaviour can be addressed and rectified, but the ageing process cannot. Thirdly, it helps to reduce the stigma resulting from labelling and categorising 'the elderly' as generically vulnerable, which in itself may reify the notion of a coherent and homogenous cohort (Fennel 1988). This culturally reproduced ageist stereotype not only informs the offender's construction of older people as 'ideal targets', but older people themselves absorb and internalise it. A 'self-fulfilling victimology' may therefore evolve, not least because 'the bully always goes for the weak' (Midwinter 1990, p. 52). Finally, it helps to prevent the exclusion of other high-risk groups from crime prevention discourses. For example, police officers interviewed by Lister *et al.* (2004) reported that younger victims of distraction burglary tend to be characterised by cognitive, health, and mobility problems.

Conclusion

This chapter has told a complex, but important, story, and in doing so it has reviewed and challenged some of the assumptions that underpin the debates over distraction burglary. Clearly, distraction burglary should not be viewed as a specific offence, but must be accepted as a family or genre of offences driven by diverse motivations, with a broadly common *modus operandi.* Some of these variations are highly organised and calculating patterns of offending behaviour that display the hallmarks of being reproduced across generations of offenders. Others, however, appear to be carried out on-the-spur-of-the-moment and are largely opportunistic. But, to complicate the typology, distraction burglars also tend to be very reflexive about their situation. So, what may start off as a distraction sometimes ends up as an aggravated burglary (barge in). The drama created by this aggravation against an 'ideal victim' makes incidents of distraction burglary highly newsworthy.

On the one hand, media sensationalism can be very productive because it informs a sympathetic public about the problem, who then drive the policy formation process. Furthermore, greater public 'knowledge' of the offence leads to an increase in levels of reporting by the public, as well as rates of recording by the police. In the case of the latter, not only are police officers themselves subject to media sensitisation, but public concerns about the offence lead to calls for the police organisation to respond. On the other hand, there is a downside to media treatment which needs to be carefully considered during policy formation because the sensationalising force of the media amplifies public perceptions of deviancy (Cohen 1972) which can also reduce the effectiveness of crime prevention initiatives. During the course of their reportage the media tend to construct only older people as the victims, rather than those with vulnerabilities linked to the ageing process. This shapes the public view of the problem by reinforcing the idea of older people as potential victims and eventually skews the formation of crime prevention policy. Moreover, this same process of construction also identifies older people and their lifestyle patterns as a low-risk crime opportunity to potential offenders. The media cycle further amplifies the problem because the increases in victim reporting and recording rates give the outward impression of rising rates of distraction burglary and the publication of the statistics becomes a newsworthy event, contributing further to the media frenzy. This chain of events creates problems for the subsequent management of public expectations of policies designed to reduce distraction burglaries, especially as it reinforces, but also 'reifies' the notion of older people as a coherent unit for the delivery of criminal justice policy.

In conclusion, the distraction burglary debate is permeated by ageism – an ideology which uncritically links together constructs such as age and risk as 'naturally' occurring – not just in the deliberation of criminal justice policy, but also by offenders in the construction of their victims. Nevertheless, although distraction burglary crime prevention resources appear to be being allocated to the right place and fairly efficiently, our concern is that this may in part be for the wrong reasons. Without a thorough understanding of the dynamics of the processes of offending and victimisation, other groups of victim may not enjoy the same level of protection – and we may not know about this.

Notes

1 As our analysis will show, distraction burglary victims are predominantly elderly, white females, living alone.

References

Anderson, S. (1998) *Older People, Crime and Crime Prevention*. Edinburgh: Age Concern.

Bennett, T. and Wright, R. (1984) *Burglars on Burglary: Prevention and the Offender*. Aldershot: Gower.

Budd, T. (2001) *Burglary: Practice Messages from the British Crime Survey*, Briefing Note 5/01. London: Home Office.

Bytheway, B. (1995) *Ageism*. Buckingham: Open University Press.

Christie, N. (1986) 'The Ideal Victim' in E. Fattah (ed.) *From Crime Policy to Victim Policy: Reorienting the Justice System*. Basingstoke: Macmillan.

Chivite-Mathews, N. and Maggs, P. (2002) *Crime, Policing and Justice: The Experience of Older People*, Statistical Bulletin 08/02. London: Home Office.

Clarke, R. (2004) 'Alternative Decision Models in Consumer Internet Commerce', Paper given at the, IFIP International Conference on Decision Support Systems, Florence (Prato), 1–3 July 2004 (http://www.anu.edu.au/people/Roger.Clarke/EC/ICDec.html).

Cohen, S. (1972) *Folk Devils and Moral Panics: The Creation of the Mods and Rockers*. London: MacGibbon and Kee.

Cornish, D.B. and Clarke, R.V. (eds) (1986) *The Reasoning Criminal: Rational Choice Perspectives on Offending*. New York: Springer-Verlag.

Cromwell, P., Olson, J. and Avary, D. (1991) *Breaking and Entering: An Ethnographic Analysis of Burglary*. Newbury Park, CA: Sage.

Donaldson, R. (2003) *Experiences of Older Burglary Victims*, Home Office Research, Development and Statistics Directorate, Findings No. 198. London: Home Office.

Fennel, G., Phillipson, C. and Evers, H. (1988) *The Sociology of Old Age*. Buckingham: Open University Press.

Home Office (2001) *Tackling Distraction Burglary.* London: Home Office.

Home Office (2002) *Tackling Distraction Burglary: A National Distraction Burglary Taskforce Report.* London: Home Office.

Home Office (2004) *Counting Rules for Recorded Crime: Instructions for Police Forces.* London: Home Office.

Jones, G. (1987) 'Elderly People and Domestic Crime', *British Journal of Criminology*, 27 (2): 191–201.

Lister, S., Wall, D. and Bryan, J. (2004) *Evaluation of the Leeds Distraction Burglary Initiative*, Home Office Online Report 44/04, available at: (http://www.homeoffice.gov.uk/rds/pdfs04/rdsolr4404.pdf). London: Home Office.

Lyon, D. (2002) 'Everyday Surveillance: Personal Data and Social Classifications', *Information, Communication & Society*, 5 (2): 242–57.

Maguire, M. and Bennett, T. (1982) *Burglary in a Dwelling: The Offence, the Offender, and the Victim.* London: Heinemann.

Maguire, M. and Kynch, J. (2000) *Public Perceptions and Victims' Experiences of Victim Support: Findings from the 1998 British Crime Survey.* London: Home Office.

Mawby, R.I. (2004) 'Reducing Burglary and Fear of Crime Among Older People: An Evaluation of a "Help the Aged" and "Homesafe" Initiative in Plymouth', *Social Policy and Administration*, 38 (1): 1–20.

Mawby, R.I. (1988) 'Age, Vulnerability and Impact of Crime' in M. Maguire and J. Pointing (eds) *Victims of Crime: a New Deal?* pp. 127–38. Buckingham: Open University Press.

Midwinter, E. (1990) *The Old Order: Crime and Older People.* London: Centre for Policy and Ageing.

Mullins, C. and Wright, R. (2003) 'Gender, Social Networks, and Residential Burglary', *Criminology*, 41: 813–39.

National Statistics (2004) *Focus on Gender,* (http://www.statistics.gov.uk/downloads/theme_compendia/fog2004/Gender.pdf). London: Office for National Statistics.

Pain, R. (2003) 'Old Age and Victimisation' in P. Davies, P. Francis and V. Jupp (eds) *Victimisation: Theory, Research and Politics*, pp. 61–72. London: Macmillan.

Ruparel, C. (2004) *Distraction Burglary: Recorded Crime Data.* London: Home Office.

Sexsmith, A.J. (1990) 'The Meaning and Experience of "Home" in Later Life', in B. Bytheway and J. Johnson (eds) *Welfare and the Ageing Experience*, pp. 110–22. Aldershot: Avebury.

Shover, N. (1973) 'The Social Organization of Burglary', *Social Problems*, 20: 54–62.

Steele, B., Thornton, A., McKillop, C. and Dover, H. (2001) *The Formulation of a Strategy to Prevent and Detect Distraction Burglary Offences against Older People*, Police Research Award Scheme. London: Home Office.

Thornton, A., Hatton, C., Malone, C., Fryer, T., Walker. D., Cunningham, J. and Durrani, N. (2003) *Distraction Burglary Amongst Older Adults and Ethnic Minority Communities*, Home Office Research Study 269. London: Home Office.

Thornton, A. and Hatton, C. (2004) *Bogus Caller Crime: A Help the Aged Survey of Britain.* London: Help the Aged.

Wright, R. and Decker, S. (1994) *Burglars on the Job.* Boston, MA: Northeastern University Press.

Yorkshire Evening Post (10 February 2002) 'Beating Bogus Callers who Prey on the Elderly'.

Chapter 8

Reassuring older people in relation to fear of crime

Alan Burnett

Introduction

The aim of this chapter is two-fold. Firstly, I will review the literature about fear of crime with particular reference to older people. Secondly, on the basis of the evidence from fear of crime studies, reassurance scheme evaluations, and other work undertaken by Help the Aged, some practical suggestions as to what can be done to reassure senior citizens will be made.

The government has set national targets to reduce fear of crime in England and Wales. There is also the Home Office Fear of Crime Reduction toolkit and E-Community in existence. In 2002 *Crime, Policing and Justice: The Experience of Older People* was published, which includes major findings from the British Crime Survey (BCS) (Chivite-Mathews and Maggs 2002). The Scottish Executive, too, has made reducing fear of crime among older people one of its 'milestones'.

National bodies such as Crime Concern, Victim Support, The Suzy Lamplugh Trust, and Help the Aged are also focusing on victimisation and fear of crime, as are the Crime Reduction Teams in the Regional Government Offices, local Crime and Disorder Partnerships, crime prevention officers and neighbourhood and street warden schemes.

In the first part of the chapter some of the key issues relating to fear of crime are discussed. The findings of research into the causes, characteristics and consequences of fear of crime amongst older people are outlined. The theoretical elements of the debate on what constitutes fear of crime are noted only in passing. It seems logical to assume that if reassurance policies and projects are to be effective then a clear understanding is required on the issues about which older people are 'fearful': of what, when, where and why.

This is followed by a discussion on reassurance, with the emphasis on enhancing feelings of safety and security on the part of older people. Reassurance, certainly from the point of view of the police, has other strands, for example public confidence in their service. The challenge is, as Singer (2004) points out, knowing what to do and how to do it: a case of what works and how it works. Also what sort of reassurance projects and schemes have been shown to be effective and which have not. And in which cases are the outputs and outcomes of reassurance programmes 'promising' or 'unknown' (Dagleish and Myhill 2004). Given the multi-faceted nature of the fear of crime concept and the diversity of older people there are unlikely to be universal panaceas found in relation to reassurance. As Singer has noted, policy makers need to ensure that reassurance schemes are tailored to the right problem (Singer 2004, p. 52). Nor are 'quick fixes' at all likely to be in evidence.

Nonetheless, this should not deter us from seeking to identify effective good practice. There is an extensive literature on some elements of these issues. For example, a lot is known about what is feared by some older people, when and why. Many crime and disorder reduction partnerships have undertaken audits/surveys into fear of crime and formulated reduction targets and strategies. The information needs of the elderly have been analysed. The effectiveness of street lighting and visible patrolling by beat police officers and neighbourhood wardens in making (older) residents less 'fearful' has been evaluated in depth. Much less is understood for example as to what can be done to reassure older people of different backgrounds, and in different circumstances. Nonetheless it is important to make connections between academic research and practical policy making and between the issues of fear of crime on the one hand and reassurance on the other. This is precisely what this chapter attempts to do.

Older people

Researchers define 'older' people in a variety of ways. In the British Crime Survey, 60 and over is used, although there is also some analysis of people aged 65–74 and 75+. Many others use 60 and over, for example Pain (1995); while others use 55 and over, for example Lee (1982) and Miethe and Lee (1984); yet others set the boundary at 65 and over, or 66 and over (Warr 1984). To a certain extent, this variation thwarts easy comparison of findings. A distinction between the 'old' (60–74) and 'very old' (75+) may be more common in the future.

As far as the demographics are concerned it has been well established that the UK has an ageing population, as elsewhere. For example, the number of people aged 65 and over in England is projected to rise from 7.8 million in 1996 to 12.4 million in 2031. Older women are more likely than older men to live alone and the proportion increases with advancing age. Seventy-one per cent of women aged 85 and over who live in private households lived alone in 2001. In private households (approximately 95 per cent of older people) 40 per cent of men and 42 per cent of women aged 65 and over reported having at least one of five types of disability. Between 1998 and 2031 the number of older people with cognitive impairment in England will rise from 461,000 to 765,000 – an increase of 66 per cent (Comas-Herrera 2003).

In 2001, Help the Aged collaborated with the then Department for Transport, local government, and the regions in the production of a pamphlet about older people and their needs for use by neighbourhood and street wardens (Neighbourhood Renewal Unit 2001). This publication included a handy fact file about UK pensioners to capture the diversity of senior citizens. Despite all the differences between individual older people and the places in which they live, a pen picture of senior citizens was attempted.

One way of doing this is to identify the characteristics of a notional ten pensioners. The following facts amongst many were reported: 82 per cent of the blind or partially sighted people in Britain are over 65 years of age; 5 out of 10 aged 75 and over say that they have difficulty in hearing, at least 1 in 10 will be treated for depression or anxiety; 5 out of 10 of those aged 80 and over will have a serious fall in any year; three tenths of all pensioners are living below the official poverty line, pensioner households spend around 40 per cent of their income on housing, fuel and food; 3 out of 10 will have lived in the same locality for many years; 6 in 10 regularly use public transport, nearly all have access to a TV and they watch on average 36 hours every week; 1 in 10 reported that they 'felt trapped in their own homes' and 3 out of every 10 people aged 75 and over 'live more or less alone and socialise with very few people'; 8 in 10 talk to their neighbours at least once a week. It should be borne in mind that variations in age, ethnic background, place of residence, income and (former) occupation are all significant factors affecting the welfare and wants of those who were born before the Second World War.

Older people's fears

Definitions of fear and related attitudes, feelings and reactions are abound. The *Oxford English Dictionary* (2004), defines fear as: 'the emotion of pain or uneasiness caused by the sense of impending danger, and as a state of anxiety derived from the concern for the safety of a person or thing'.

Everyone has his or her own fears and older people are no exception. Indeed, we know that ageing brings its own worries (and actual risk) in relation to ill health, mobility, isolation and loneliness (Victor *et al.* 2002), physical frailty and economic vulnerability (Ramsden and Anderson 1998). In addition, specific anxiety disorders affect a minority of people, especially into older age (Whalley 2000, p. 89). There are a number of psychiatric conditions that predispose sufferers to express inordinate levels of anxiety in many areas of their lives. Perhaps as many as 5 per cent of the population suffers from *general anxiety syndrome.*

The particular life worries which may be associated with ageing include for example: illness and frailty; retirement and loss of companionship at work; being isolated and lonely; dependence; dying; losing one's driving licence and becoming less mobile; having a fall or accident; not having enough money to pay the bills; local environmental problems such as noise, litter and graffiti; and last, but certainly not least, being a victim of an attack or burglary.

It is important to note that some of these, what are sometimes called 'non-crime worries', have also been shown to be powerful predictors of fear of crime. It is generally accepted that perceived risk and fear of crime cannot and should not be treated as separate from other anxieties, such as the phobias and worries noted by Singer (2004, p. 35). These included fear of the dark, going into hospital, enclosed spaces, and certain animals and insects, as well as heights and crowds. The fear of becoming a victim of crime remained consistently the second highest ranked worry after 'something bad happening to a loved one' (Burnett 1995).

Fear of crime

The term 'fear of crime' has gained almost universal use. Some believe it is overused and misused (Ferraro and La Grange 1987). Pantazis (2000) points to the confusion that exists in the literature on the precise meaning of fear of crime and how it should be measured.

Nevertheless, it is widely accepted as a short-hand term to refer to a whole range of attitudes, feelings, reactions and emotions that (older) people have towards crime and victimisation. It can include worry and anxiety (Hough 1995, cited by Pantazis 2000); terror, panic and unease (Bannister and Fyfe 2001) as well as annoyance and anger (Ditton *et al.* 2000).

Wurff and colleagues (1988, p. 136) suggest that three components play a part in fear of crime, namely: the existence of a certain element of well-being; the perception of a threat to that well-being, and a feeling of inability to cope with that threat. The first of these is rarely mentioned, but it refers to the possession of valued objects, a way of life one cares for or people one loves, which are variously described as the *sine qua non* of fear.

> In essence, people experience a range of 'emotions' about crime (and other threats to their well being) – emotions that vary in nature, duration, and from one situation to another. (Bannister and Fyfe 2001, p. 85)

Smith makes the point that 'fear is an experience that is not discrete or clearly bounded, unlike crime itself. Anxiety about crime is not so much an event as a persistent and recurring sense of malaise' (Smith 1987, p. 2).

We should, of course, try to be as precise as possible when using the term fear of crime. So, for example, perceived risk should be separated analytically from feeling safe/unsafe and perceptions and judgements of the seriousness and prevalence of crime should be distinguished from the emotions of being afraid, worried or angry. Warr differentiates between fear of crime and perception of risk by defining fear of crime as 'an emotion, a feeling of alarm or dread caused by an awareness or expectation of danger'. It involves:

> a variety of emotional states, attitudes or perceptions (including mistrust of others, anxiety, perceived risk, fear of strangers, or concern about deteriorating neighbourhoods, or declining national morality). (Warr, 1990, p. 892)

He contends that fear is a 'reaction to the perceived environment' and the perceived risk of harm is a proximate cause of fear of crime. There is ample evidence that actual and perceived risk should not only be conceived of as different analytically, but also that establishing cause and effect between them is not a simple matter and cannot be taken for granted. Gates and Roe (1987) cite researchers who have found that perceived levels of crime can be independent of fear of crime. Those who perceive higher levels of crime, for example, are not necessarily more fearful of victimisation.

There seems little option but to treat the whole range of attitudes, perceptions and views displayed by older people about crime and anti-social behaviour as 'fear of crime' as is commonly the case, at the same time bearing in mind that most observers would differentiate between general perceptions of crime and anxiety about becoming a victim.

Justified or not?

One very obvious explanation for some older people's fear of crime is, of course, that it may be justified. An older person may have been a victim of a crime or know other people, friends or neighbours, who have been victims. They may live in an area with a high crime rate. In some cases, all three may be true. Fear then, is quite a reasonable response, either to what they have experienced or to what they know or both.

Where fear of crime is not a response to experience or factual knowledge, we can say that it is 'not justified' but still it may be understandable given a number of inter-related personal, economic, environmental and societal factors. Some of these factors may also contribute to fear of crime, for reasons outlined above.

Ultimately of course, the point of showing that some fear is justified and some is not is not to make judgements about older people's views and attitudes. Rather, the aim is to attempt to understand why older people are afraid so that we can formulate policies and introduce measures that are effective in reducing both crime and fear of crime.

First, this section looks at whether the commonly held idea that older people have high levels of fear of crime, but relatively low risk of becoming victims, is true. Second, in attempting to understand why some older people are more afraid than others, sometimes apparently with 'no justification', we look at who is afraid, of what and whom, and in what circumstances, i.e. when and where. We do this by examining some of the key personal, environmental and societal factors that can contribute to fear of crime among older people and which researchers in this field have identified.

129

High fear, low risk – reality or myth?

The conventional wisdom is that older people taken as a whole are at relatively low risk of being victims of crime in the UK, certainly when compared to younger age groups and in relation to most property and personal crimes (Chivitte-Mathews and Maggs 2002).

It is also well known that older people are probably more likely to be the victim of a fire or fall at home or to be involved in a traffic accident than they are to be burgled or mugged. As Pain notes, in the literature on fear of crime older people are usually discussed as a group who experience high fear of crime but paradoxically low risk of victimisation: '... the discovery of this "irrational" fear has been very influential on ensuing research and policy' (Pain 1997, p. 119).

Some of the 'generalised' statistics would appear to support the idea that there is indeed a mismatch between older people's expressed levels of worry about crime, particularly violent crime and their antecedent levels of objective risk. Analysis of responses in national surveys certainly reinforces the view widely held by people in the criminal justice system that many older people's fears are not justified.

Psychologically, the impact of a crime, particularly a violent crime, burglary or a crime of deception, such as doorstep conning or distraction burglary, may serve to damage an older person's self-esteem, heighten their perceptions of their own vulnerability and increase their levels of fear still further.

It is clear then that we cannot simply assume that older people's fears and anxieties about crime are 'irrational' or 'unjustified'. At the very least, we should investigate their experiences of crime as well as local levels of actual and reported or recorded crime and anti-social behaviour. Hough suggests that the BCS findings confirm that worries about crime are often firmly and intelligently grounded in direct or indirect experience (Hough 1995, p. 43).

It is also possible for us to agree with Brogden and Nijhar (2000) that the 'received criminological wisdom' – that older people are among those least likely to be victims of crime but who nevertheless fear crime the most – is flawed. The idea is based on a false homogenisation of older people and fails to take account of differences in how susceptible they are to crime according to their older age 'band' (within the wider categorisation of old age) as well as their gender, ethnicity, lifestyle and location (Scarf *et al.* 2002).

Key factors contributing to fear of crime

Researchers have advanced at least three models to explain fear of crime among older people. It is fair to say that no single approach predominates. These approaches can be characterised thus:

- Fear as the product of actual direct or indirect victimisation, as discussed above. How an older person perceives such an experience will have a strong bearing on their level of fear of crime and of different types of crime.

- Fear as determined in relation to an older individual's (perceived and/or real) ability to exercise control over their own life and the behaviour and activities of others and their (perceived and/or real) inability to prevent or cope with the consequences of victimisation, i.e. actual or perceived vulnerability.

- The (urban) environment as a barometer of risk and protective factors.

People read visual evidence to determine likely levels of criminal risk and the likelihood of intervention on their behalf.

Three key explanatory factors can be highlighted. These are:

1. *Perceived vulnerability* amongst older people, especially the very old, many of whom are women living alone, who may therefore perceive themselves to be particularly vulnerable.

2. *Perceived inability to cope with the impact of crime* which involves some older people's perceived inability to cope with the impact or consequences of being a victim of crime, particularly physically and financially.

   Although many older people are healthy and active, the physical consequences of a push, fall or serious attack are likely to be far more traumatic for them than for younger people. More serious injuries are recorded with half of older victims requiring medical care compared to only a quarter for younger ones (Brogden and Nijhar 2000, p. 58). Moreover, a recent analysis of the impact of crime on victims on the basis of the 2000 Scottish Crime Survey reports that in 60 per cent of incidents the victim or someone else in the household had an emotional reaction to victimisation

– 33 per cent recorded 'distressing' emotions such as shock, fear, intimidation, vulnerability or numbness.

Midwinter (1990) has pointed out that older people living on low incomes (will) find it more difficult to replace belongings that have been stolen or damaged in a burglary – they are often not insured. Older people may worry particularly about the loss of items of lifelong sentimental value. Even the thought of replacing a pension book, library tickets, bus pass, chequebook or banker's card and other documentation after a snatch theft may be overwhelming.

3. *Poverty and deprivation* is another factor that is consistently associated with greater anxiety about crime; for the population as a whole and for older people specifically, low income is often combined with living in a deprived neighbourhood.

Not only do older people have difficulty replacing items, but also their lack of material resources can limit their ability to protect themselves against risk in the first place. 'For example, people with limited income may be unable to afford to install security devices such as burglar alarms or secure locks' (Scharf *et al.* 2002, p. 79).

All this can lead to older people's heightened perceptions of their own vulnerability and increase their fear of crime. Indeed, writing about the impact of poverty on fear of crime among the population as a whole, Pantazis (2000, p. 420) demonstrates that people living in low-income households are more than twice as likely as rich people to feel unsafe – 54 per cent compared to 25 per cent. She also found that poor women are one and a half times more likely to feel unsafe than women in rich households and poor older people are more prone than younger people to feel unsafe – 62 per cent and 46 per cent respectively. In addition, Pantazis found that older people living in circumstances of multiple deprivation were seven times more likely to feel unsafe in comparison with older people in less deprived surroundings.

Thus the main 'parameters' of fear of crime amongst older people are reasonably well known, even if there are disagreements over definition and measurement. Which older people are 'fearful' of crime? When, where, and why must be taken into account by those who seek to offer reassurance.

Reassurance

Reassurance is a term which is usually defined in terms of 'restoring confidence', 'dispelling apprehension', 'encouraging and heartening' and 'putting someone's mind at rest or at ease'. An example given in one source was – 'The Minister reassured the public regarding the safety of public transport'!

In Home Office and police circles, reassurance is seen as being multi-faceted. It is suggested that the concept of reassurance policing was coined in the US by Charles Bahn (1974) and became a catch-all term encompassing a variety of police actions and reactions. Visibility, accessibility and familiarity on the part of the police are key elements, and reassurance is seen as a desirable outcome. Singer (2004), for example, identifies and bases his analysis on four key strands – public engagement, feelings of safety and security, satisfaction with the policing provided, and public confidence in the policing expected. In his study of reassurance policing undertaken in Milton Keynes a broad definition was used including crime reduction and fear of crime foci. Feelings of safety and security amongst neighbourhood residents was one element explored and reassurance initiatives to reduce concern/fear about crime and anger with disorder were analysed. In their review of international reassurance interventions, Dagleish and Myhill (2004) see reducing fear of crime as but one aspect of reassurance. They examine the efficacy of schemes which improve the visibility and familiarity of police officers – usually on patrol. They also evaluate improvements to the physical environment as a mechanism to enhance reassurance.

So the question to be addressed in this section of the chapter is what strategies, initiatives, research projects, key messages can be suggested which have a sound basis for reassuring older people in relation to crime?

In the absence of theory in relation to the issue of reassurance the empirical studies noted above are useful and there are a number of useful sources from which lessons can be drawn, for example the Home Office Fear of Crime toolkit and E-Community.

On the basis of the findings of existing research, project evaluations and in conjunction and consultation with older people some suggestions for good practice can be made. It should be borne in mind that those tasked with reassuring older people about crime and associated problems are likely themselves to have plenty of experience. Many will be serving or retired police officers. But the point to be made is that local projects will only succeed if they are delivered at the right time, in the right place and in the right way. Below four 'case topics' are briefly outlined by way of illustration.

(a) Befriending and other schemes to reduce isolation and anxiety

One of the clear pointers to emerge from the review of evidence on fear of crime amongst older people was that such anxieties should not be 'detached' from other life concerns and worries. Old age often brings ill health, bereavement, isolation and loneliness and perceived vulnerability. Some older people are of an 'anxious disposition' and others suffer from cognitive impairment.

For those who for one reason or another are generally anxious, measures to reassure about crime alone are unlikely to succeed. There is a strong case that safety and security advice and assistance should be combined with or contained within wider social provision. Befriending and home-sharing schemes, for example, have been shown to reduce risk and isolation amongst vulnerable older people, who themselves are very likely to be fearful of being a victim of crime. Andrews (2004) evaluated a befriending scheme and found that, on the basis of comments made by older participants, it was effective. Likewise, Burnett (2004), reviewing the research evidence on local homesharing schemes in England and Australia found that such domestic arrangements had positive results. Having a younger person staying with them or visiting them regularly has proved to be beneficial to many older people, and reduces in general their anxieties.

(b) Purposeful patrolling

When older people are asked what they would like to see done to make them feel safer they often say they want more police on the beat. The numbers of police officers, community support officers and neighbourhood and street wardens have grown in the last decade. Neighbourhood policing in all its variants has become a reality in the cities, towns and villages in Britain.

The evidence reported by Dagleish and Myhill (2004), and Singer's (2004) evaluation of local safety and reassurance schemes, show that increased foot patrols produce positive results. The presence of uniformed officers, especially on foot, enhance perceptions of safety and reduce anxiety. Singer quotes an older man in Beanhill, Milton Keynes – 'Walking around the estate, just talking to people and finding out what people's fears are and what they would like done about it' (Singer, 2004, p. 22). Thus there is evidence that patrolling can not only deter criminal activity (Burnett 1995), but also reassures the population in general and older people in particular. The only caveat that should be added is that it is purposeful patrolling that works, not just wandering around chatting to each other. There may be operational reasons for patrolling in pairs, but presumably twice as many older people could see and be contacted by single officers operating independently. There is a case for a review of operating procedures in relation to patrolling to maximise beneficial impacts.

(c) Mapping older people and crime

Amongst the wealth of evidence summarised earlier in this chapter perhaps the most compelling was that the fears of older people of becoming a victim of crime and anti-social behaviour are often fully justified. There are areas in which high risk and high fear coincide. The Office of the Deputy Prime Minister published its latest Index of Multiple Deprivation in 2004. (Help the Aged 2004). Contained therein for the first time were data and maps at various scales on not only 'a crime domain' but also 'a supplementary index of income deprivation affecting older people'. From those data it is feasible to pinpoint precisely in any locality where older people have to endure a double whammy of low income and high crime. The evidence is that senior citizens in such circumstances are likely to be anxious, as well as probably angry, about crime and disorder. It is suggested that such areas should be plotted, and targeted for crime prevention and reassurance. Reassurance measures which have had a proven impact should be implemented taking into account local characteristics and the views of local (older) residents.

(d) A judicious menu of mechanisms and messages

A series of proposals was made in *Tackling Older People's Fear of Crime* produced by Help the Aged's Senior Safety Campaign in 2002. They included collecting data on crime hot spots and 'feared' areas; involving older people in crime and disorder audits and strategies, increasing support for home security schemes; promoting responsible reporting of crime in the media, improving the local environment/ removing signs of disorder and setting up intergenerational schemes to build up trust between older people and teenagers. To this list can be added a plea for reassurance to concentrate on older victims. In high crime areas older people are often victimised including by distraction burglars. Accurate and up-to-date statistics should be collected from a variety of sources on how, when and where older people become victims and appropriate actions taken to reduce crime and the consequences of crime. Crime statistics should be used to alert but not alarm. Finally some key axioms should be borne in mind in any presentations made to older audiences. Events should be held in daylight hours and at places which are readily accessible. A 'workshop' style format for meetings is preferable with care being taken to ensure that speakers can be heard clearly. Reassuring words should be combined with practical suggestions, for example self defence and home security. Trouble should be taken to outline what is being done and/or will be done by those in authority to tackle the issues raised by older people. On no account should older people be patronised or accused of irrationality and overreacting in relation to anxieties over crime. Lastly, the active involvement of older volunteers should be solicited in such initiatives as local surveys and contacting those that are 'hard to reach'.

Conclusion

Fear of crime is a contested concept and it is hardly surprising that there is little unanimity amongst academics and even practitioners about how it should be defined, characterised and measured. Thus, there is bound to be ambivalence over the whole issue of reassurance. Nonetheless there are some clear pointers for those interested. That some older people are fearful of being victims of certain sorts of crime at certain times and in certain places is not in doubt. The main dimensions of anxiety about becoming a victim of crime on the part of older people are well established. Not all of them have been pursued here. But who it is that needs to be reassured – be their fears justified or not – is clear. There is also limited empirical research evidence as to which reassurance policies and practices work.

What is needed now is for more studies to be undertaken which link fear of crime amongst older people *and* reassurance projects. A good example of this type of work is the evaluation studies that have been conducted on improved street lighting. Certainly any local reassurance strategy or scheme should be rigorously evaluated in terms of costs and benefits. And the same goes for the practical measures to reassure older people that have been suggested in the latter part of this chapter.

References

Bahn, C. (1974) 'The Reassurance Factor in Police Patrol', *British Journal of Criminology,* 12 (3): 338–45.

Comas-Herrera, A., Wittenburg, R., Pickard, L. and Knapp, M. (2003) *Cognitive Impairment in Older People.* London: Alzheimer's Research Trust.

Bannister, J. and Fyfe, N. (2001) 'Introduction: Fear and the City', *Urban Studies* 38, (5/6): 807–14.

Brogden, M. and Nijhar, P. (2000) *Crime, Abuse and the Older People.* Cullompton: Willan Publishing.

Burnett, A. (1995) *In the Wrong Place? Urban Facilities and Crime Patterns,* Unpublished paper. Institute of British Geographers' Annual Conference, University of Northumbria.

Burnett, A. (2004) *I've Got Company Tonight: Does Homeshare work? Review of the Evidence.* Help the Aged in conjunction with the Oxford Institute of Ageing.

Chivite-Mathews, N. and Maggs, P. (2002) *Crime, Policing and Justice: The Experience of Older People.* Home Office Statistical Bulletin/02. London: Home Office Research, Development and Statistics Directorate.

Dagleish, D. and Myhill, A. (2004) *Reassuring the Public: A Review of International Policing Interventions.* London: Home Office: Research, Development and Statistics Directorate.

Ditton, J. and Farrall, S. (2000) 'Crime Surveys and the Measurement Problem: Fear of Crime' in V. Jupp, P. Davies and P. Francis (eds) (2000) *Doing Criminological Research,* pp. 142–155. London: Sage.

Ferraro, K. and La Grange, R. (1992) 'Are older people most afraid of crime? Reconsidering Differences in Fear of Victimization', *Journal of Gerontology,* 47 (5): 233–44.

Gates, L. and Rohe, W. (1987) 'Fear and Reactions to Crime', *Urban Affairs Quarterly.* 22 (3), 425–53.

Hough, M. (1995) *Anxiety About Crime: Findings From the 1994 British Crime Survey.* Research Study 147. London: Home Office.

Lee, G. (1982) 'Sex Differences in Fear of Crime Among Older People', *Research on Ageing,* 4 (3): 282–98.

Midwinter, E. (1990) *The Old Order: Crime and Older People.* London: Centre for Policy on Ageing/Help the Aged.

Neighbourhood Renewal Unit (2001) *Neighbourhood and Street Wardens' Programme*: Guidance on How Wardens Can Help Older People, DETR.

Smith, S. (1987) 'Fear of Crime: Beyond a Geography of Deviance', *Progress in Human Geography,* 11: 1–23.

Scharf, T. Phillipson, C., Smith, A. and Kingston, P. (2002) *Growing Older in Socially Deprived Areas: Social Exclusion in Later Life.* London: Help the Aged.

Singer, L. (2004) *Reassurance Policing: An evaluation of the Local Management of Community Safety*. London: Home Office, Research, Development and Statistics Directorate.

Pain, R. (1995) 'Local Contexts and Fear of Crime: Older People in the North East of England, *Northern Economic Review*, 24: 96–111.

Pantazis, C. (2000) 'Fear of Crime: Vulnerability and Poverty', *British Journal of Criminology*, 40: 414–36.

Victor, C., Bowling, A., Bond, J. and Scambler, S. (2002) 'Loneliness in Later Life: Preliminary Findings from the Growing Older Project', *Quality in Ageing*, 3 (1): 34–41.

Warr, M. (1984) 'Fear of Victimisation: Why are Women and the Older People more afraid?', *Social Science Quarterly*, 65: 681–702.

Warr, M. (1990) 'Dangerous Situations: Social Context and Fear of Victimisation', *Social Science Quarterly*, 3: 891–907.

Chapter 9

Local responses to elder abuse: building effective prevention strategies

Jill Manthorpe

Introduction

To some extent interests in crime and older people, and interests in the abuse of older people occupy parallel universes. Different emphases and terms are encountered and different stakeholders reflect and influence the work and concerns of different systems. This chapter takes a local focus in the hope that discussion of adult protection working will shed some light on what it means to put into operation a protective and preventive response to the abuse of individual older citizens.

This chapter takes the English policy guidance *No Secrets* (Department of Health 2000) as a watershed. This guidance sets out local authority and other public services' responsibility to work with their wider communities, such as the voluntary sector and commercial providers of care, to tackle mistreatment and neglect among vulnerable adults. Local authorities have lead responsibility but the emphasis of the guidance was that such responsibility would be through partnership, and the setting up of an Adult Protection Committee was strongly recommended as a means of bringing together the key agencies as well as representatives of vulnerable adults. All local areas were required to produce policies and procedures for their staff and the following years have seen these structures and partnerships become working relationships.

Some brief outline of what is meant by the term elder abuse and how this differs from adult protection may form a useful backcloth to discussion. The term 'elder abuse' is one that is increasingly recognised, but hard to define precisely. It may include abuse, mistreatment or neglect, but it is differentiated from specific crimes or offences by its context, generally presuming that those affected are 'vulnerable' citizens and that the harm they suffer is in the context of a relationship where there is an expectation of trust or care. *No Secrets* sets out these general definitions and, in particular, argues that among the different forms of abuse: physical, sexual, emotional, financial and so on, is discriminatory abuse. It is amidst this context of the social problem of adult protection that elder abuse is situated in the UK. Brogden (2001) is one of a number of authors who is critical of the distinct framing of elder abuse outside criminological definitions. However, this chapter, while conscious of the lack of clarity and lack of consensus over the area, explores current systems evolving from *No Secrets*. The consideration of operational and practice issues, of course, may throw some light on abstract definitions.

The abuse of older people, or elder abuse, is a term that is used in the professional and service communities of social care and health services. *No Secrets*, as noted above, relates to the abuse of vulnerable adults, not all of whom are older people. Many older people are not vulnerable, or share the vulnerabilities of other individuals. While levels of disability, poverty and illness are high among some older people, and those who use social care and health services are likely to be vulnerable to an extent, elder abuse sits in the context of wider concerns about vulnerable adults. At local levels this means that policies and procedures need to cover a range of care and treatment settings, to involve a number of service and professional groups, and to consult and listen to a wide number of service user, advocacy and representative groups of local citizens. Briefly, adult protection is now a strategic goal, while elder abuse is a term that refers more to specific instances. In the UK, the work of the pressure group Action on Elder Abuse (Manthorpe 1999) has focused attention on older people's risk of abuse and their vulnerabilities. In order to work at local levels, organisations of and services supporting older people collaborate with those working with other communities of vulnerable adults.

This chapter draws on my interest in elder abuse, much of it initially crystallised in my research for the Age Concern (1986) Report *The Law and Vulnerable Elderly People* and my current role as Chair of the Hull and East Riding Adult Protection Committee. Over these two decades, adult protection has moved from a position of being a minor to a major policy goal, with developments in training, professional practice and research. Understanding too has developed, with a range of evidence and theoretical perspectives shaping strategies and activity. In order to comment on such developments from a local perspective, four themes form the main discussions of this chapter; adult protection work at local level, in small groups, among local citizens and in respect of prevention.

Before *No Secrets*

While *No Secrets* remains at the level of government policy and has not led to legislation, it has made, nonetheless, a major impact at local level in England. This is not to say that many local areas had not previously considered their responses to practitioners' concerns, pressure group campaigning and earlier policy initiatives. In many areas a variety of protocols, policies and procedures had evolved; however, these were inconsistent and their variability extended both to content and levels of enforcement. Without a legal or regulatory framework, initiatives at local level can be sporadic or may be partially implemented. Surveys of policies and procedures prior to *No Secrets* indicate the variability of local policies (see Brown and Stein 1998).

While policies and procedures may indicate to staff the extent of their responsibility, early research on adult protection suggested that practitioners often had an incomplete picture of their roles and the new importance being accorded to adult protection could not build on existing professional training. Most practitioners admitted little knowledge and confidence (Brown, Kingston and Wilson 1999; Taylor and Dodd 2003). Among non-professionals, those staff in most frequent personal contact with highly vulnerable people, such as care assistants or home care workers, the 'training gap' was visible and, of course, related to the low levels of training and high turnover among this sector as a whole (Balloch *et al*. 2004). It would not be fair to argue that thinking about training was negligible: over the 1990s a variety of initiatives occurred, some promoted by pressure groups, many with government funding (see for example, Action on Elder Abuse 1995; Pritchard 1996).

However, while the 1990s saw numerous training initiatives, often around 'awareness raising', these were often directed towards a relatively narrow sector. Mainly focused on social care, within local authority social services and voluntary providers, such initiatives were not always inclusive of all health professionals or the growing commercial sector of residential and home-based (domiciliary) care.

A lack of central government direction provided initial excuses for inaction. Pressure group politics centred on raising the profile of the issue of adult protection, drawing attention to individual cases and wider concerns about the quality of care and responses from the criminal justice sector. With the benefit of hindsight, the impetus for reform had to address multi-faceted issues related to the low priority of older people, unlike reform of other similar areas, such as child protection where individual 'scandals' have done much to provoke government reform or response (Butler and Drakeford 2003). It was also not always clear what changes various stakeholders or pressure groups were wanting: other than 'action' or reform. The founding of the organisation Action on Elder Abuse in 1993 enabled greater precision around the priorities for reform (for a general history of developments of the issue of elder abuse, see Manthorpe 1999), notably those calling for government insistence on local responses.

No Secrets can be set in the context of accumulations of concern about the abuse of older people in settings ranging from their own home to care homes, day care and hospital provision. As noted above, it used the term 'vulnerable' people or adults and not older people as the category to whom adult protection systems would apply: a term that is difficult to define in anything other than in relative terms. The definition of 'vulnerable' is a person 'who is or may be in need of community care services' (Lord Chancellor's Department 1997), a category that can contract or expand according to legislation and in line with movable eligibility criteria. At the time, geographical variations in service thresholds were widely acknowledged, a situation that subsequently was tackled by government direction in Fair Access to Care Services (Department of Health 2002).

The use of the category vulnerable adult also reduces the reliance on the terminology of client or service user group. Adult protection has been used as an umbrella term to bring together concerns over the abuse of people with learning disabilities, people with mental health problems, people with physical disabilities, and older people. Clearly though, these are not the totality of the adult population and the evolution of the term 'vulnerable adult' brings together disabilities or poor health status that might be also termed mental or cognitive impairment, chronic sickness or profound/multiple/complex needs. Community care services, however, do extend to people with lower levels of need for social care and their status as 'vulnerable' is more arguable. *No Secrets* takes a firm line, however, on rights to self-determination and the need for any actions to be agreed by the aggrieved or 'injured' party. Such values differentiate the world of adult protection from child protection.

In the criminal justice sector, however, the report of the Interdepartmental Working Group on the Treatment of Vulnerable or Intimidated Witnesses in the Criminal Justice System (Home Office 1998) proposed greater protection for witnesses defined as vulnerable. Under the Youth Justice and Criminal Evidence Act 1999, a vulnerable witness is seen as one suffering from mental disorder, or impaired intelligence or social functioning, or physical disability, including the elderly and frail. This means that there is much overlap in the definitions of vulnerability, and at local level, one of the continued prompts to partnership working appears to be a fairly constant flow of such initiatives requiring joint thinking, shared training and protocols. Thus, while the next section focuses on the aftermath of *No Secrets*, already this document is being superseded by other policy imperatives. The risk of policy overload may therefore be reduced by strong yet flexible partnerships that can adapt to new initiatives, such as these changes in the treatment of witnesses in the criminal justice system.

After *No Secrets*

From the year 2000 local organisations implemented *No Secrets*, their main tasks being to formulate multi-agency adult protection policies and procedures, to consider setting up an adult protection committee and, for local authorities, taking on the role of lead agency in this area and agreeing what this entailed. As early research into implementation has revealed (Mathew *et al.* 2002) that implementation has varied, although an overview of local authority activity (Sumner 2003) found generally good progress. Four main developments mark these early days. The first is a levelling up of some local systems to a baseline of provision. Clearly, in some areas, systems were already well developed at the time of *No Secrets*, but there has been a reduction in the number of areas where little work or priority had transpired. Second, *No Secrets* does not simply expect greater 'awareness' among staff: its systems require more sophisticated responses by those who are responsible for investigation, decision-making and casework. As a result, greater specialism has occurred. In respect of work with older people, some of this seems to have been influenced by work with people with learning disabilities where systems and practice appear to have been better developed overall. Court craft, for instance, and long-term therapeutic support for those who have been subject to abuse (see, for example, Hollins 1994 and the work of the Ann Craft Trust) have been specialisms in this area of work for over a decade. Third, while appointing local authorities' social services departments as lead agencies, *No Secrets* put great emphasis on the importance of partnership between a broad range of agencies, to include the local Crown Prosecution Service, for example, not just the twin peaks of health and social services. Finally, *No Secrets* eradicated any excuse for inaction. This represented a challenge to pressure groups that had to move to discuss in more detail the design and workings of adult protection systems. It also provided an impetus to bring together activity at local level and examine it in the light of government aspirations (for an example of a systems model from West Sussex, see Doonan 2002). The following sections outline local responses to these general achievements.

What works at local level?

The need to produce multi-agency policies and procedures compels communication and negotiation. One legacy of the policy vacuum before *No Secrets* was a set of policies and procedures that could overlap at local level, leading to possible confusion, but also to a sense that these were voluntary and could be used or not according to professional discretion, or inertia. Such policies relied on good will and ownership was not always clear or confirmed. *No Secrets* prompted moral and organisational force to agree local systems and responsibilities. These explicitly included services and practitioners that traditionally placed high value on their own organisational and professional autonomy, such as hospital services and the private sector of care. While many of the latter are in contractual relationships with the statutory sector, they do not always have to abide by policies unless these are an explicit part of the contract. Beyond health and social care, *No Secrets* was able to wield the power of a government directive to indicate to other organisations that they too had a role in adult protection, for example, the local Department of Work and Pensions. Other key members of the local adult protective organisational systems generally include the police, the voluntary sector, and legal services. Such agencies provide a wealth of experience and are also important links in the chain of communication. Legal advice on the options available to organisations or the committee can be invaluable, issues can be discussed in the light of numerous perspectives, and information that is not yet in the public domain can be discussed in confidence. Specific local pressures or incidents may also be shared between organisations that may be centrally involved, or more peripheral. It is the communication with and involvement of those on the apparent periphery that may be the strength of the multi-agency approach. Common concerns may be recognised and resolved.

Such communication may be one positive result of *No Secrets* and it also reflects the growing range and number of co-ordinating bodies or partnerships that relate to the government's modernisation agenda (Department of Health 1998). This sees value in sharing resources, in working differently and breaking down agency barriers. But, unlike many modernisation initiatives, *No Secrets* was not linked to pump priming or allocation of financial resources. Thus local level adult protection work has often been primarily funded by the statutory health and social care sector from existing budgets.

Who should fund a local adult protection system? While local authorities are lead agencies, the multi-agency approach has led in many areas to 'packages' of funding. In the Hull and East Riding area (at the time of writing covering two local authorities, three large NHS Trusts; (one hospital [multi-site and acute], one mental health facility and one ambulance), a segment of the area served by another hospital Trust, four primary care trusts and one police force (itself covering two further local authorities), the potential for complex funding arguments was extreme. Fortunately, these statutory stakeholders of local authorities and primary care trusts with the police were willing and able to agree joint responsibility and to make use of a formula already in operation for the division of financial responsibility for the local (co-terminous) area child protection committee. While the 'source' of this formula was not, of course, valid in respect of work or numbers, it represented an agreeable and workable formula. Pragmatism at local level appears a highly effective lever to producing resources, although despite agreements in principle, it still remains challenging to extract sums at the right time. One lesson, quick to emerge, was that annual funding collections were time-consuming and made planning very difficult. This has since been resolved by agreement to commit funds 'in principle' over a three-year cycle. Clearly such resources are not always forthcoming and this may explain the continuing local variations in development of adult protection. But what are resources for? At local level one commitment may be around the funding of individual staff to take responsibility for the delivery of an adult protection service. Prior to *No Secrets* some local authorities had established the post of an adult protection co-ordinator to develop a service (for example, in Gloucestershire and Sheffield). This model requires resources, particularly if a co-ordinator is to have back-up in respect of administration. Other costs, for instance office space or administrative costs, may be contributed by host organisations, with or without a charge. Running an adult protection service is not cost-free. In some areas it appears that resource constraints have simply meant that adult protection is placed on the shoulders of an existing member of staff with an already high workload.

Thus in speaking of commitment to developing adult protection services, local agencies have had to find extra resources and, perhaps, expand existing resources. Such outlays appear distinctly unlikely to save money, more likely to increase demand. In the continued absence of central government performance indicators, necessitating a response from local government, it is not surprising that local authorities may feel that the argument for this to be a priority is not compelling. As yet we have little knowledge of how priorities are agreed, but from my local experience it appears that a helpful and constructive foundation has been the commitment of middle managers who have worked together over the years and have been able to take on leadership roles and to 'find' new or unused resources to spread and share costs. Such managers appear to have met a receptive ear among senior levels: we do not yet know much about local politicians' understanding of and commitment to the subject of adult protection.

Local developments thus require commitment when they are not under central government scrutiny or compulsion. A lack of resources means that there is little to do by way of financial accountability to central government, and any suggestions by central government that progress is laggardly may be met with a retort that this is to be expected. Commitment, it seems, is not only around creating and launching new policies, but having the ability to sustain interest, to deal with difficulties and to continually revisit what can be achieved at the level of local working. In our area we decided to review adult protection policies, to produce a report after the first six months and then an annual report from the adult protection committee, and to revise the committee's terms of reference and strategy through an iterative consultation of agreeing aims and goals. The work of any committee obviously depends on its members' commitments: hard, but not impossible, to sustain over time as numerous competing priorities emerge.

Local systems face considerable challenges. While resources are easy to identify as a problem, and the difficulty of keeping going is an organisational truism, local experience also raises the importance of personnel and their strength when forming a loose network across agencies. This type of informal network seems to have the potential to survive changes in membership if these are not simultaneous, and to bring to bear members' experiences and contacts. Thus in forming the policies required by *No Secrets* in our area, staff were able to draw in colleagues who had similar or related backgrounds in the detail of multi-agency policy making. They were also able to link with colleagues in neighbouring authorities, a welcome move to avoid 're-inventing the wheel', and also ensuring wider consensus of approach.

Two problems remain to be explored. First, there is the challenge of involving 'vulnerable' adults, or users of services. There is wide recognition that this is neither simple nor easy (Andrews *et al.* 2002). Vulnerable adults are not 'represented' by any agency, and many organisations within the voluntary sector do not now see themselves as mandated to be their representatives. At local level, this continues to be a dilemma, how to make involvement meaningful and to respond to individuals' priorities? Research into methods of participation needs to inform thinking and practice in this highly emotional area. The 'creative tension' Wilkinson (2004) identified in relationships between the voluntary/community sector and the government may also exist between voluntary groups who claim to speak on behalf of older people.

The involvement of the private sector of care needs careful consideration too. As the major provider of social care, particularly care homes and domiciliary care, this sector provides support for many of the most vulnerable people. However, this is a sector that contains a wide range of providers – from large multi-national chains to small 'cottage' businesses. There are few organisations representing providers and much competition between providers in some areas. Recent regulatory reforms, such as the Care Standards Act 2000, have also increased responsibilities among such providers to heighten their safeguards against abuse and mistreatment. These may be their focus of change, not the development of local services to identify and respond to abuse. How to provide a forum for discussion at local level remains a challenge, particularly if one of the benefits of discussion at adult protection committees, for example, might be a confidential discussion of investigation into services that are evoking concern. Commercially sensitive information may impact upon commissioning bodies, such as local authorities or primary care trusts, but these systems may be removed: we do not know whether such 'firewalls' exist within the private sector to keep such information confidential. The workings of small groups at local level form the focus of the next section.

What works in small groups?

While the adult protection committee is the most public face of local services, such a committee, meeting perhaps quarterly, cannot run a system. To do this a parallel group of operational staff has been an effective means of managing day to day business, translating aims into concrete tasks, organising programmes of training, for example, and dealing with on-going investigations and issues. In the Hull and East Riding area, for instance, such a group meets regularly and is chaired by a senior manager who provides line management to the adult protection co-ordinator. At this forum, arrangements for joint agency activities are planned, issues emerging from the interpretation of policy are resolved or acknowledged, and new initiatives are discussed to assess their relevance. Such a forum keeps a service grounded in the requirements of local agencies, it also sets some limits on the apparent predilection to involve more and expand further.

Information sharing is clearly one central role and purpose of an adult protection service. Information may be politically or commercially sensitive, it may also be regular, routinised data that assumes greater importance only if it is explored in the context of adult protection. Other information may be central government policy, or information from regulatory bodies, that has implications for adult protection services.

Such a context may prove a foundation for problem solving. Issues that may benefit from airing between agencies can be apparently minor, but the addressing of problems facing individual citizens or practitioners makes a local adult protection system visible and constructive. Not that small issues or problems are by any means easy to resolve, many of them represent long-standing difficulties, but an adult protection service may provide the opportunity to seek greater information and to confirm its validity. At another level, in our experience, an adult protection service may choose to tackle major issues, such as setting up an inquiry into an 'incident' or significant cause for concern (Manthorpe 2003).

At a small group level three main challenges remain. These include the potential for activity around abuse and neglect to heighten the anxiety of service users, carers and members of the public. Portrayal of services as locations of potential abuse or as housing abusers may evoke fear unintentionally. Other possible risks include refusing or delaying access to care that may be much needed. While these are hypotheses, caution may be needed not to over dramatise or sensationalise abuse.

Second, such alarm may not only affect potential or current service users and carers. Existing staff or potential members of the workforce may find that an emphasis on care settings as abusive undermines their already low status. The shortages of staff in all care settings may well contribute to care being poor quality: if we are to improve staffing the social care workforce needs to be motivated and their activities may need to be supported rather than criticised. Again we need to consider how reported incidents of abuse impact on the workings of local care services. In one of the few studies of this topic, Pritchard uncovered great concern among front-line staff about how they could find the support and time to respond to the needs of victims of abuse (Pritchard 2000).

Third, local groups' work may give a false sense of security that all is working well and that a network of support and good quality care operates at a local level. Salutary reminders that, at best, risks of abuse can be only minimised may need to be voiced rather than comfortable reassurances about safety. One of the main outcomes of casting light on adult protection may be that more cases of abuse are exposed. While this does not mean there is more abuse, it is an outcome that needs to be managed, particularly if a climate of anxiety is created.

What works for local citizens?

The argument above suggests that one role for a local protection service is to ensure that 'good news' stories are disseminated. While it is difficult to establish that prevention works, some confidence can be given to staff and service users that it is worth raising issues and that new policies can support people who wish to discuss situations of concern. Locally, this can extend to the use of case studies, 'anonymised' but based on local events. This provides credibility in training and sets out a positive message. In our area, the use of video recording of a vulnerable person, while in hospital, was seen as a very constructive and respectful way of collecting evidence. It gave a clear example of the joint working between police, health care practitioners and social services' staff.

New methods of raising awareness may also make an impact. Locally, as other areas have done, we have commissioned drama productions that focus on the way in which people with learning disability can raise issues of abuse. Performed in community centres and social care settings, these productions have reached people who might not necessarily have been interested in or provided with accessible written material or information. Their local roots enable the performances to reflect the area's geography, language and culture. Scripts were seen and debated by representatives from a variety of agencies to reduce the risk that unintentional coincidence of name or ongoing issues (e.g. investigations of certain incidents) could be misinterpreted.

Such publicity takes on the form of consultation to a degree. While consultation with people using services and their carers is still under-developed, it has to be seen as part of awareness training in my view. Consultation without a system for offering support would be unethical, but it is also important not to use awareness raising events or publicity as 'fishing expeditions' to unearth more stories of abuse without regard to the capacity of services to cope with the anxiety these will provoke or to respond to situations not already recognised or being resolved. This is not to condone abuse. but to acknowledge that responses such as staff suspension and service closure have an impact on service users and may leave them vulnerable to other harms.

For local citizens, the portrayal of services and staff as potential abusers may be positive in that it strips away any false sense of safety. Early publications such as *It Could Never Happen Here* (ARC/ NAPSAC 1993) or *Care Betrayed* (Counsel and Care 1995) or feelings that abuse was more likely in large institutional settings than group homes (see Cambridge 2004) have laid to rest these notions that 'places of safety' exist. In a climate of concern however we know little about service users' reactions to such distrust. Finally, we know even less about the evidence for prevention of abuse: it is this subject that forms the final section of this chapter.

What works in prevention?

Prevention of harm is a more feasible aim than protection, since prevention is less likely to infantilise or treat vulnerable people as in need of extra layers of surveillance or control. We still know little of what prevents people from becoming abusive, what systems mean that organisations do not foster or condone abuse, or what prevents low level abuse from escalating. At the moment we can help at a local level by making seeking help more acceptable. This may be achieved if the language of abuse, with terms such as 'victim' and 'perpetrator', is used more cautiously. Inadequate care may be a euphemism, but it may mean individuals are able to admit this is happening without being seen as 'abusers' or 'abused'. Language in respect of local services may be important here.

At local level, it may also be time to place greater attention on effective and sustained responses and sources of help, turning attention to these areas instead of narrowly concentrating on identifying and assessing abuse. In the UK, Pritchard (2001) is one of the few who has described in detail what elements of a service, post abuse, might look like, how it may operate and the resources it will entail. Few areas have a 'service map' of sources of help. This omission needs to be addressed, particularly within information for vulnerable older people and the public in general.

Prevention may have much to learn from the partnership activity referred to earlier, links may be established with community safety work (as described in this volume, Lister *et al.* 2006) and with agencies working with adults around domestic violence issues. Such work may make strong connections between local systems and existing or planned resources.

Prevention needs to assume a higher profile in my view. It would be helpful if this were community orientated and thus related to wider groups of older people, other than those in care settings. Engaging with older people's organisations so that they can assess the relevance of messages from professionals is one key step. Working across issues relating to community safety may also provide greater impetus to development in advocacy, particularly citizen advocacy (Croft and Beresford 1999).

Conclusion

This chapter has focused on local developments in adult protection. Three challenges have been highlighted: how agencies and systems are to take on responsibilities in the context of no extra resources; second, how practitioners, managers and service commissioners are to join up protection and prevention; and third, how to draw on communities' own strengths and solutions. Work on such questions may help to set the agenda, but also provide a vision for this latter part of the decade. The chapter started by suggesting that interests in crime and older people and interests in elder abuse occupy parallel universes to some extent. In research and policy making, this may well be so, but at a local level the chapter has revealed ways in which these universes are being drawn closer together, in their shared territories of responses to crime and the promotion of community safety and the search for ways to prevent the abuse and mistreatment of vulnerable older citizens.

References

Action on Elder Abuse (1995) *Everybody's Business: Taking Action on Elder Abuse*. London: Action on Elder Abuse.

Age Concern England (1986) *The Law and Vulnerable Elderly People*. London: Age Concern.

Andrews, J., Manthorpe, J. and Watson, R. (2002) 'Involving Older People in Intermediate Care', *Journal of Advanced Nursing*, 46 (3): 303–10.

ARC/NAPSAC (1993) *It Could Never Happen Here*. Bradford: Thornton and Pearson.

Balloch, S., Banks, L. and Hill, M. (2004) 'Securing Quality in the Mixed Economy of Care: Difficulties in Regulating Training', *Social Policy and Society* 3 (4): 365–74.

Brogden, M. (2001) *Geronticide: Killing the Elderly*. London: Jessica Kingsley.

Brown, H. and Stein, J. (1998) 'Implementing Adult Protection Policies in Kent and East Sussex', *Journal of Social Policy*, 27 (3): 371–96.

Brown, H., Kingston, P. and Wilson, B. (1999) 'Adult Protection: An Overview of Research and Policy', *Journal of Adult Protection* 1 (1): 6–17.

Butler, I. and Drakeford, M. (2003) *Social Policy, Social Welfare and Scandal*. Basingstoke: Palgrave.

Cambridge, P. (2004) 'Abuse Inquiries as Learning Tools for Social Care Organisations', N. Stanley and J. Manthorpe (eds) *The Age of the Inquiry: Learning and Blaming in Health and Social Care*, pp. 231–54. London: Routledge.

Counsel and Care (1995) *Care Betrayed*. London: Counsel and Care.

Croft, S. and Beresford, P. (1999) 'Elder Abuse and Participation: A Crucial coupling for change', in P. Slater and P. Beresford (eds) *Elder Abuse: Critical Issues in Policy and Practice*, pp. 73–88. London: Age Concern.

Department of Health (2000) *No Secrets – Guidance on Developing Multi-agency Practice and Procedures to Protect Vulnerable Adults from Abuse*. London: Department of Health.

Department of Health (2002) *Fair Access to Care Services*. London: Department of Health.

Department of Health (1998) *Modernising Social Services*. London: HMSO.

Doonan, S. (2002) 'Working in Partnership With *No Secrets* – A Whole System Approach to Consultation', *Journal of Adult Protection* 4 (1): 33–9.

Hollins, S. (1994) *Going to Court*. London: Gaskell.

Home Office (1998) *Interdepartmental Working Group on the Treatment of Vulnerable or Intimidated Witnesses in the Criminal Justice System*. London: Home Office.

Lord Chancellor's Department (1997) *Who Decides? Making Decisions on Behalf of Mentally Incapacitated Adults*. London: HMSO.

Manthorpe, J. (1999) 'Putting Elder Abuse on the Agenda: Achievements of a Campaign' in P. Slater and M. Eastman (eds) *Elder Abuse: Critical Issues in Policy and Practice*, pp. 24–37. London: Age Concern.

Manthorpe, J. (2003) 'Informing Local Inquiries: Developing Local Reviews in Adult Protection', *Journal of Adult Protection* 5 (4): 18–25.

Mathew, D., Brown, H., Kingston, P., McCreadie, C. and Askham J. (2002) 'The Response to "No Secrets"', *Journal of Adult Protection* 4 (1): 4–14.

Pritchard, J. (1996) *Working with Elder Abuse: A Training Manual for Home Care, Residential and Day Care Staff*. London: Jessica Kingsley.

Pritchard, J. (2000) *The Needs of Older Women: Services for Victims of Elder Abuse and Other Abuse*. Bristol: Policy Press.

Pritchard, J. (2001) *Male Victims of Elder Abuse: Their Experiences and Needs*. London: Jessica Kingsley.

Sumner, K. (2003) *No Secrets: The Protection of Vulnerable Adults from Abuse: Findings from an Analysis of Local Codes of Practice*. London: Department of Health.

Taylor, K. and Dodd, K. (2003) 'Knowledge and Attitudes of Staff Towards Adult Protection', *Journal of Adult Protection* 5 (4): 26–32.

Wilkinson, M.D. (2004) 'Campaigning for Older People: A Case Study Approach to the Input of Voluntary and Community Organisations in the Policy Process', *Social Policy and Society* 3 (4): 343–52.

Chapter 10

Global developments in relation to elder abuse

Bridget Penhale

Introduction

This chapter will provide an overview of elder abuse. The issues and developments that have occurred globally will be briefly explored. Over the last ten years there has been an increasing global recognition of the abuse and neglect of vulnerable older adults as a social problem in need of attention. A number of European countries have been working in this area, but are at different stages of development. The identification of abuse remains problematic. Techniques of intervention are in quite early stages of development, although some recent progress has been made.

A number of national and international organisations have been established. Various research initiatives are underway. Education and training for professionals is taking place concerning recognition and awareness of abuse and intervention skills. In discussion about the issues involvement of the public, and in particular service users themselves, is an essential next step in the process.

The chapter aims to examine some of the pertinent issues. Responses to the problem of elder abuse from several countries across the world will be explored, although there will be a concentration on those from Europe.

Throughout the 1990s in the UK there was a gradual increase in concern about the abuse and neglect of older people. The principal focus initially was on abuse and neglect of elders in the domestic setting. However, increasingly there has been consideration of abuse and neglect occurring within institutional settings (Glendenning and Kingston 1999; Stanley *et al.* 1999).

Elder abuse and neglect are not new concerns (Stearns 1986) and appear to be global in nature (World Health Organisation (WHO) 2002). Although the phenomena were initially recognised by English doctors in the mid-1970s (Baker 1977) it was not until the late 1980s that the issue was really concentrated on in the UK. This was largely due to a national conference organised by the British Geriatrics Society (a group of physicians concerned with older people) held in London in 1988. However, in the USA the problem was identified from the mid 1970s and has been researched from that time to try and clarify the issues and to provide solutions to it. Other countries such as Australia, Norway and Sweden have similarly approached the problem largely during the late 1980s and 1990s, although as we shall see later, some countries are only now beginning to consider the issues.

The amount of research and material published about the subject has been increasing fairly steadily. Yet, in many ways in a number of different countries, the stages of identification of the problem and the development of responses to it are still evolving. For example, it was not until 1993 that there was any clear sign from the UK government that elder abuse was a problem in need of attention (Department of Health 1993), although there has been a consistent approach from successive governments since that time (Department of Health 1999). The abuse of older people in institutions is an area where there has been even less research into abusive and neglectful situations. Whilst there has been a lengthy tradition in the UK of scandals in institutional care these tend to have been investigated and treated as separate inquiries into standards of care rather than concerned with abuse and abusive situations.

Undoubtedly, elder abuse and neglect are complex and sensitive areas to explore. This was also the case with child abuse and domestic violence against younger women. Additionally, there have been difficulties in establishing a sound theoretical base. This is partly due to the lack of agreement concerning definitions, but also due to problems with researching the topic (Ogg and Munn-Giddings 1993; Penhale 1999).

How prevalent is elder abuse? There is at present insufficient evidence concerning the prevalence and incidence of abuse in the UK and many European countries share this difficulty. In most countries where work has been conducted to establish the prevalence of elder abuse (for example, US, Canada, Australia, Finland), a figure of 5 per cent of the older population likely to be affected has been obtained and it is accepted on a global basis that 4–6 per cent of the population of older people in any country are likely to be affected (WHO 2002). This may however relate *either* to those individuals who experience abuse *or* to those who are at risk of abuse. The figures derived may well be an under-estimate as a proportion of older people is 'hard to reach' as they may be housebound, isolated, or have communication difficulties and so are often excluded from research samples.

Elder abuse is the most recent form of interpersonal violence to have been recognised as a problem in need of attention. It is also, however, an area that has been hidden from public concern and has been regarded as a 'taboo topic'. Much of the abuse that occurs, even within institutions, happens behind closed doors and is not open to public scrutiny (see Bennett *et al.* 1997). Making what happens in private a matter for public concern is not an easy task. This is in part due to societal ageism and ambivalence about older people and their care and well-being. It has not been easy to challenge this taboo nor to encourage people to discuss situations, let alone to disclose abuse. Throughout the 1990s in the UK, however, social care and health professionals raised issues concerning violence towards older people on a consistent basis and the taboo has been challenged and gradually eroded.

Elder abuse is now increasingly being acknowledged as an important problem and one in need of solutions. This is in part due to the existence of rapidly ageing populations in many countries. In overall terms, by 2025 the global population of older people aged 60 years and older is predicted to be 1.2 billion, which is more than double the number that existed in 1995 (542 million) (WHO 2002).

Differing forms of abuse

Despite the lack of agreed or standard definitions of abuse, commented on by McCreadie (1996) and others (Penhale *et al.* 2000), a number of definitions of elder abuse have developed. Early attempts at defining abuse in the UK context were relatively specific as seen in the following example:

> A single or repeated act or lack of appropriate action occurring within any relationship where there is an expectation of trust,

which causes harm or distress to an older person. (Action on Elder Abuse 1995)

However, later definitions tend to have been more widely drawn, as in the more recent government document, *No Secrets*, in which the definition is given as:

Abuse is a violation of an individual's civil or human rights by any other person or persons. (Department of Health 2000)

Given the lack of consensus concerning definition, which ultimately may not result in any major difficulty (Penhale 1993), it is at least reassuring to find that most people concerned with the issue agree on the different types of abuse that can happen. These types are broadly similar to those found with other forms of violence (WHO 2002). The usual types of abuse included within most definitions are physical abuse; sexual abuse; neglect; psychological and emotional abuse, and financial abuse (also referring to exploitation and misappropriation of an individual's property and possessions). It is financial or economic abuse which is not always found in other types of violence. When considering neglect, separate, stand-alone definitions do not usually appear, with neglect often appearing as a sub-type of abuse. Thus in the Social Services Inspectorate (1993) definition, elder abuse is described as:

... physical, sexual, psychological or financial. It may be intentional or unintentional or the result of neglect. (Department of Health 1993, para. 2.1)

More recently, draft guidance issued by the Social Services Inspectorate indicates that abuse may occur:

... as a result of a failure to undertake action or appropriate care tasks. It may be physical, psychological, or an act of neglect ... (Department of Health 1999, para 2.7)

Neglect and acts of omission are then further delineated as:

... including ignoring medical or physical care needs, failure to provide access to appropriate health, social care or educational services, the withholding of the necessities of life, such as

157

medication, adequate nutrition and heating. (Department of Health 1999, para 2.8)

To these may be added such categories as enforced isolation and deprivation of necessary items for daily living (warmth, food or other aspects, such as teeth). In general, however, situations of self-neglect by an older person would not be considered within the UK perspective of elder abuse. Although many practitioners work with older individuals who self-neglect, usually this is not considered within an elder abuse or indeed an adult protection framework.

However, definitions often do not make any reference to the location in which the abuse occurs. There are a number of different types of settings in which abuse and/or neglect may take place. From an institutional perspective, these are: nursing or residential homes; day care settings of all types; and hospital settings. Abusive or neglectful situations may happen in any of these places. Health and social care practitioners who work with older people therefore need to be aware of this possibility when visiting patients/clients in such locations.

Abuse within institutions can also encompass situations that arise because of the regime or system that operates in the unit in addition to individual acts of abuse that occur therein. Such abusive acts may include a failure to provide adequate care to meet needs, the use of physical restraint or deprivation of dignity, respect or choice. Within institutions, there may also be abusive situations that arise between a resident and a member of care staff, initiated by the older person as protagonist, so there could be dual directionality of abuse, or uni-directional abuse from resident towards staff member (McCreadie 1996).

In addition to different types of abuse and different settings, it is also necessary to be aware that there may be a range of different participants involved in abusive situations and in different locations: residents; staff; relatives, friends or volunteers. We must also recognise that a change of setting (from home to institution, perhaps) does not necessarily mean that pre-existing abuse will cease altogether. It may mean that a different type of abuse then occurs or that the nature of the abuse is transformed somewhat. As the UK government guidance indicates:

Assessment of the environment, or context, is relevant, because exploitation, deception, misuse of authority, intimidation or coercion may render a vulnerable adult incapable of making his or her own decisions. (Department of Health 2000, para 2.16)

Different responses and interventions to alleviate or prevent institutional abuse and neglect (rather than abuse and neglect in the domestic setting) may be necessary, depending on the type of abuse that is happening within the institutional setting and the numbers of individuals involved. The location of the abuse, whether the situation is occurring in a private or a public area of the unit is also of relevance within such considerations.

The consequences of abuse

The effects of abuse on older people will vary, depending on the type of abuse experienced and the characteristics of the victim, including the physical and mental health status of the individuals involved. However, it is important to recognise that for many elders, the effects of abuse can be particularly severe and serious because even quite minor injury can lead to permanent damage and recovery from illness or injury takes longer for older people. In addition, the psychological *sequelae* of abuse should not be under-estimated: one longitudinal study from the US indicated that the mortality rate for elders who have been abused is very much higher than that for non-abused individuals (Lachs *et al.* 1998). If we also take into account that continuing mental health difficulties occur for many victims and survivors of all forms of abuse and violence, then we must acknowledge the serious nature of many of the consequences of elder abuse for individuals on a long-term basis.

National guidance, local approaches

As we saw earlier, government guidance relating to adult protection does not appear to have been a priority area of concern until comparatively recently. Yet as we have seen, this is likely to be an important aspect of prevention of abuse and violence towards vulnerable individuals. However, it was not until 1993 that any guidance concerning elder abuse was forthcoming from the Department of Health, and from the Social Services Inspectorate. This document did not consider situations occurring beyond the domestic setting. The provision of guidance, albeit limited, is, of course, both important and necessary. Practitioners do not operate in a vacuum from the wider society and therefore need the direction of national government and employing bodies to ensure that standards of practice are clear and at an appropriate level.

The Social Services Inspectorate began work in 1998 to rectify the lack of guidance concerning other vulnerable adults (for example, adults with physical disability, sensory impairment, or mental health difficulties, who might also have needs relating to vulnerability and protection) in order to produce necessary guidance on adult protection for authorities and organisations to adopt in their work. The process of working party participation and development of guidance was understandably lengthy given the need for involvement across the spectrum of adult protection. In late 1999, a draft guidance document was produced for consultation purposes (Department of Health 1999), with a final document appearing during the year 2000 (Department of Health 2000). The final document produced guidance concerning the roles and responsibilities of differing organisations and disciplines and the processes that should take place in relation to abuse. Social services departments were designated as the lead agency within adult protection, and the guidance itself had sufficient status that it was a requirement for the guidance to be implemented by authorities. The implementation date for the guidance was the end of October 2001.

It is important to acknowledge that policies and procedures are important to inform practitioners of the actions that should be taken at particular points in the process of responding to a situation that is potentially related to abuse and/or neglect. However, policies and procedures alone cannot ensure good practice. How these are put into practice is absolutely crucial to consider here (Penhale 1993). Most policies and procedural documents detail what should happen from the initial referral, or notification of an alleged abuse of a vulnerable adult and the subsequent stages of investigating, or assessing the circumstances within that situation and determining whether abuse has occurred or not. There will then be a further stage in which decisions will be taken about whether there is a need for any ongoing work or monitoring and review of the situation (Penhale *et al.* 2000). However, specific strategies of intervention and how these are applied are unlikely to be entirely prescribed by procedures. Good practice in this area now needs to evolve in the next few years beyond just the development of regulation and documentation designed to guide practitioners through a sequence of processes. There are different types of responses that have been developing in relation to elder abuse. Many of these relate to health and social care initiatives, although some may be linked to the sphere of legislation and criminal justice. However, a proportion of these developments is as yet under-developed in many areas, partly because of a lack of funding for specific projects. Responses to abuse and abusive situations also need to develop further to ensure that they are multi-sectorial in range and scope.

European developments

Although as stated, English doctors originally identified elder abuse and neglect in the mid-1970s, for a number of reasons it was not until the late 1980s that the issue was concentrated on in the UK. Whilst a number of Western European countries such as Sweden, the Netherlands and France similarly recognised the existence of abuse at about the same time as the UK, there are others such as Spain, Italy and Belgium where the existence of abuse has only been acknowledged in recent years. Others still (Iceland, Czech Republic, Slovenia) are only now beginning to consider issues relating to elder abuse. Of course there are yet other countries (Denmark and some of the accession countries) that do not really appear to have recognised elder abuse up until this time.

For the purposes of this chapter, it would appear useful to provide brief information concerning the development of responses to elder abuse from a selection of European countries. My thanks are due to a number of contacts that I have established in Europe, through the International Network for the Prevention of Elder Abuse (INPEA), who have provided information concerning the situation in their countries.

France has been concerned about issues relating to elder abuse since the late 1980s. Small amounts of research have been taking place in recent years. ALMA France (ALlô MAltraitance) was created in 1994 by Professor Robert Hugonot, a retired professor of geriatric medicine. ALMA France has several objectives to:

1. develop a national elder abuse helpline network;
2. support and protect the isolated, excluded and vulnerable elderly;
3. recruit and train helpline listeners/counsellors among the community and from the students and professionals of its institutions;
4. evaluate and document the work in the form of statistics, research, and publications;

5. inform the general and professional press, radio and TV networks.

ALMA France is developing a national network of ALMA helpline centres, with the aim of having one in each of the 98 French departments. So far, 54 ALMA helpline centres have been opened and each functions according to its specific local needs. The system is quite different from that which Action on Elder Abuse has developed in the UK. The work of ALMA brought the topic 'elder abuse' into the open and to public awareness and ALMA France now receives some funding from the French government. Limited amounts of research have been taking place in recent years. In 2002 several official policy texts and laws were passed to fight elder abuse. A 'Comité de Vigilance' was created by the 'Secrétariat d'Etat des Personnes Agées' (State Secretariat for the Elderly) in December 2002. A free 08 number (national helpline number) was established in the summer of 2004. ALMA France's overall goal is to find ways to identify the risk factors both in institutions and in the home setting which lead to elder abuse and then to prevent it from happening.

Germany has been developing responses in recent years since the mid-1990s and has seen developments in a number of different areas. There are no laws which specifically and explicitly deal with the topic of elder abuse. However, there have been recent changes (and improvements) in laws pertaining to elder care and quality of care: (Pflegequalitätssicherungsgesetz – Law on Quality Assurance in Nursing Care; Heimbewohnerschutzgesetz – Law for the Protection of Nursing Home Residents). One example is that residents' family members can now become members of residents' councils. At the level of federal policy, elder abuse is not a dominant topic. However, there are some activities which specifically address the problem of elder abuse. The Federal Ministry for Family, Senior Citizens, Women, and Youth (BMFSFJ) funded a model project on 'Violence Against Elderly People in Domestic Settings' (1998–2001); and a study on 'Crime and Violence in Old Peoples' Lives' was commenced in 2004. There are a number of activities aiming at improvements in elder care. The BMFSFJ and the Federal Ministry for Health have started a 'Round Table on Care' where experts from different institutions and disciplines meet.

There are a number of NGO-helplines, most of which operate at a local level. The helpline run by 'Handeln statt Misshandeln' based in Bonn is probably the most important. These local helplines have formed a kind of national network. Most elder abuse helplines focus explicitly on problems with elder care, mainly in residential settings. Other contexts, in which elderly people are victimised, remain rather hidden (e.g. domestic violence in old age). Since 2003, there has been a slight shift away from the very strong focus on elder care towards linking the topic of elder abuse with broader concepts and actions in the fields of crime and violence prevention. The Prevention Council of the federal state of North Rhine-Westphalia has taken up the issue, so has the German Forum on Crime Prevention (DFK). Additionally, there is a long tradition of police crime prevention targeted at the elderly. Traditionally, these programmes covered offences like burglary, fraud, and robbery of handbags. Increasingly, the police are 'discovering' other areas of elder abuse and neglect.

There has been a small number of studies on elder abuse in Germany, most of them either from the field of caring science or from criminology – each with their own specific focus, terminology, methodology and theoretical background (see for example, Görgen 2004). Starting in 2005, a new study on elder victimisation ('Crime and Violence in Old People's Lives') is being undertaken by the Criminological Research Institute of Lower Saxony (KFN).

Norway has been concerned about the issue of elder abuse since the mid–late 1980s. Early research work in Oslo led to the development of pilot projects to test out interventions and responses to elder abuse. These were based on an Action-research methodology, which meant that the projects could change and develop as necessary. At the end of the 1990s, it was decided that the model of intervention teams of specialist social workers, which had developed through the pilot projects, would be established throughout Oslo and then progressively, but incrementally, throughout the country. This is now in process (Juklestad 2004). The Ministries of Justice, Health and Social Affairs and Children and Families provided funding in the mid-1990s to establish the Norwegian Resource Centre for Information and Studies on Violence, based in Oslo. This centre was unique in that it considered child abuse (and protection), sexual violence and violence towards young women, and elder abuse and protection. The model has been successful and from January 2004, the centre has been combined with three other institutions within Oslo University, forming the National Centre for Knowledge about Violence and Stress. The results of the intervention projects on elder abuse continue to inform the work of the centre.

Israel[1] has an established history of research and work in this area, which dates back to the late 1980s. Work has taken place in a number of different areas and on a number of different levels since that time. In some of the larger municipalities, special units to deal with elder abuse have been established and the Ministry of Welfare, together with ESHEL (the Association of Planning and Development of Services for the Aged in Israel) runs annual training courses for welfare officers. A large-scale national survey on elder abuse co-ordinated by the University of Haifa was completed in 2004. This included a qualitative study of families involved in abuse and findings are in the process of dissemination. Work also continues on violence between couples/partners in later life (Lowenstein and Ron 2000) and on the development of training for professionals.

In **Belgium**, there has been consistent work since the 1990s, consisting of both research and service development. A branch of the French organisation ALMA has been developed (ALMA Wallonie-Bruxelles) and several helplines have been developed in the past seven years. A number of conferences and symposia have been held to assist in the training of professionals, students and volunteers and in 2003 a training programme for frontline doctors was established. Also in 2003, a pilot project, Libr'age, was established by three different organisations (CAPAM, URGEDES and EMPAGE) to provide a specialist service on elder abuse in each province. This consists of a telephone helpline, training programmes for professionals and also campaigns concerning the prevention of elder abuse. Despite the lack of any specific legislation in relation to elder abuse, certain laws have been found to be useful at times. These include laws in relation to well-being and also relating to competence and mental health. Attention has also been paid to institutional settings through regulation, complaints procedures and organisations to assist elders in choice of residential placements and associations that link with residents.

In **Ireland** there have been a number of developments since the late 1980s. These have included short articles in professional journals, some media attention including reporting of fatal cases, and also some enabling legislation (Enduring Power of Attorney Act 1996; Domestic Violence Act 1996; Health (Nursing Homes) Act 1990. In 1996 the Minister for Health requested the National Council on Ageing and Older People (a Ministerial advisory body) to provide a report on elder abuse. This report was produced in 1998 (O'Loughlin and Duggan 1998) and included a literature review, survey of professionals and service providers, a review of policy and the legal framework and recommendations for a way forward. The major recommendation was for the setting up of a Working Party on Elder Abuse at the Department of Health.

A Working Group on elder abuse was established by the Irish Department of Health in 1999 and was published in 2002 (Ministry of Health 2002). Recommendations included: the establishment of a national implementation group at the Department of Health to oversee the implementation of the recommendations of the Working Group; formulation of a national policy on elder abuse; development by each health board of a strategy to implement the policy; setting up of a steering group in each health board with a dedicated officer responsible for policy development and implementation; recruitment of a senior case worker in each community care area to respond to all referrals; law reform; the establishment of a National Centre for research and training on elder abuse; and a campaign in relation to financial abuse and a public awareness programme. So far the main development has been the establishment of the national implementation group at the Department of Health and Children in December 2003 (one year after publication of the report). One Health Board has developed a draft policy on adult abuse and another has appointed a person to develop policy in relation to this area. However, this report was launched at a time of serious cutbacks in the health service including a ban on recruitment and therefore little further development has happened so far.

A number of other countries, such as **Greece**, **Poland**, the **Netherlands** and **Portugal** were involved in initiatives concerning elder abuse during the 1990s, but no recent news has been forthcoming about subsequent developments. Other countries such as the **Czech Republic**, **Slovenia** and **Iceland** have recently been involved in progressing work in this area, particularly in relation to awareness raising and developing professional responses.

As is apparent from the information provided above, different levels of development occur throughout countries in Europe and there are undoubtedly some countries, which have yet to begin to tackle the issue of elder abuse and neglect. Whilst a number of committed individuals and organisations in the UK have been working in this area to develop knowledge, information and assistance concerning abuse and neglect since the late 1980s, there is no room for complacency. Effective guidance at strategic and national levels is yet to be fully seen. Much remains to be achieved for and on behalf of elders who experience or are at risk of experiencing abuse, no matter where it occurs. This is where the work at a global and international level is imperative and it is to this area that we now turn.

International Network for the Prevention of Elder Abuse (INPEA)

INPEA is an organisation dedicated to the global dissemination of information as part of its commitment to the worldwide prevention of the abuse of older people.

The organisation was established at the 16th World Congress of Gerontology, which was organised by the International Association of Gerontology (IAG) and was held in Adelaide, Australia in 1997. At this Congress, there was an opportunity to emphasise issues relating to elder abuse and neglect. As part of a number of sessions that provided a focus on elder abuse from a more global perspective, a roundtable discussion was held to discuss the feasibility of setting up an International Network for the Prevention of Elder Abuse. Representatives of 12 different countries from across the world were present at this session and overwhelming support for the establishment of a network was attained from over 75 people who attended the session. Within the Congress as a whole, more prominence was given to elder abuse than at any previous World Congress. Elder abuse also featured as a keynote lecture and the Adelaide declaration, produced as an outcome of the Congress, included mention of elder abuse as an issue of growing concern.

A subsequent meeting of a small ad-hoc group of interested parties was held in Sydney, Australia in August 1997. This group discussed plans for the next stages in the establishment of a network. Some preliminary work was undertaken at this meeting concerning the aims and objectives for the organisation, which were produced as part of the next step approach to the process.

The agreed aims of the organisation, which were subsequently ratified, are as follows:

- to promote knowledge and awareness about elder abuse and neglect;
- to disseminate information;
- to stimulate research into the causes, consequences, prevalence, treatment, and prevention of elder abuse and neglect;
- to promote education and training of professionals and para-professionals;
- to assist in the development of responses to elder abuse and neglect in different countries.

The principal goal of INPEA is to increase society's ability, through international collaboration, to recognise and respond to the mistreatment of older people in whatever setting it occurs, so that for individuals the later years of life will be free from abuse, neglect, and exploitation. Each individual should be able to achieve an optimal quality of life. This should be one that is consistent with that person's traditions and cultural values.

At subsequent meetings, a Board was established in order to reflect the intent of the organisation to cover the globe and charitable status was agreed on. A system of regional representatives was also developed in order to co-ordinate the organisation on a global basis. These representatives cover the following regions: Africa, Asia, Europe, Oceania, North America and South America. Membership categories, for organisations, groups and individuals was established, initially on a free basis. A newsletter and web page have been introduced in order to assist with dissemination of information and communication in general.

Since the initial meetings to establish the organisation, INPEA has participated in a number of congresses and conferences at both international and national levels. For example, INPEA participated in the first World Conference on Family Violence, which was held in Singapore in September 1998. The contribution of the organisation to this conference was significant, and the issue of elder abuse managed to achieve as much recognition as the other major forms of family violence, which were discussed during the conference.

In total, there were 15 presentations (free papers) concerning elder abuse and the countries represented included USA, UK and Japan. In addition, INPEA held a half-day roundtable entitled, 'Building an International Network for the Prevention of Elder Abuse'. The organisation made a major impact at this first World Conference on Family Violence and was asked to support and help develop recognition of the issues involved. Subsequent conferences have been assured of having the topic of elder abuse fully represented within the programme.

Rapid growth

The United Nations Year of the Older Person, which took place during 1999, saw rapid development concerning elder abuse in a number of the different regions covered by INPEA. A significant IAG Congress of Geriatric Medicine and Gerontology in Argentina followed by an IAG Congress in Havana, Cuba in September 1999 meant that the South American region saw the largest increase in membership (particularly of individuals) and of interest in the issue generally. Similar responses were, however, noted following the IAG European Congress in Berlin in July 1999 and a series of significant conferences and events held in Australia and Africa during 1999. Additionally during that year, the organisation was honoured with the acceptance of Dr. Alexandre Kalache, (Chief of Ageing at WHO) to be a Special Observer to INPEA. Since that time, the organisation has continued to see rapid growth and development, with members spread across the world and a system of national country representatives established to assist the regional representatives.

A global organisation

During its comparatively short existence, INPEA has developed into a global organisation, raising awareness about the issues of elder abuse and neglect. The organisation contributed to two reports concerned with the issue of older people and violence, which have been produced by WHO and the United Nations (UN). Further developments concerning the INPEA website and collaboration with WHO on research work in developing countries are underway (see: www.inpea.net for details). The Brazilian Congress of Gerontology, held in June 2000, highlighted elder abuse, and the IAG World Congress held in Vancouver in 2001 also provided further prominence for the issue. Additional congresses, held in Europe, Latin America and Asia since 2001 have also extended this prominence. Additionally, in the autumn of 2003, INPEA achieved NGO (non-governmental organisation) status with the UN. Further to this, a UN World Elder Abuse Awareness Day has been agreed on to take place on 15 June 2006.

Whilst this century should provide many answers to previously unsolved questions concerning ageing, elder abuse is likely to provide further challenges to us all. Gerontologists active in this field are committed to continue their work in coming years at all levels, local, regional, national and international. This will be in order to investigate the phenomenon further and to attempt to achieve solutions to some of the most pressing questions. The international network, and the opportunities that this will provide to facilitate working together at international levels, will assist in tackling the problems posed by elder abuse, and also improving the quality of life for all older people, everywhere.

Note

1 Israel is included within the European region of INPEA and interesting developments have been taking place there, and therefore it is included, within this chapter concerning European perspectives.

References

Action on Elder Abuse (1995) 'New Definition of Abuse', *Action on Elder Abuse Bulletin*.

Baker, A.A. (1977) 'Granny Battering', *Modern Geriatrics*, (8): 20–4.

Bennett, G., Kingston, P. and Penhale, B. (1997) *The Dimensions of Elder Abuse: Perspectives for Practitioners*. Basingstoke: Macmillan.

Department of Health (1993) *No Longer Afraid: The Safeguard of Older People in Domestic Settings*. London: HMSO.

Department of Health (1999) *No Secrets: The Protection of Vulnerable Adults – Guidance on the Development and Implementation of Multi-agency Policies and Procedures* (consultation document). London: HMSO

Department of Health (2000) *No Secrets: The Protection of Vulnerable Adults – Guidance on the Development and Implementation of Multi-agency Policies and Procedures*. London: HMSO.

Görgen, T. (2004) 'A Multi-method Study on Elder Abuse and Neglect in Nursing Homes', *Journal of Adult Protection*, 6 (3): 15–25.

Glendenning, F. and Kingston, P. (eds) (1999) *Elder Abuse and Neglect in Residential Settings: Different National Backgrounds and Similar Responses*. New York: Haworth Maltreatment and Trauma Press.

Juklestad, O. (2004) 'Elderly People at Risk: A Norwegian Model for Community Education and Response', *Journal of Adult Protection*, 6 (3): 26–33.

Lachs, M. Williams, S.C., O'Brien, S., Moen, P. and Charlson, M.E. (1998) 'The Mortality of Elder Mistreatment' *Journal of the American Medical Association*, 280: 428–32.

Lowenstein, A. and Ron, P. (2000) 'Adult Children of Elderly Parents Who Remarry: Aetiology of Domestic Abuse' *Journal of Adult Protection*, 2 (4): 22–32.

McCreadie, C. (1996) *Elder Abuse: An Update on Research*. London: HMSO.

Ogg, J. and Munn-Giddings, C. (1993) 'Researching Elder Abuse', *Ageing and Society*, 13 (3): 389–414.

Ministry of Health (2002) *Protecting our Future: Report of the Working Group on Elder Abuse*. Dublin: Ministry of Health and Children.

O'Loughlin, A. and Duggan, J. (1998) *Abuse Neglect and Mistreatment of Older People: An Exploratory Study*. Dublin: National Council on Ageing and Older People.

Penhale, B. (1993) 'The Abuse of Elderly People: Considerations for Practice', *British Journal of Social Work*, 23 (2): 95–112.

Penhale, B. (1999) 'Research on Elder Abuse: Lessons for Practice' in M. Eastman and P. Slater (1999) (eds) *Elder Abuse: Critical Issues in Policy and Practice*. London: Age Concern Books.

Penhale, B., Parker, J. and Kingston, P. (2000) *Elder Abuse: Approaches to Working with Violence*. Birmingham: Venture Press.

Stanley, N., Manthorpe, J. and Penhale, B. (1999) (eds) *Institutional Abuse: Perspectives across the Lifecourse*. London: Routledge.

Stearns, P. (1986) 'Old Age Family Conflict: The Perspective of the Past' in K.A. Pillemer and R.S. Wolf (eds) *Elder Abuse: Conflict in the Family*. Dover, Massachusetts: Auburn House.

World Health Organisation (WHO) (2002) *Report on Violence*. Geneva: WHO.

Chapter 11

'No problems – old and quiet': imprisonment in later life

Azrini Wahidin

Introduction

This chapter draws upon ongoing research examining the needs and experiences of women and men who are over 50 and in prison, on both sides of Atlantic. The chapter will landscape the older prison population and will identify the needs of this older population and the challenges the group poses to the prison estate. American researchers such as Ron Aday have led research in this area, and it is only in the last ten years that researchers in the UK (see Manthorpe 1983; Phillips 1996; Wahidin 2004) have examined the relationship between ageing and crime.

We are unaccustomed to thinking about people in later life as criminal offenders. Usually, when older offenders receive publicity, they are represented as the victims of crime, not its perpetrators. Some women and men in later life, nevertheless, do commit crimes; some are arrested, some are convicted, some are sent to prison, and some grow old in prison. A decade ago we would not have imagined it possible that people were committing crimes in later life and growing old behind bars, and that prison nursing homes would be a feature of the prison landscape.

Background

Much of the debate on older offenders is over how to define 'old'. The definition of 'elderly', 'elder' or older, can produce information which at first appears contradictory. Official statistics on the age breakdown of offences and prison statistics (see Home Office 1997a, 1997b, 1999) give a cut-off point anywhere between 21 and 59 or simply give figures for offenders aged 21 and above. An extensive review of the literature reveals that some previous researchers have defined older prisoners as those 65 years of age and older (Newman 1984a; Grambling and Forsyth 1988), some 60 (Kratocoski 1990) and some 55 (Goetting 1992). However, the majority of studies such as Aday, (2003), Wahidin, (2002), Phillips (1996), the American Department of Justice, and older units for older prisoners in the UK and in the States have used the age 50–55 as the threshold age to define when one becomes an older offender. Aday (1994), conducted a national survey of State prison departments and found that 50 years of age was the most common criterion for old age that prison officials utilise. Similarly, Wahidin (2002, 2004) found in a national study of men and women who are over 50 in prison in the UK that prison officers, health care personnel and governors running older units, defined older offenders as 50 and over. Furthermore, UK health care statistics show that from the 50–80+ age group, the 50–59 is the most costly age cohort in terms of bed-watches required and medications consumed (Wahidin 2005), underlining the usefulness of a cut-off point which enables this age-group to be included within the definition of 'older'. This definition is further supported by the fact that offenders experience what is known as 'accelerated' ageing so that a typical offender in their 50s has the physical appearance and accompanying health problems of someone at least ten years older in the community. Studies have shown that on average the cost of keeping an elder in prison runs over three times that of a young adult in prison (Dubler 1988). The specialised medical care for elders varies from simple needs such as hearing aids and dentures to more expensive items such as high-cost prescription medication, prosthetic devices and wheelchairs. At the far end of the cost spectrum are the needs of Alzheimer's sufferers and critically or terminally ill prisoners. For these reasons, Morton (1992), and prison health care personnel and prison officers in the UK (Wahidin 2004, 2005) stipulate that 50 is the ideal starting point to initiate preventive health care and is the point to take appropriate measures to reduce long-term medical costs for older offenders.

For the purpose of this chapter the terms 'older' or 'offender in later life' or 'elder' will be used interchangeably, to denote a person aged 50 or over. Within gerontological literature the blanket label of 'the elderly' perpetuates a stereotype that the elderly population constitutes a homogeneous social group. The term culturally reproduces 'ageist' stereotypes and equates older-age with weakness, infirmity and vulnerability. The term 'the elderly' has deliberately been avoided in this chapter because the adjective has become 'misappropriated as a noun' which, as Fennel *et al.* (1988) argues, leads to people becoming treated as 'things'. Hence the term 'elder' will be used in recognition of the positive aspects that older age can confer (Bond *et al.* 1993; Cole *et al.* 1993; Bytheway 1994).

Age breakdown of prison population

When thinking about elders as perpetrators of crime we associate them with relatively minor offences such as breach of the peace, shoplifting or driving under the influence of alcohol. We are unlikely to associate this group with crime serious enough to result in prison sentences continuing into old age. Ageing, in criminological literature, is not seen to be an issue, which in itself reflects how the age and crime relationship has been constructed. Contrary to popular belief, the most common offences for the older female age group are not perpetrated by the menopausal shoplifter; they are not theft and handling or fraud and forgery, but violence against the person and drug offences (see Figure 11.1). The most common offences for men in this group are sexual offences, violence against the person, and drug offences (see Figure 11.2).

UK profile

Women in prison of all ages form only a very small proportion of the total prison population (6 per cent) and women over 50 represented only 4 per cent of the total female prison estate in 2005. Out of the total prison population for both men and women, 13 per cent are over the age of 50 (Wahidin 2005a). Men in prison constitute 94 per cent of the total prison population and men over 50 represent 8 per cent of the male estate. In terms of actual numbers, there were 170 women and 4,513 men in prison who were over the age of 50 in January 2005 (*ibid.*). To break this down even further, there were only 20 women over the age 60. In comparison there were 1,507 men who were over the age of 60. More than 1 in 10 male older prisoners who are over 60 belong to a minority ethnic group, which is far higher than the proportion of the general population (Prison Reform Trust 2003). From 1995 to 2003, the female over-50 population rose by 98

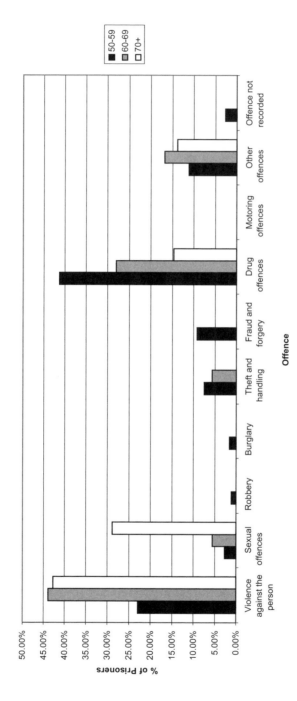

Figure 11.1 Older Female Prisoners by Offence and Age (January 2005)
Source: Wahidin 2005a (© Crown Copyright. Data provided by the Research, Development and Statistics Directorate of the Home Office).

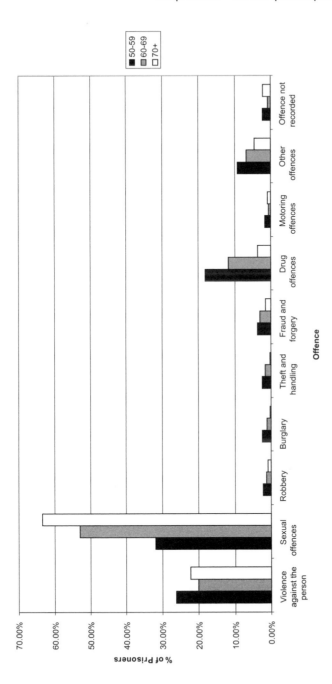

Figure 11.2 Older Male Prisoners by Offence and Age (January 2005)
Source: Wahidin 2005a (© Crown Copyright. Data provided by the Research, Development and Statistics Directorate of the Home Office).

per cent and for men by 82 per cent. The overall increase over this seven-year period is 83 per cent. From 1999 to 2005, the older prison population doubled from 3,000 to almost 6,000. Furthermore, the over-60 male population more than trebled over 13 years from 442 in 1992 to 1,507 in 2005. In 1992 those aged 60 and above made up 1 per cent of the male population over the age of 18, compared to 3 per cent in 2002, and the 80+ male population has become the fastest growing section of the male prison estate, increasing by 375 per cent between 1995 and 2003. In the female estate the sentenced prison population of prisoners aged 50 and over in the female estate has increased by two and a half times over the last ten years (Wahidin 2005).

The graphs below show the increase in the prison population by age group over an eight-year period, 1995–2003. Each graph demonstrates that the 50+ age groups in prison are growing at a faster rate than the younger age cohorts.

It is evident from the Thematic Report of 2004, 'No Problems – Old and Quiet: Older Offenders in England and Wales' and from the above statistics that the older prison population in the UK is indeed a fast growing group and that no comprehensive policy or strategy is in place to address their needs. In particular, the Home Office Prison Department in England and Wales has no overall policy or strategy for dealing with older females in prison, although the Home Office does have three older units for men (see also HM Chief Inspector of Prisons (HMCIP 2004). So far there has been no discussion or plan for similar arrangements to be made for women. Notwithstanding the existence of the older units for men, the Home Office Prison Department and the National Probation Service still have no overall policy or strategy for dealing with older offenders, despite having policies in place for groups of similar numerical significance (Home Office 1995; HMCIP 1997, 2004).

Growing old in prison: imprisonment in later life

The largest concentration of male prisoners aged 50+ (at the time of writing) are at the following prisons: HMP Kingston–E Wing and, subsequent to its closure in 2005, HMP Norwich, HMP Frankland and HMP Wymott have replaced the role of E Wing. HMP Holloway and HMP New Hall have the highest percentage of women in the 50+ categories in the female prison estate although they have no facilities or formal policies in place to address their specific needs.

If more and more people are receiving longer mandatory sentences,

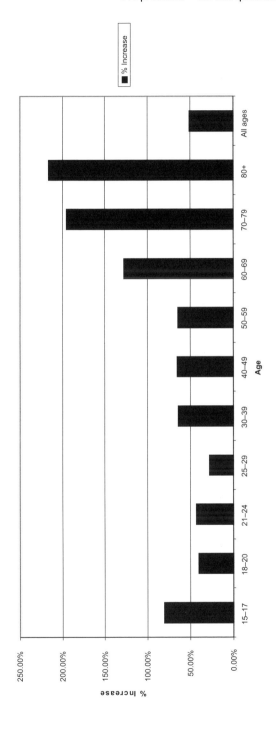

Figure 11.3 Percentage increase from 1995–2003 for Both Males and Females by Age Category
Source: Wahidin 2005a (© Crown Copyright. Data provided by the Research, Development and Statistics Directorate of the Home Office).

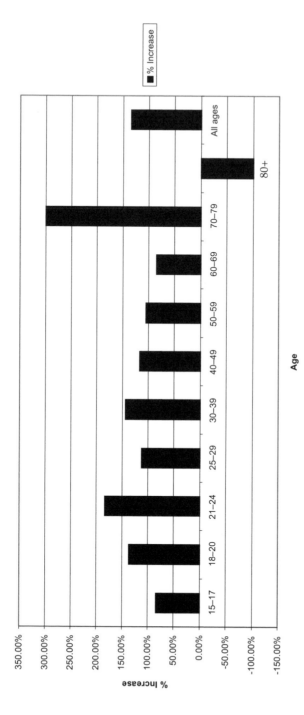

Figure 11.4 Percentage increase from 1997–2003 for Females by Age
Source: Wahidin 2005a (© Crown Copyright. Data provided by the Research, Development and Statistics Directorate of the Home Office).

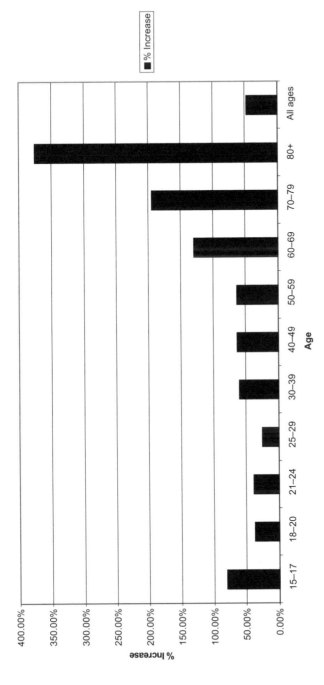

Figure 11.5 Percentage increase from 1997–2003 for Males by Age
Source: Wahidin 2005a (© Crown Copyright. Data provided by the Research, Development and Statistics Directorate of the Home Office).

this will mean that some will remain imprisoned until they are old. This phenomenon is known as the 'stacking effect' (Aday 2003). Partly for this reason, those serving life sentences in general are older than the average age of the prison population as a whole. From 1996 to 2000, the over-50 lifer female population rose by 45 per cent and the lifer male population rose by 66 per cent (Wahidin 2004). Changes in arrest and prosecution practices, revised sentencing policies such as bifurcation, the war on drugs, the incremental extension of the life sentence; historical offences, the introduction of natural life for certain prisoners; the times served by people subject to mandatory sentences are getting longer, and ageing in wider society are additional variables that have led to an increase in the older prison population.

This growing forgotten minority will surely pose particular challenges to the current physical environment, health care facilities and regime. Moreover, the lack of adequate provision for this cohort will contravene the Disability Discrimination Act 2004 and the Human Rights Act 1998, (implemented in October 2000), which was heralded by the Home Secretary Jack Straw as 'the most significant statement of human rights in domestic law since the 1968 Bill of Rights' (cited in Sim 2000, p. 186).

Old age and crime

> Old criminals offer an ugly picture and it seems as if even scientists do not like to look at it for any considerable amount of time … On the other hand, if the thesis of the interrelationship between age and crime is to hold, an investigation of all its implications has to yield results, and with the tendency of our population to increase in the higher age brackets, a special study of criminality of the aged seems to meet a scientific as well as a practical need. (Pollak 1941, p. 212)

The absence of elders in the criminological imagination mirrors where the study of female offenders in criminology was 30 years ago. The lack of research in this area is an implicit form of ageism that implies that the problems of this group can be disregarded, or that ageing criminals are simply not worth discussing. The explanation frequently given for the lack of statistical information on this topic is that at present the numbers involved are too small to yield statistically significant information, with the implication that this justifies excluding and ignoring the rights of elders in prison.

Yet there has been no assessment of the implications of this, or recognition that England and Wales, like the USA, are facing an ageing prison population. This phenomenon has become known as the 'geriatrification' of the prison population.

If Pollak's view was correct in 1941, it is even more so today, over 60 years later. With the elder prison population representing the fastest growing age group in our prison system, we have reached an important juncture in the disciplines of gerontology and criminology.

What do we know about the needs of older prisoners?

The literature available on elder offenders is restricted to predominantly American-based research (Newman 1984). The work of Aday (1994, 1994a 2003) has been instrumental in raising the profile of older offenders in the US. In contrast, there has been only one study in the UK that addresses the needs of the elder female and male prison population (Wahidin 2004, 2005). The arguments and recommendations which this section addresses are based on the findings of this research which includes the views expressed by older prisoners themselves.

There are different types of offenders, ranging from the:

- older first time offender currently serving a term of imprisonment;
- the older offender who has had previous convictions, but not served a prison sentence before;
- the recidivist who may have spent a significant amount of her or his life in and out of prison;
- prisoners fulfilling a life sentence and who have grown old in prison;
- long-term inmates.

Typically, the crimes committed by the above groups of offenders mirror those of young offenders. However, in all five groups, the ageing prison population is a special one in terms of health and social care needs, individual adjustment to institutional life, maintaining kinship networks, and end of life issues (Gallagher 1990). This group challenges the structure of the prison system regarding purposeful activity, rehabilitation, and the resettlement needs of offenders in later-life.

Elders in prison

The increase in the proportion of elders is having far reaching effects on all components of the criminal justice system. This section will examine how prisons can begin to address the needs of the older prison population. Once in prison, the vulnerabilities of age are exacerbated by the lack of adequate facilities to enable prisons to fulfil their statement of purpose where elders are concerned, namely, to enable them to lead 'law abiding and useful lives in custody and after release' (this statement can be found at every prison in England and Wales). The lack of facilities catering for individual need increases the pain of imprisonment where the prisons focus resources and facilities such as training, education, and resettlement programmes on the young and able-bodied. This is a good example of how the discourse of ageism and the idea of less eligibility operate when faced with limited resources: prison personnel fail to place elders on educational or training programmes because they assume that, due to their age, they are less likely to find employment.

The lack of help and rehabilitation exacerbates the almost inevitable poverty that they will face as a result of their imprisonment. Once prisoners are released, the effect of the discontinuity of pension contributions will leave them with insufficient contributions and consequently they will be in receipt of either a partial pension or none at all.

Although little research has been undertaken in England and Wales into the health of older female and male prisoners, Aday, Krabil and Wahidin (2004) found that more women than men over 50 considered themselves disadvantaged in preventive health and wellness schemes. Similarly, in the USA, Kratocoski and Babb (1990), (cited in Kerbs 2000, p. 219), found that older female prisoners were less likely than men to participate in recreational programmes, and reported significantly higher levels of poor or terrible health (46 per cent versus 25 per cent), with depression and generalised 'worry' being the two most persistent health problems they experienced. McDonald's (1995) study identified several conditions that have forced prison health care costs in the US to rise. A similar pattern is emerging in the prison system in England and Wales. The factors influencing the increase in expenditure are the following:

- the rising cost of health care in society at large;
- the increasing number of prisoners in the prison system;
- the general ageing of the prison population;

- the higher prevalence of infectious diseases among prison populations.

As long as these trends continue, prison health care costs will continue to increase. Like prisoners in general, ageing prisoners have not had proper access to health care on the outside. They often come into the prison system with numerous chronic illnesses and consume multiple medications. Jonathan Turley, Director of *The Project for Older Prisoners* (POPS), noted that: 'the greatest single contributor to the high costs of older prisoners is medical expenditures' (Turley 1990, p. 26). On average prisoners over the age of 50 suffer at least three chronic health problems, such as hypertension, diabetes, and emphysema (Turley 1990; Acoca 1998). Prisoners, as a population, traditionally have medical and social histories that put them more at risk of illness and disease than their non-inmate peers (Marquart *et al.* 1997, 2000). As the number of older prisoners increases, the prison system will be even more challenged to provide adequate health and social care. (Rothman *et al.* 2000).

The health needs profile of the ageing offender is hard to map in the absence of statistical information relating to health care costs in prisons in England and Wales. We know that in the US daily medical care for the general prison population costs $5.75 per offender. On average, for an offender over 50 years of age, the cost of incarceration is approximately three times as much as for a prisoner aged under 50 (Neeley, Addison and Craig-Moreland 1997; Fazel *et al.* 2001). Statistics for 2001, provided by the Florida Corrections Commission, support the above findings and demonstrate that prisoners over 50, despite making up only 9 per cent of the total prison population, were responsible for 19 per cent of the costs paid for ambulatory surgery episodes, 17 per cent of costs for non-emergency room episodes, 31 per cent of costs for ancillary care episodes, 20 per cent of costs for speciality care episodes, and 29 per cent of costs for inpatient care episodes.

With a predicted rise in the number of offenders who are older, sicker, and serving longer sentences, coupled with institutions' stretched resources, it is reasonable to argue that if we fail to address the needs of elders in prison, we will be facing an inevitable crisis (Prison Reform Trust 2003). As more cohorts enter the later stages of life, the age revolution will significantly affect all facets of the criminal justice system.

Recommendations

To alleviate some of the pains of imprisonment, the prison authorities should be turning their attention to literature relating to residential homes (Atherton 1989; Hockey 1989; Coleman 1993). There are many simple measures that could be taken which would allow elders control over their immediate physical environment; for example, installing doors and windows which they could open easily and radiators which they could adjust themselves, replacing the harshness of the prison corridors with appropriate carpet tiles, use of electricity sockets which would allow all elders the opportunity to listen to the radio, and replacing the glare of the strip light with something less harsh. Such measures would at once make prison a less hostile and a more accessible place. In addition, due to the impairment of sight, hearing, memory and reflexes, and also the general slowing of movement and mental responsiveness, elders need to be cared for by staff members who are specifically trained in the needs of elders in prison.

Segregation versus integration

Opinions on special prisons/units for elders vary. In Europe, Germany has only one such prison, called Singer, in the State of Baden-Württemberg. In the UK there is only one specialised unit with 24-hour medical care for elders, at HMP Norwich. The other units or special wings such as the ones at HMP Frankland and HMP Wymott are located within the main prison. In contrast, the American criminal justice system has been at the forefront of delivering special programmes for older offenders (Krajick 1979; Aday and Rosenfield 1992). 'Special programmes' here constitute the distinctive treatment of the older prisoner housed in an age-segregated or in an age-sensitive environment. Segregation provides a concentration of specialised staff and resources for elders, thereby reducing costs (Florida Corrections Commission 2001).

Previous research supports the notion that participation in a specific group increases self-respect and increases capability to resume community life once released. Age segregation or age integration provides older prisoners with the opportunity for forming peer networks, whilst also reducing vulnerability and the violence they may encounter in the mainstream of prison life. Fattah and Sacco state:

Concern for their safety and the need to protect them against victimisation, exploitation and harassment outweigh any stabilising effect their integration may have. (Fattah and Sacco 1989, p.101)

However, what is ideally needed is the flexibility of having accommodation and provision reserved for elders, without creating a separate prison or excluding elders from the main prison environment. Aday succinctly states: 'Like the elderly in the free world, they are familiar with life in the general population and perceive that it has a mark of independence' (Aday 2003, p. 146).

This approach would mean that the needs of ageing prisoners could no longer be regarded as an 'add-on', but would need to be considered throughout every aspect of prison provision and the planning of facilities. Equally, it implies responding to prisoners as individuals each with a unique profile of needs, which may include some or all the following: physical, mental and preventive health care; custody allocation to special housing, educational, vocational or recreational programmes, physical exercise, and rehabilitation programming; dietary considerations and long-term geriatric and nursing care.

An emerging theme within the integration versus segregation debate is that the way forward is to provide flexible accommodation, not through segregation, but through integration, within a framework of tolerance, understanding, and adaptability.

The way forward

The ageing prison population poses a true dilemma, and deserves recognition both among those interested in the well-being of those in later life and those executing prison policy. Age, in time, will be considered as one of the biggest issues that will continue to affect the criminal justice system and prison health care in the future. With the continued increase in criminal activity among the older population as a whole, learning more about crime and ageing, and about institutional adjustment, recidivism and release, seems imperative. As more cohorts enter the latter stages of life, the age revolution will significantly affect all facets of the criminal justice system.

In the absence of relevant policies and because of the lack of planning in this area, the prison service of England and Wales should be turning its attention to addressing the recommendations made in this chapter (for an in-depth discussion see Aday 2003; Wahidin 2004, 2005), and to special older units in the States, if we are to respond adequately to the growing number of elders who find themselves in the criminal justice system. A call for future research integrating gerontological and criminological theory is necessary in order to understand the needs of elders in the criminal justice system (Wahidin and Aday 2005). This research will need:

- to examine existing formal and informal practices regarding elders in prison as the first step in developing an explicit and integrated set of policies and programmes to address the special needs of this group;

- to begin to develop a comprehensive and gender sensitive programme for elders that fosters personal growth, accountability, and value-based actions that lead to successful reintegration into society;

- to prepare all personnel of the criminal justice system to understand and appropriately address elder-specific topics and issues;

- to address work-based prison programmes in order to develop and enable older prisoners to maintain their maximum levels of productivity and self-worth;

- to have information on their health problems and needs so that prison and health service managers can plan to provide a standard of care equivalent to that available in the community.

In terms of being able to address the needs of elders in the criminal justice system, the Prison Policy Unit should institute the changes recommended below:

- adoption of the age of 50/55 as the chronological starting point in a definition of the older offender;

- compilation of comprehensive data on the over-50s in the criminal justice system, from arrest to custody through to re-entry into wider society;

- adaptation of existing institutions to assure equitable treatment of the aged, thus complying with the Disability Discrimination Act 2004 and the Human Rights Act 1998;

- introduction of specific programmes geared towards the health, social and care needs of the elders in prison. This means providing more than: (a) health care; (b) the kind of social care that is intended to help with activities of daily living (ADLs);

- functional assessment tools should be utilised to determine both how the older prisoner perceives his or her own functioning and to assist in the implementation of an effective case management strategy;

- pre-release planning is particularly important for those who are in later-life, chronically ill, terminally ill or who have special health care needs. This will commonly include chronic mental health issues requiring assessment by appropriate practitioners with units to the community and mental health care teams;

- greater attention should be given to proper staffing for the care of elder and infirm inmates and special training for staff is critical;

- since only a few terminally ill prisoners are granted compassionate release, policy should receive more consideration as the number of terminally ill inmates increases;

- health promotion activities that encourage prisoners to live healthier lifestyles should be implemented along with programming to enhance quality of life for prisoners who will spend the remainder of their years incarcerated.

From nothing works to something works

Prisons are not the panacea for social ills; instead prison exacerbates the problems that offenders have to encounter once released. The modern prison has fulfilled a number of roles such as incapacitation, punishment, deterrence, reform, and rehabilitation. However, these goals have often sat uneasily together and depending on the political pressures of the day one or more of these goals has taken precedence over the others. For example, the 1950s–1960s were characterised by the belief in rehabilitation. By the 1980s the Thatcher Government was emphasising notions of deterrence and retribution. However, at the same time, ministers recognised that for less serious offenders, using prisons was 'expensive and ineffective' (Crow 2001, p. 104). It is only with well-funded alternatives to custody, changes in sentencing, and a concerted effort to divert offenders from custody, that curbing the growth of the prison population can be achieved. Jackson (1972) stated that:

> The ultimate expression of law is not order – it's prison. We have hundreds upon hundreds of prisons, and thousands upon thousands of laws, yet there is no social order, no social peace. (Jackson 1972, p. 1)

Elders in prison are less likely to be a risk to society, and less likely to re-offend, and this allows for the possibility of designing future prisons/alternatives to prisons with the older person in mind. In a report produced by the Florida Corrections Commission (1999), it was found that older prisoners have the lowest recidivism rate of any group examined. In England and Wales, the only figures to compare release by age are in relation to the Home Detention Curfew (HDC) (HDC was introduced across England and Wales in 1999). It allows short-term prisoners to spend up to the last two months of their custodial sentence in the community and subject to an electronically monitored curfew for at least nine hours per day. The figures suggest that the release rate on HDC tends to increase with age and it is more likely to be used for the 50+ groups. The association here is that there is a higher risk of reconviction for younger offenders (Home Office 2001; Johnson and Alozie 2001; Long 1992).

Whilst further research is needed to ascertain how these figures break down for the female and male prison population, one could certainly imagine a future in which the imprisonment of older women was a rarity, reserved for those who are convicted of abnormally serious crimes of a nature indicating a continuing risk to society. Male and female prisoners are not comparable; they have different criminal profiles, both in terms of types of offences committed and previous offending history, and have different adjustment patterns to imprisonment. It has been argued that a gender-specific policy based on substantive equality will improve the plight of women in prison across the life-course (NACRO 1993, 1994; Carlen 2002). By using this group to explore alternatives to imprisonment, what is for sure is that there are savings to be made on both a humanitarian and a fiscal level.

A good example of diverting or reducing custodial sentences for elders is an early release scheme orchestrated by *The Project for Older Prisoners* in the US. Candidates must be over 50 years of age, have already served the average time for their offences, and have been assessed as low risk and thus unlikely to commit further crimes. Another unique requirement of this programme is that the victim, or the victim's family, must agree to early release. As a result of these strict standards, no prisoner released under the Project for Older

Prisoners has ever been returned to prison for committing another crime (Turley 1992). The programme helps them find employment and housing, and ensures that they receive their full entitlement to benefits. Such a scheme could beneficially be extended to England and Wales, to include a large number of older prisoners and, if successful, could foster a willingness within the penal system to consider shorter or non-custodial sentences for this low-risk group.

Conclusion

The title for this chapter, 'No Problems – Old and Quiet', was taken from the first Inspectorate Report on Older Offenders (2004) and the irony of the title is that this group is in a system that fails to acknowledge the specific health, social, and care needs for just under 5,000 people who are in prison. In these circumstances the needs of elders must be taken into account to avoid accusations of injustice and lack of care.

Yet the structure of prisons in organisation, architecture, and training fails to address the diversity of need of those who are other than able-bodied. The kinds of problems women and men in later life may, and do, experience in the prison system largely result from the fact that the prison is geared for the able-bodied young male. The majority of prisons in England and Wales have not been designed with the disabled or the older prisoner in mind. It is the absence of basic facilities, such as having a 24-hour medical centre on site, ground floor rooms, adequate resettlement programmes, activities for daily living etc., that results in a situation where women and men in later life are left behind the prison walls without any form of purposeful activity. By ignoring the harms generated by the prison machinery and consequently it's perverse consequences we are compounding and reproducing social inequality. If we continue to fail to recognise this 'significant majority' (Wahidin 2004), we are compounding the pains of imprisonment far beyond the recognised intentions of sentencing.

Professionals in the field of criminology and gerontology can provide a greater awareness and understanding of the problems facing persons who encounter the criminal justice system in later life. The problems of offending, prison adjustment, and successful re-entry to society of the aged can be fully addressed in the context of an awareness of ageing in general. Policymakers must respond to this significant minority and address the special needs of prisoners who will spend the remainder of their lives in prison as well as those who will be released in late old age.

References

Acoca, L. (1998) 'Defusing the Time Bomb: Understanding and Meeting the Growing Healthcare Needs of Incarcerated Women in America' in *Crime and Delinquency,* 44: 49–70.

Aday, R.H. (1994) 'Ageing in Prison: A Case Study of New Elderly Offenders', *International Journal of Offender Therapy and Comparative Criminology,* 1 (38): 79–91.

Aday, R.H. (1994a) 'Golden Years Behind Bars: Special Programs and Facilities for Elderly Inmates', *Federal Probation,* 58 (2): 47–54.

Aday, R.H. (2003) *Aging Prisoners: Crisis in American Corrections.* Westport, CT: Praeger Publishing.

Atherton, J.S. (1989) *Interpreting Residential Life – Values to Practice.* London: Tavistock/Routledge.

Bond, J., Coleman, P., and Peace, S. (eds) (1993) *Ageing in Society – An Introduction to Social Gerontology.* London: Sage.

Bytheway, B. (1994) *Ageism.* Buckingham: Open University Press.

Carlen, P. (2002) *Women and Punishment: The Struggle for Justice.* Cullompton: Willan Publishing.

Cole, T., Achenbaum, W., Jokobi, P. and Kastenbaum, R. (1993) *Voices and Visions of Aging – Towards a Critical Gerontology.* New York: Springer.

Coleman, P. (1993) 'Adjustment in Later Life' in J. Bond, P. Coleman and S. Peace (eds) (1993) *Ageing in Society – An Introduction to Social Gerontology.* London: Sage.

Crow, I. (2001) *The Treatment and Rehabilitation of Offenders.* London: Sage.

Dubler, N.N. (1998) 'The Collision of Confinement and Care: End-of-life Care in Prisons and Jails', *Journal of Law, Medicine and Ethics,* 26: 149.

Fattah, E.A. and Sacco V.F. (1989) *Crime and Victimisation of the Elderly.* New York: Springer.

Fazel, S., Hope, T., O'Donnell, I., Piper, M. and Jacoby, R. (2001) 'Health of Elderly Male Prisoners: Worse than the General Population, Worse than Younger Prisoners', *Age and Ageing,* 30: 403–7.

Fennel, G., Phillipson, C. and Evers, H. (1988) *The Sociology of Old Age.* Buckingham: Open University.

Florida Corrections Commission (1999) *Annual Report Section 4: Status Report on Elderly Offenders,* Florida Corrections Department.

Gallagher, E. (1990) 'Emotional, Social, and Physical Health Characteristics of Older Men in Prison', *International Journal of Aging and Human Development,* Vol. 31 (4): 251–65.

Goetting, A. (1992) 'Patterns of Homicide Among the Elderly', *Violence and Victims,* 7: 203–15.

Gramling, R. and Forsyth, C. (1988) 'Elderly Crime: Fact and Artifact' in B. McCarthy *Older Offenders*, pp. 75–86. New York: Praeger Publishing.

Her Majesty's Chief Inspector of Prisons (1997) *Women in Prison: A Thematic Review*. London: The Home Office.

Her Majesty's Chief Inspector of Prisons (2004) 'No Problems – Old and Quiet: Older Prisoners in England and Wales'. London: HMSO.

Hockey, J. (1989) 'Residential Care and the Maintenance of Social Identity: Negotiating the Transition to Institutional Life' in M. Jefferys (ed.) (1989) *Growing Old in The Twentieth Century*, 201–18. London: Routledge.

Home Office (1995) *Managing the Needs of Female Offenders*. London: Home Office.

Home Office (1997a) *Understanding the Sentencing of Women*, Research Study 170, The Research and Statistics Directorate.

Home Office (1997b) *The Prison Population in 1997: A Statistical Review*, Research Findings No. 76. London: HMSO.

Home Office (1999) *Statistics on Women and the Criminal Justice System – A Home Office Publication Under Section 95 of The Criminal Justice Act 1991.* London: HMSO.

Home Office (2001) *Prison Statistics of England and Wales*, National Statistics Cm.5743.

Jackson, G. (1972) *Blood in My Eye*. London: Penguin Books.

Johnson, W. and Alozie, B.O. (2001) 'The Effect of Age on the Criminal Processing: Is There an Advantage in Being "Older"?', *Journal of Gerontological Social Work*, 35: 47–62.

Kerbs, J. (2000) 'The Older Prisoner: Social, Psychological and Medical Considerations' in M. Rothman, B. Dunlop, and P. Entzel (eds) (2000) *Elders, Crime and The Criminal Justice System – Myth, Perceptions, and Reality in the 21st Century*. New York: Springer.

Kratocoski, P. (1990) 'Circumstances Surrounding Homicides by Older Offenders', *Criminal Justice and Behaviour*, 17: 420–30.

Long, L.M. (1992) 'A Study of Arrests of Older Offenders: Trends and Patterns', *Journal of Crime and Justice*, 15: 157–75.

Manthorpe, J. (1983) 'With Intent to Steal in the New Age', *Journal of Offending Counselling Services and Rehabilitation*, 13 (Spring): 25–8.

Marquart, J.W., Merianos, D.E. and Doucet, G. (2000) 'The Health Related Concerns of Older Prisoners: Implications for Policy', *Aging and Society*, 20: 79–96.

Marquart, J.W., Merianos, D.E., Herbert, J.L. and Carroll, L. (1997) 'Health Condition and Prisoners: A Review of Research and Emerging Areas of Inquiry', *Prison Journal*, 77: 184–208.

Morton, J. (1992) *An Administrative Overview of the Older Inmate*, US Department of Justice National Institute of Corrections.

NACRO (1993) *Women Leaving Prison*. London: NACRO.

NACRO (1994) *Prison Overcrowding – Recent Developments*, NACRO Briefing No. 28 (July). London: NACRO.

Neeley, L.C., Addison, L. and Craig-Moreland, D. (1997) 'Addressing the needs of elderly offenders', *Corrections Today*, August, 59: 120–4.

Newman, E., Newman, D. and Gewirtz, M. (eds) (1984) *Elderly Criminals*. Oelgeschlager, Massachusetts: Gunn and Hain Publishers, Inc, Cambridge.

Newman, E. (1984a) 'Elderly Offenders and American Crime' in E. Newman, D. Newman and M. Gewirtz (eds) *Elderly Criminals*, pp. 25–51. Oelgeschlager, Massachusetts: Gunn and Hain, Publishers Inc., Cambridge.

Phillips, J. (1996) 'Crime and Older Offenders', *Practice*, 8 (1): 43–55.

Pollak, O. (1941) 'The Criminality of Old age', *Journal of Criminal Psychotherapy*, 3: 213–35.

Prison Reform Trust (2003) *Growing Old in Prison: A Scoping Study on Older Prisoners*. London: PRT.

Rothman, M.B., Dunlop, B.D. and Entzel, P. (2000) *Elders Crime and the Criminal Justice System*. New York: Springer.

Sim, J. (2000) 'One Thousand Days of Degradation: New Labour and Old Compromises at the Turn of the Century', *Social Justice*, 27 (2): 168–92.

Turley, J. (1990) 'Long-term Confinement and the Ageing Inmate Population' in US Department of Justice, Federal Bureau of Prisons *Form on Issues in Corrections, 'Alternative Solutions'*. Washington, D.C: U.S Government. Printing Office.

Turley, J. (1992) 'A Solution to Prison Overcrowding', *USA Today Magazine*, November 121: 80–1.

Wahidin, A. (2002) 'Reconfiguring Older Bodies in the Prison Time Machine', *Journal of Aging and Identity*, 7 (3): 177–93, September 2002.

Wahidin, A. (2004) *Older Women in the Criminal Justice System: Running Out of Time*. London: Jessica Kingsley.

Wahidin, A. (2005) 'Older Offenders, Crime and the Criminal Justice System' in C. Hale, K. Hayward, A. Wahidin and E. Wincup (eds) *Criminology*, pp. 403–23. Oxford: Oxford University Press.

Wahidin, A. (2005a) 'Not Old and Quiet: Older Prisoners in the Criminal Justice System in England and Wales', The British Society of Criminology Conference, 'Re-Awakening the Criminological Imagination', 12–14 July 2005: Unpublished paper.

Wahidin, A. and Aday, H.R. (2005) 'Managing the Needs of Older Offenders: An International Perspective', *Prison Service Journal*, July No. 160: 13–23.

Chapter 12

'Unregarded age in corners thrown': an answer to the issues of healthcare for older prisoners

Debby Jaques

This chapter aims to demonstrate that appropriate and adequate healthcare for elderly prisoners can be and is achieved within the custodial setting. This is based on my own experience as head of healthcare within HMP and YOI Norwich (employed by Norwich Primary Care Trust). It should be noted that this is based on my own experiences and observations as a practitioner and does not necessarily represent the views of either the prison or the Trust. Comments by prisoners/patients will also be included.

It could be argued that it is easy to disregard the needs of older people in prisons (Prison Reform Trust 2003; HM Chief Inspector of Prisons (HMCIP) 2004; Wahidin 2004). Statistically they represent a small percentage of the prison population – 2.6 per cent of the male population in 2002 (HMCIP 2004) – and an even smaller percentage of the wider population. But can a humane society really disregard the needs of the elderly – even in prison? Just as the elderly population in society is increasing, the old are getting older (Department of Health 2001) – so too they are in prison. Male prisoners over the age of 60 are the fastest growing population in the prison estate – representing 1.3 per cent in 1992, compared with 2.6 per cent in 2002. Clearly, the number of older people in prison will continue to grow, especially as sentences lengthen and more indeterminate sentences are passed. Of the older prisoners, many have committed serious offences, and as a result some will grow old in prison until such time as they no longer pose a risk to the public, and some will spend the rest of their lives in prison. Prison represents a microcosm of society. Just as the needs of older people in society are highlighted both by government and the media – so too are the needs of the elderly in prison now beginning to be highlighted. In the community there are many examples of excellent care for older people, but until the publication of the National Service Framework for Older People (2001), there had been no national focus on the needs of older people. There had, however, been reports of poor, unresponsive, insensitive, and discriminatory services (Department of Health 2001). This has been reflected in the prison population and highlighted by HMCIP (2004). The proper care and treatment of older prisoners is not just an issue for the prison service and probation, the National Service Framework places firm responsibility on all agencies involved with the care of the elderly – regardless of whether they are in prison. These responsibilities do not cease merely because someone is a prisoner.

In the joint report by the Prison Service and the Department of Health – 'Report of a Working Group on Doctors Working in Prisons' (Department of Health/HM Prison Service 2001), a recommendation was:

> As part of the health needs assessment process, prisons, health authorities and primary care groups/trusts review the needs of older prisoners and those with a disability and take steps to ensure that they have access to the same range of professionals and services that are available to these groups in the community. There needs to be a greater emphasis placed on providing both groups with a healthy and suitable regime.

The report highlights further that the health needs of older prisoners are often long term and chronic in nature, and that social care and support may be required just as in the community.

No matter what a person has done (the criminal justice system has already meted out its punishment) the role of prison healthcare is not to punish but to provide an equivalent level of healthcare to which all society is entitled and enjoys. We live in a civilised society where health is a priority for all regardless of gender, ethnicity or age. Health/ill health is no respecter of persons – free or in prison. Pain is pain and old age is old age regardless of status.

It has been documented that there is a dearth of research in this field (Prison Reform Trust 2003; HMCIP 2004; Wahidin 2004) and the evidence base demonstrating good practice is sadly lacking. However, it should be noted that there are individual areas of good practice (HMCIP 2004) which have not been publicised. It would appear that it is not publicly popular to demonstrate that decent healthcare is provided for prisoners. This will be demonstrated further on in the chapter.

The aim of prison healthcare is to provide prisoners with access to the same range and quality of services that the general public receives from the wider National Health Service: these must include appropriate health services for elderly prisoners (Department of Health/Home Office 2002). In September 2004, HMCIP published a thematic review on the conditions and treatment of older prisoners, their healthcare and resettlement, in the light of the requirements of the Human Rights Act 1998, the Disability Discrimination Act 2004 and the National Service Framework for Older People (*ibid.*). The review reported that a few prisons were taking seriously the needs of older prisoners and that some examples of good practice were found. However, it remarks that there is no overarching strategy throughout the prison estate for assessing and providing for the needs of older prisoners. The review was published after the unit at Norwich was opened in August 2004, but recognised that the unit was planned. The Department of Health's National Service Framework for Older People (*ibid.*) stresses the need to provide adequate health and social care for prisoners over the age of 60. The Prison Reform Trust, with the Centre for Policy on Ageing, produced a scoping study on older prisoners in 2003, which also highlighted the lack of a national strategy for meeting the needs of older prisoners. On speaking with colleagues around the country, there are obvious areas of good practice with dedicated interest and concerted effort: however conversations substantiated the lack of national strategic working.

The Elderly Lifer Unit at HMP Norwich was planned in 2003. At that time, it would appear that Norwich was chosen as it had ground floor space available to provide an appropriate facility. The unit was planned with 15 single cells to accommodate elderly life serving prisoners. At the time of the appointment of the head of healthcare the plans had already been drawn for the unit, but no criteria had been devised. Therefore, on appointment, a priority was to draft criteria and a plan. It was envisaged that the unit would provide nursing/residential home type facilities for elderly life serving prisoners.

In light of all of the legislation and guidance with regards to nursing home and residential homes and the above noted legislation and available reviews, excepting the HMCIP thematic review which had not at the time been published, criteria for the unit were drafted. These were then submitted to the prison and the Trust, bearing in mind the size of the unit, the regime of the rest of the prison and the supporting structures that would be required to facilitate decent healthcare. There was an awareness of the lack of strategic input – the dedicated healthcare unit being very much the 'first of its kind' in the country. It was imperative that the unit would be manageable from all aspects, including consideration being given to the local National Health Service secondary care facilities and necessary financial constraints. It was also important to address the workforce issues, the location of Norwich as a national resource and the possible demands on so few beds, given the information received as to there being an intense demand for places.

The process

Although the architectural drawings had already been done, there was a need to review them in light of the anticipated client group. Alterations were made with guidance drawn from Department of Health, 'Care Homes for Older People' (Care Standards Act 2000), the National Service Framework for Older People (2001), and evidence-based areas of good practice. Whilst much consideration was being given to the new unit, raising the profile of elderly prisoners generally highlighted the need for a focus on elderly prisoners across the prison. With this in mind a named senior nurse for elder care was identified to address the needs of the existing population, and to utilise tools such as the single assessment process to inform practitioners of their existing and ongoing needs, through care and aftercare. Provision of a named senior nurse/manager was later published as a recommendation by HMCIP (2004).

As stated, the unit is specifically for elderly life serving prisoners with *healthcare* needs. The criteria reflect this. It is appropriate that elderly prisoners who do not have healthcare needs are integrated into the wider population of the prison – as a reflection of wider society. Outside of the prison environment older people are not segregated from the rest of the population merely because of age, but move to nursing/residential homes as their health/social needs dictate – the unit is, therefore, based on a similar model. There are older prisoners across the rest of the prison whose needs are met with regards to environment/location, but who do not require constant nursing care. It was imperative from the outset that the criteria be adhered to. HMCIP (2004) expects that healthcare beds are not used as general purpose beds. This has not been a problem locally, but may be a consideration for some prisons given the pressure on prison spaces. The beds within the Elderly Lifer Unit are protected from this – however, there has been increased pressure and interest from prisons around the country for availability of places, thus proving the demand for beds.

It must be stated that the prison was entirely receptive to the plans for the unit, accepting the recommendations that needed to be incorporated for a fit for purpose healthcare facility. There were challenges however, in that this was a venture that had never been addressed before within a custodial setting. The challenges were not those that had been anticipated, one example being that furnishings should be appropriate for the client group, i.e. round tables instead of square. The Prison Service makes its own furniture, but only square tables! After explanation (older people have a tendency to falls and knocks), it was accepted that round tables were more appropriate. Furthermore, it was agreed that older people should have seating that is appropriate for their needs, i.e. wing-backed armchairs, and dining chairs with arms to facilitate standing from a seated position. This, too, was later published as a recommendation by HMCIP (2004). Whilst this may seem common sense and obvious, as this had not been approached previously, each issue required explanation and justification. Furnishing within cells was also given careful consideration – it would have been inappropriate to provide traditional low level 'prison' type beds. The cells are all single cells equipped with King's Fund hospital type beds, with a number of cells having electric profiling beds for those most infirm/unwell and requiring the most nursing care. Provision was made for three dedicated 'disabled cells' with hand rails etc. as would be seen externally. It should be noted that older prisoners are not accepted to the unit solely by virtue of disability, as facilities are available across the prison estate for the 'well' disabled. However, older prisoners with disablement as an ongoing health problem are accepted, e.g. 'stroke' patients, amputees as a result of systemic vascular disease. Bathing/showering facilities also reflect that which is available 'outside', with both able bodied facilities and bathing facilities wherein patients/prisoners can be assisted in/out of the bath with the aid of an electric hoist, and showers on level ground, all with hand 'grab' rails. Previous evidence has reported that older prisoners do not have access to 'in-cell' privileges such as televisions (Wahidin 2004; HMCIP 2004), and that prisoners perceive that they are penalised for having healthcare needs. All cells in Norwich are equipped with in-cell television, some with teletext for the hard of hearing. Facilities within what is traditionally called the 'association room', now locally called the 'day room', also reflect that which would be seen in a

National Health Service nursing/residential facility – library area (with large print books and books on tape), relaxation area, activity area and television. There are some who may criticise, and indeed do, that the facilities are 'too nice' for prisoners. This was reflected in the media when the unit first opened, with some public opinion stating that the unit is better than facilities outside. However, it is argued that the unit reflects the Prison Service/Department of Health aims to provide prisoners with access to the same range and quality of services that the general public receives from the wider National Health Service. This does not mean that the unit is better than that which is available outside, but that it reflects what is appropriate. By observation, however, it does provide a facility which is better than that which has traditionally been seen within a custodial setting. Visitors, including the media, observe that the unit has the 'feel' of a nursing home with 'bars'. There remains an awareness that although the unit provides 24-hour nursing care to older prisoners/ patients, the client group are prisoners. There remains a constant and necessary balance between the obvious requirement for security and nursing care. It is necessary to be aware that this particular unit caters for the healthcare needs of elderly life serving prisoners (elderly lifers), who by virtue of their sentence are not in prison for minor misdemeanours. This too has been highlighted publicly: that they are perhaps the least deserving in society. It could be argued that if a 75-year-old man in wider society was neglected and unwell, and died that way, that there would be an outcry. If however, the same happened in prison, would there be the same level of public outcry and concern – if not, why not? In a civilised society, decency and health are paramount.

The regime within the unit has to conform to the prison regime. However, consideration has been given to the healthcare needs of the prisoners/patients, i.e. access to cells at night for healthcare interventions. The daytime regime also reflects the needs of older people – activities which are time limited, physical ability appropriate, and reflecting the mental capacity (e.g. Alzheimer's). Activities include physical instruction (through the prison PE department), music therapy with a reflective, contemplative theme, table top games, and computer skills. Physical rehabilitative therapy as required is supplied through the Primary Care Trust. The prisoners/patients remain subject to the prison rules, and Incentives and Earned Privileges Scheme (IEP).

On admission to the unit, each prisoner/patient is fully assessed with regards to their healthcare needs, physically and mentally, social needs, and nutritional and pressure area scores are assessed and recorded. These are reviewed regularly by the named nurse. This initial assessment is undertaken by the nursing team, and then by the GP. They are risk assessed for safety for equipment in cells (e.g. kettles) and ability to manage in/out of bed, bath and shower. They are also risk assessed as to whether it is appropriate for them to have their medication held in possession – as for some this is suitable to promote independence and self care. A complete assessment is also undertaken with regard to activities of daily living utilising recognised assessment tools, such as the need for adapted cutlery for those with arthritic joints.

It was also necessary to address the workforce issues – this being a healthcare facility it was appropriate to reflect that which is necessary in the wider National Health Service. Whilst always bearing in mind that the unit is within a prison setting, and that the patients are prisoners, nonetheless the skill mix meets the needs of both disciplines – trained nurses, healthcare assistants and healthcare officers who provide both a healthcare and a discipline presence. Medical cover is provided by the medical officer/general practitioner and visiting specialists as required. Other visiting specialists, i.e. psychiatrist, optician, radiographer, dentist, chiropodist, and physiotherapist, contribute to the overall care available.

The unit

The aim of the unit is to provide a needs-based in-patient facility for older life sentence prisoners. The unit provides a service that specialises in the care of older life sentence prisoners (lifers) with healthcare needs. Care programmes are provided to maximise and maintain each individual's potential quality of life. Patients/prisoners who are admitted should not continuously require acute hospital services or the continuous services of a specialist National Health Service team. They are managed to the same standard of care and range and quality of services as the general public receives from the National Health Service. Care programmes and systems of care reflect the standards outlined in the National Service Framework for Older People (Department of Health 2001).

It is recognised that currently there are over 1,200 people aged 60 or over in prison in England and Wales (Home Office 2003). The overall percentage of older men in prison remains small. Most of them have grown old during their imprisonment. Although offender units for older persons are increasingly common in the USA, there are few in the rest of the world, an exception being a wing for frail and elderly prisoners at HMP Kingston. It is suggested that people age quicker when in prison than in the wider community (Better Government for Older People 2004). The Prison Reform Trust suggests that existing prisons cannot provide adequate healthcare provision for prisoners over 60 years of age, the fastest growing group in Britain's jails, and further that the Prison Service may have to consider the kind of 'nursing home prisons' that exist in America in order to care for older prisoners and cope with their unique healthcare needs (Prison Reform Trust 2003).

In the 2003 report 'Growing Old in Prison' published by the Prison Reform Trust, funded by the Nuffield Foundation, indicated that there were over 1,200 prisoners over the age of 60, of which one fifth were male lifers, i.e. 240. Of this number it indicated that 80 per cent (192) had a chronic illness or disability. Of these, one third (64) have cardiovascular disease, one fifth (38) had respiratory disease and over half (120) suffered from some form of mental disorder.

The Elderly Lifer Unit at Norwich has been designed around the specific needs of these prisoners. It is recognised that not all older lifers will have healthcare needs that require admission to an in-patient facility. Therefore, the assessment and admission criteria reflect this, in order to provide a service to those most in need of this specialist service.

The criteria

In order to provide an effective and appropriate service, it is necessary to outline admission and discharge criteria based on clinical need and the ability of the local service to meet the needs of this group. Admission is at the sole discretion of the head of healthcare (or named deputy) in conjunction with the governor, and based on clinical need and documented in the clinical record (Health Services for Prisoners 2002).

* the service is available to those aged 60 years and over, who are life-sentenced prisoners, whose healthcare needs meet the admission criteria;
* the decision to admit rests with the head of healthcare or deputy and is based on the following:
  (i)   assessment by the head of healthcare;

(ii)   medical status;
(iii) bed availability;
(iv)   overall dependency of patients currently within the unit;
(v)   legal status.

In order to provide an appropriate service it is also necessary to outline those for whom the service would be inappropriate, and who should therefore not be admitted:

• those who require continuous admission to the acute National Health Service Trust services;
• those who require continuous observation due to an acute psychiatric illness or disturbed behaviours;
• those who require specialist treatments or investigations that cannot be met within this care setting;
• those who are applying for early release on compassionate grounds.

Note, although the above may appear to be discriminatory, it allows the limited number of places to provide for those most in need of the service.

Further, although the age criterion rests at 60 years of age, this is discretionary – as in the wider community a person can be 'old' at 50 or 'young' at 70, depending on physical and mental health factors. Also, it is generally believed that prisoners tend to age up to ten years more than their biological age.

Medical and nursing care is provided as previously described. Care programmes are co-ordinated utilising a multi-disciplinary approach, in liaison with the services within the Primary Care Trust. The unit provides non-acute medical care for patients/prisoners who are unable to be managed within their normal environment because of complex needs of care and their need for ongoing observation, assessment, and treatment. They are admitted for a period of assessment, treatment and therapeutic input. Prisoners, who, because of their age, may require an extended period of nursing care or rehabilitation, may be admitted following an acute intervention. Physiotherapy may be provided following a needs assessment. Patients/prisoners are admitted requiring palliative care necessitating symptom relief, assessment or terminal care, but who do not require the ongoing services of an acute National Health Service team. Liaison and care planning is done in conjunction with the National Health Service palliative care team. The patients/prisoners will not have an ongoing application for release on compassionate grounds. Care that can be facilitated within the unit includes blood investigations, extensive dressings, catheterisation, gastrostomy feeding, syringe drivers, nebulisers and oxygen concentrates, ECGs, subcutaneous fluids, and rehabilitation following an acute intervention or illness (e.g. surgery or stroke). Patients/prisoners are placed on the chronic disease register for automatic recall where necessary, and for vaccinations such as the annual flu vaccination as clinically indicated.

The regime in the unit offers care, stimulation and purposeful activity appropriate to the needs of the individuals. The unit functions as a community with activities provided suitable to the age and abilities of the patients, e.g. where able, they eat together in a communal dining area. A suitable garden area is, at the time of writing, being constructed. This was designed by young offenders, with the needs of elderly people in mind, and includes appropriate access, raised flower beds and a water feature, providing dedicated external space to enhance the therapeutic environment.

Applications for places in the unit are submitted by way of an application form, indicating medical problems and needs, by the healthcare team from the referring establishment, together with documentation from the clinical record, as needed. The applications are collated and assessed by the head of healthcare and discussed with the referring healthcare team. An assessment visit is made to the referring establishment, together with a representative from the lifer management team within HMP Norwich. Currently a waiting list exists for places on the unit.

Outcomes

The unit provides a service to older life sentenced prisoners, respecting them as individuals and managing their care needs. This:

- respects their privacy and dignity;
- enables older people to make informed choices by involving them in decisions about their needs and care;
- provides a co-ordinated and integrated service.

Good holistic assessment and active care management for older prisoners supports individuals in their wish to remain independent (within an appropriate setting), and reduces costs of providing services which are not appropriate. Assessment of older prisoners is comprehensive ensuring that they receive properly integrated needs-based services in an appropriate custodial setting.

The standards focused on in the National Service Framework for Older People (2001) will be met by:

- rooting out age discrimination;
- providing person-centred care;
- promoting older people's health and independence;
- fitting services around people's needs.

The current profile of the population within the unit indicates that all (100 per cent) have multiple health problems, all of whom if not in prison, would require nursing home/residential home accommodation. Table 12.1 illustrates the diversity and prevalence of health problems.

Whilst this table illustrates very basic data, analysis of it indicates that 33 per cent have diabetes and problems related thereto, 66 per cent have musculoskeletal problems, including joint replacements, arthritic conditions affecting mobility, peripheral vascular disease requiring amputations, 40 per cent have respiratory disease, including chronic obstructive pulmonary disease, previous TB, 46 per cent have mental health problems including Alzheimer's disease, paranoid schizophrenia, 73 per cent have cardiac disease including previous myocardial infarctions, angina, poorly controlled hypertension, 33 per cent have gastro-intestinal problems ranging from gastric reflux

Table 12.1

	Diabetes/ endocrine disorders	Musculo-skeletal	Respiratory disease	Mental health problems	Cardiac disease/ circulatory problems	Terminal disease/ palliative care
No. of patients	5	10	6	7	11	1

	Gastro-intestinal disease	Urology problems	Cancers	CVA (Stroke)	Other	
No. of patients	5	2	2	1	4	

Source: Jaques, 2006.

to gastric ulcers, diverticular disease, epigastric hernia, 14 per cent have prostate/urology problems, 7 per cent have diagnosed and treated cancers, 14 per cent have had strokes. Other problems include glaucoma, hepatitis C and general frailty. The most staggering statistic reveals that 93 per cent have multiple health problems with 26 per cent having five health problems or more. Most (80 per cent) require assistance with normal activities of daily living (ADLs). To date, it has been possible to manage, care and treat all the prevailing health needs, facilitated by appropriate interventions and links with the wider National Health Service. It has been possible to rehabilitate those who have had major surgery – including bilateral below and above knee amputees, to the extent that sentence progression can be managed. This has been achieved due to the fact that a fit for purpose facility has been provided, together with appropriately qualified staff and skill mix levels of those providing care.

Whilst these data indicate the prevalence of disease or ill-health, the level of applications and the types and multiplicity of disease, suggests that this may be higher. Applications for places within the unit are received on a weekly basis, with a diversity of need from the frail who simply find it difficult to cope in the general prison population to those with a number of health problems.

The opening of the unit drew media attention. Prisoners/patients within the unit were interviewed by the media four months after it opened. Responses received ranged from it being a superb facility, with nothing matching it in the prison service, to others who commented that the Prison Service itself has changed with regard to attitude and treatment of prisoners. All who were interviewed suggested that more facilities like Norwich should be available across the country. Patients/prisoners have been accepted for the unit from as far apart as Cornwall and Northumberland. This may suggest that for the purpose of social needs this would be detrimental; however, experience has shown that as prisoners are so used to being moved around, to progress sentence plans etc., that to date movement in itself has not been an issue. Public response to the media indicated displeasure – with opinion ranging from providing a facility 'too good' for prisoners, to comments that old people should not be locked up. Whilst consideration is given to their social needs, when allocating prisoners to the unit the overriding factor has been their health needs. In reality, as the unit cares for life serving prisoners, some who have been in prison for many years, if not a number of decades, have already lost contact with family and friends, and receive few, if any, visitors for reasons other than distance. However, in the future, if the elderly population within prison continues to increase, and it is deemed necessary to open further units, the distance issue should be addressed more directly.

The future

In 2004 HMCIP published its thematic review of older prisoners in England and Wales 'No problems – Old and Quiet', which in its conclusion made both key recommendations and immediate recommendations with regard to environment, regimes and relationships, healthcare and resettlement. It also highlighted areas of good practice, which although fairly limited, clearly demonstrate that individual areas are taking seriously the health and social care needs of elderly prisoners. The key recommendations highlight the need for the National Offender Management Service (NOMS) and the Department of Health to develop a national strategy for older and less able prisoners that conforms to the requirements of the Disability Discrimination Act 2004 and the National Service Framework for Older People (2001). This level of recognition and joint working must serve to highlight the growing need for facilities and care for this group of prisoners. It also serves to recognise that this is an issue which is forecast to increase both in terms of numbers and need. The recommendations for immediate action focus on national policy and local policy. However, it is perceived that without the national drivers, the local policy may be more difficult to implement, as, throughout the public sector, there are many targets to achieve – not just within the elderly prison population, which represents a small percentage, but across the entire prison estate and the National Health Service. The key recommendations for the national strategy focus on a phased programme of providing sufficient suitable and accessible accommodation in each prison. It could be argued that given the numbers involved and the costs that would be incurred, it may be appropriate to provide a smaller number of specialist units strategically sited across the prison estate in preference to each prison. However, as further research is also recommended in the review, this may yet be identified. The review further recommends that the national strategy should also include the development of standards for the care of older prisoners, using the national policy recommendations identified and building on the good practice already recognised, to include regime differentiation for older prisoners and training for staff, involving specialists from health and social care sectors. Although it is highlighted in the review recommendations, it is imperative that inter-agency co-operation between prisons, the National Health Service, probation, social services and relevant statutory and voluntary community agencies is perceived as pivotal to provide support for older prisoners both in custody and on return to the community. Historically, agencies have worked in isolation. However, in this regard the importance of inter-agency co-operation is perceived as pivotal to successful working – primarily for the appropriate care for prisoners, but further in terms of the wider community. It is worthy of note that care of older people in the wider population has had high priority and focus for some time, including the publication of the National Service Framework for Older People in 2001, but the focus for older prisoners has only recently been addressed. Whilst the National Service Framework made brief mention of healthcare provision for older prisoners, it would appear that the real focus has only been established with the transfer of commissioning responsibility for prisoners' health to the National Health Service.

The review highlights that further research should be carried out into the general health of prisoners aged 45 years and over, to establish their likely health needs if they remain in prison into old age, the extent of mental health problems in older prisoners, the specific needs of older women prisoners, more appropriate and flexible ways of confronting offending behaviour and the resettlement needs of older prisoners, in order to inform the development of the national strategy. It has been highlighted previously that there is an absence of research in this area; this recommendation therefore should be welcome news to professionals working in the field. The development and launch of the Prison Health Research Network (2005) further highlights the need for research into these and other prison health issues, and should inform the specific research required. Those areas that are recognised as being providers of good practice should also inform the research process and the evidence base.

With specific regard to healthcare, the review recommends: that nationally all prisons have chronic disease registers and management clinics to ensure that prisoners with chronic medical conditions have care in line with best practice; that there should be specific mental health protocols for older prisoners; that all healthcare centres have a palliative care policy which has been developed in partnership with local palliative care service providers; and that there should be a review of the criteria for compassionate and early release on the grounds of old age or ill-health to ensure an appropriate balance between risk and humane care. Although these are recommendations for national policy, many of these, excepting the criteria for early release, are achievable at local levels, with the drivers for implementation being at national level. All palliative care and mental health Trusts have local strategies addressing these issues, in which prisons should now be included. There is also national evidence-based guidance available in areas such as palliative care, for example the 'Liverpool End of Life Care Pathway'.

The recommendations for local policy development and implementation include:

- a lead nurse/manager with responsibility for the overall care of older prisoners, ensuring that:
  - healthcare needs for older prisoners are separately assessed;
  - age-based healthcare policies are reviewed;
  - medications are formally reviewed in conjunction with the pharmacist at least every six months, ensuring that medications are issued to prisoners without gaps or delays and ensuring effective delivery for those who have mobility difficulties to reach healthcare centres;
  - full consideration of mental health needs, including a review of clinical records;
  - prisoners who require it are given help with incontinence problems;
- training specific to the needs of providing healthcare for older prisoners is provided, including recognition for signs of mental illness;
- formal local arrangements with local health agencies for loan of equipment and specialist nursing advice;
- a patient forum with representation from older prisoners;
- patients/prisoners should not be deprived of mobility and health aids;
- older prisoners should be actively encouraged to have the Hepatitis B vaccination as part of initial screening on arrival in prison.

These recommendations have already been implemented locally and in other prisons that have evidenced areas of good practice, prior to the publication of the review. However this endorses the need for a shared vision and national strategy.

It may be perceived that these recommendations are already given in other documents, such as the National Service Framework for Older People (2001). However, it pulls together a prison service/health strategy for the holistic care of older prisoners, which informs practitioners and prison service managers in a joint framework.

It is worthy of note that other national developments are being implemented which will assist in the development of prison healthcare, including the older population, such as electronic clinical information systems which will assist in areas such as the facilitation of automatic recall for clinics (e.g. well-person, vaccination).

This chapter, is very much from a practitioner viewpoint and is based on the experiences of service providers and recipients. It demonstrates that with informed planning, joint co-operation and working, appropriate healthcare for this minority and apparently unregarded group can not only be achieved, but provided and managed within the custodial setting to the same quality and range as that which is available in the wider community – the aim to which all are striving.

Only time will tell the story of the successful implementation of national strategy and recommendations – time, which of course for the existing elderly prison population is, as Wahidin (2004) aptly describes, running out.

Note

1 William Shakespeare *As You Like It*, Act 2, Scene III.

References

Centre for Policy on Ageing and Prison Reform Trust (2003) *Growing Old in Prison – A Scoping Study on Older Prisoners*. London: Prison Reform Trust.

Department of Health (2001) *National Service Framework for Older People*. London: Department of Health.

Department of Health and HM Prison Service (2003) *Prison Health Handbook*. London: Department of Health.

Department of Health (2003) *Care Homes for Older People – National Minimum Standards, Care Homes Regulations*, 3rd edn. London: TSO.

Her Majesty's Inspectorate of Prisons (2004) *A Thematic Review by HM Chief Inspector of Prisons. 'No Problems – Old and Quiet': Older Prisoners in England and Wales*. London: HMCIP.

Her Majesty's Inspectorate of Prisons (2004) *Expectations: Criteria for Assessing the Conditions in Prisons and the Treatment of Prisoners*. London: HMCIP.

Wahidin, A. (2004) *Older Women in the Criminal Justice System – Running Out of Time*. London: Jessica Kingsley.

Chapter 13

Managing the special needs of ageing prisoners in the United States

Ron Aday

Introduction

Since the 1980s, prison officials, policymakers and researchers have observed an astonishing phenomenon in the US: increasing numbers of older adults are entering the prison system, finding themselves locked behind steel doors and razor wire fences. Countless older prisoners sit in wheelchairs or feebly shuffle back and forth to receive medication waiting for their life sentences to end. This fact has mobilised prison staff and other public officials to examine policy issues such as economic costs, housing and institutional management, humanitarian and other end of life concerns. Factors contributing to the ageing prison population include the ageing of the general population, the increase in older adults committing violent offences, the harsher sanctions now given for crimes committed, and the war on drugs. The numbers of older Americans entering federal and State institutions is not anticipated to diminish in the near future. In fact, researchers have estimated that during the next half century, we will continue to witness judges issuing stringent prison sentences to the elderly.

The greying of America's prisons became particularly noticeable during the 1990s as the number of prisoners 50 years of age and older in federal and State institutions more than tripled (33,499 in 1990 to more than 125,000 in 2002 (*Corrections Yearbook* 2003). In 2002, the 50 and older population comprised 8.2 per cent of the total prison population, nearly double the 4.9 per cent statistic of 1990. To further illustrate the tremendous growth of this sub-group of prisoners, older men and women comprise over 10 per cent of the total prison population in 19 States, a growth from 7 States in 1990. Lifers and prisoners with a 20-year-sentence now constitute one quarter of the total prison population (*Corrections Yearbook* 2003).

Women constitute only a small percentage (5 per cent) of the older prison population, but their numbers are growing rapidly (American Correctional Association 2003). Only in recent years have policymakers, prison officials, and academicians begun to assess and provide for the needs of this small population. Similar to their male counterparts, most women spending later adulthood behind bars are non-married Caucasians who have limited educational backgrounds and work skills. Women growing old behind bars are more likely than their male counterparts to have entered the prison system after enduring years of physical and/or sexual abuse, have numerous physical and mental health problems for which they require medical treatment, and be serving time for first (often violent) offences.

Typologies

Approximately 40–45 per cent of older prisoners are housed in federal and State prisons in the US are 'new elderly' offenders who never violated the law, but committed first offences (primarily murder and sex crimes) against relatives or close acquaintances after the age of 50 (Beck 1997). Formerly regarded as 'model citizens', these prisoners frequently have difficulties adjusting to life in prison, abiding by prison policies, living with a potentially violent population, and being away from family and former friends. The pains of imprisonment can leave some feeling guilty for disappointing loved ones, lonely, apprehensive about the future, and anxious about surviving in a total institution. As a result, many begin to exhibit symptoms of depression: withdrawal from prison staff and prisoners, change in sleep and eating patterns, and suicidal ideations. Remorseful for the crimes committed, other 'new elderly' offenders are appreciative of the free food, shelter and clothing they now have, and adjust rather well to institutional living.

Other ageing prisoners who require unique programming include long-term inmates who first offended early in life and received 20-year+ prison sentences. Often young, uneducated, poor black men who pleaded guilty to the sentence given and never requested release, these prisoners typically have grown old behind bars. Since imprisonment, many have severed any contact with members of the free world, and would have no home where they could return if released. Long-term prisoners require special consideration since many will lose motivation to participate in prison activities, obsess over visible signs of deteriorating health, and contemplate dying in prison. If these inmates were to receive parole and could tomorrow return to the free world, they would first require extensive resettlement preparation, including assistance obtaining financial support, affordable lodging, and inexpensive healthcare services since many have become heavily dependent on the prison as an institution to meet all of their needs for basic survival.

As previous research has shown, ageing prisoners are a diverse population (Aday 1994; Douglass 1991; Krebs 2000). Most older inmates are unmarried, are male (95 per cent) and have fewer than 12 years of formal education. With the exception of southern States, where older black prisoners outnumber their white counterparts, a slight majority of the ageing prisoners in America is white. The average age of inmates 50 and older is 57. A significant number were either unemployed or working in unskilled labour at the time of offence, had no access to preventive healthcare, and thus now require extensive medical treatments for poor health conditions.

Management challenges

Health care issues

Prisons have not traditionally been constructed to house older persons, whose physiological changes include progressive losses of strength, agility, physical mobility, hearing, and sight. In addition, deterioration of mental and emotional capacities (i.e. dementia and short-term memory loss), and the ability to provide self care will require additional services for these prisoners. As a result, health care tends to be the most critical concern of elder prisoners and those responsible for managing their needs while in prison. Prisoners as a population traditionally have medical and social histories that put them at greater risk of illness and disease than their non-inmate counterparts (Edwards 1998). Lifestyle choices such as widespread tobacco use, extensive drug and alcohol use, and high-risk sexual behaviour contribute to their greater need for health services.

Research conducted in several States (Aday 1995; Aday 2001; Colsher, Wallace *et al.* 1992; Douglass 1991) has found that older male prisoners frequently suffer from a variety of chronic health problems.

Older inmates frequently suffer from arthritis, hypertension, heart problems, ulcers, diabetes, emphysema, and stroke. As a whole, they have a higher incidence of chronic disease and significant functional disability compared to similar age groups on the outside. The majority of this group reported that their health was poor when compared to others their age and that their condition had worsened in the past two years (Edwards 1998). Older female offenders are generally in poorer health than their male counterparts and are more likely to suffer from depression and other mental disorders (Aday 2003).

The 1976 *Estelle v Gamble*[1] ruling stated that prisons have an obligation to provide for the medical and personal needs of all prisoners including the 2,500 dying behind bars every year (Byock 2002). America's courts do not mandate prisons to release terminally ill older, infirm prisoners, but some federal and State prisons do provide compassionate release for prisoners who have medical records and physicians' statements documenting their prognoses, low-risk security classifications, and future economic security (Anno *et al.* 2004). Sending minimal risk, terminally ill prisoners home to die reduces prison medical expenditures (Yates and Gillespie 2000), but placing prisoners in the care of others is not always possible. For example, the Texas Criminal Justice Department reported that two elderly prisoners in their 70s suffering from chronic heart and lung failure require around-the-clock intensive medical care that is costing taxpayers nearly $1 million a month (Moritz 2004). Prison officials cannot release the two men to a nursing home where their medical bills would be lower because Texas law forbids the early release of those convicted of sex crimes. In many cases, ageing relatives often do not have the strength, stamina or time adequately to support a frail, elderly inmate, and nursing home staff generally do not want to assume the liability of caring for former prisoners (Aday 2003). Therefore, prison officials must provide in-house health services and treatment programmes for prisoners who have no other option but to spend their final days behind bars.

Most prison departments see the rising cost of providing adequate health care as the biggest challenge in meeting the needs of an ageing prison population. Prisoners come into the system bringing a variety of high-risk behaviours requiring immediate attention. Health care and security for prisoners over the age of 60 typically cost in the region of $70,000 (Shimkus 2004). That is three times as much as for younger inmates. There are additional services the State has to cover beyond what they would for a non-offender citizen. Once a prisoner is incarcerated, eligibility for national health care programmes such as Medicaid and Medicare benefits are no longer accessible and each State has the responsibility for providing health care. If prisoners are not housed in a health care facility or a special geriatric unit, there are additional costs of transporting a prisoner with an armed guard (Brunner 2002).

Due to the debilitating conditions that may accompany the ageing process, older prisoners are frequently housed where they have the availability of health care staff and emergency care 24 hours a day. Medical professionals are needed in some cases for the basic activities of daily living (ADLs) such as bathing, feeding, physical therapy, medication management and rehabilitation. Numerous States also offer chronic care clinics with the hopes of encouraging health promotion activities. Some older inmates who are too frail and too weak to attend to their own personal needs are more likely to receive treatment in a nursing home environment or in an infirmary (Anno *et al.* 2004). The vast majority of prison systems now require inmates to provide a medical co-pay when receiving health services. For those systems that do mandate a co-pay plan, the rates are primarily in the $2 or $3 range, while a few systems charge $5 to $8 for each prisoner requested office visit (*Corrections Compendium* 2004).

The Americans with Disabilities Act of 1990 (ADA) prohibits discrimination against disabled prisoners. This means that all inmates must have access to the same programmes, services and other activities. Those who are formally considered disabled are defined 'as individuals with a physical or mental condition that substantially impairs one or more life activities' (e.g. caring for one's self, completing basic tasks, seeing, hearing, breathing, walking, or working) (Morton 1992, p. 10–11). In the Oregon Department of Corrections geriatric unit (Anno *et al.* 2004), prisoners are provided with hospital-style beds equipped with extra padding, toilets, sinks, and showers that comply with ADA, and older prisoners also have a therapeutic gym equipped with a pool table configured at a lower height to accommodate wheelchairs. Closed-captioned television and specially equipped phones are available for the hearing impaired. Failure to respond to prisoners with special needs could prove costly to American prison systems including legal expenditure as well as staff resources. According to prison officials, expenditure is significantly reduced when housing older offenders in an environment where a specially trained health care staff can recognise and treat problems before they become severe.

Segregation v Mainstreaming

Elder housing placements are typically based on clinical criteria and the issues concerning the care of this population are similar to those for prisoners who have a physical disability. Rather than relying strictly on age, most States take the length of sentence and physical condition into consideration when prisoners are classified, custody graded, and given work programmes or housing assignments (Flynn 1992). The main question for prison administrators concerning ageing offenders in prison is whether to mainstream or segregate this population. While prisoners in good health care live in the general population, facilities designed for physically active people may be problematic architecturally.

One argument for segregated housing is that older prisoners may not fit in well with the younger, aggressive prisoner. For example, Walsh (1989) found that older male prisoners expressed a greater need for privacy and for access to preventive health care and legal assistance than the younger men. Older inmates are often unable to cope with the fast pace and noise of a regular facility (Anderson and Morton 1989). Wilson and Vito (1986) also found that older inmates reported difficulties with a lack of privacy and complained they could not escape from the continuous level of noise and distracting activities of other inmates. As a consequence, several prisoners in later life reported heightened levels of anxiety.

Other studies have found that older prisoners report feeling unsafe and vulnerable to attack by younger inmates and express a preference for rooming with people their own age (Marquart et al. 2000; Walsh 1990; Williams 1989). This can be particularly true for the new older offender coming into an unknown environment late in life and ripe for potential victimisation. Vega and Silverman (1988) reported that abrasive relations with other prisoners were the most disturbing incidents elder inmates had to cope with while incarcerated. Fifty-five per cent of their respondents indicated that abrasive situations occurred on a daily basis. These factors, among others, often result in fear and increasing stress for the older prisoners. Therefore, separate units that provide a more sheltered environment and accommodation may be worth considering.

Opponents of segregation have raised questions about the detrimental effects that could hinder inmate adjustment when placed into specialised units or facilities (Shimkus 2004).

Housing for older prisoners may not be universally welcome by prisoners who have worked hard to get assigned to preferred facilities, such as those near family. Elder inmates might also be deprived of services and enrichment opportunities available only in the general prison population. Being grouped into a special facility, ageing prisoners may be viewed as old, weak, helpless, and in need of specialised care. Thus, a negative label could be associated with segregated prison housing designed for the aged and infirm. In this regard, removing frail inmates from mainstream prison life and work opportunities may only serve to heighten their sense of inadequacy and enhance their institutional dependency. For some older prisoners, this move may have the same symbolic meaning as entering a nursing home in the free world and would be viewed in negative terms. Prison administrators have also consistently stressed the stabilising effect older prisoners can have on the general prison population, but certainly using older prisoners for this purpose while risking victimisation from younger inmates should receive consideration.

Facility accommodation

Despite the arguments for mainstreaming, an increasing number of States do routinely house the more frail older inmates apart from the general population and offer them unique programming and services. Special units provide a concentration of specialised staff and have the potential for saving money by focusing on preventive health care. As Table 13.1 suggests, numerous nationwide surveys conducted during the past several years have found a proliferation of separate housing and services for the prisoner in later life (Aday 1999; American Correctional Association 2004; Flynn 1992; National Institute of Corrections 1997). It is evident that an increasing number of prison systems do routinely house older prisoners apart from the general population, and offer them unique programming or services. In specific States (including Alabama, Georgia, Florida, Oklahoma, Wisconsin, Illinois, Kentucky, West Virginia, Virginia, Tennessee, Louisiana, Pennsylvania, Mississippi, North Carolina, Texas, Ohio, Wisconsin, and New Mexico) stand-alone facilities or secure nursing homes have been established to accommodate the increasing number of older inmates. In a number of other States, prisoners over the age of 50 are either grouped together or housed in separate medical units. In some cases, these units may mix older prisoners with younger disabled ones.

Whenever possible, same aged prisoners are grouped together in dormitory style cells with lower level bunks. The most frequent approaches used to provide specialised medical care for the older prisoners include preventive care, chronic care clinics, and increased physical examinations. A number of assisted living units are maintained for the chronically or terminally ill. Of course, handrails, lower bunks on main-floor tiers, elevated toilets and wheelchair accessibility are provided in most specialised units. When prisoners have low security risks, the facilities often permit the older offender increased privacy by designing rooms with doors and staffing fewer officers. Additional amenities include prison-controlled thermostats, fluorescent lighting, strobe lighted fire alarms, and non-slippery flooring surfaces (Falter 1999). To further accommodate the needs of ageing frail prison populations, some State and federal prison systems have begun requiring prison staff to undergo simulations representing the various visual, auditory and sensory changes normally associated with the ageing process (Neffe 1997).

While many older prisoners may strongly desire to live with inmates of similar ages, this option is not always possible. The prisoner's work skills, medical condition, security level are all factors that must be taken into consideration before he or she is placed in an aged-infirm unit. If the prisoner meets these criteria, the proximity of the desired facility to the prisoner's living relatives becomes a significant factor in the decision-making process. Not all older prisoners reaching this point will be assigned to geriatric facilities, as slots are frequently limited, with some units having long waiting lists. Others may actually wish to live in mainstream facilities as such placement permits them to remain engaged, to mentor younger peers, and to feel younger themselves (Gallagher 2001). Ageing prisoners housed with younger prisoners frequently have more opportunities to participate in educational, recreational and vocational activities than do prisoners housed in geriatric facilities, while inmates housed in geriatric prisons are often more likely to become bored, feel isolated, and use medical services to compensate for having excessive unstructured free time (Marquart *et al.* 2000).

Programming for older offenders

Although Goetting (1983) reported earlier that prison staff were unwilling to place older prisoners in educational and vocational programmes, numerous States have now expanded these programmes to accommodate the older offender (Aday 2003; Anno *et al.* 2004). The most important consideration in determining programme assignments for older prisoners is their physical limitations (Anno *et al.* 2004). Issues such as reduced physical strength, hearing and

Table 13.1 Available facilities, services and challenges for older prisoners

	Grouped or in geriatric facilities	Programmes or recreational opportunities	Chronic care clinics	Hospice/End of Life Programmes	Special needs and pressing problems in responding to needs of ageing inmates
Alabama	✓	✓		✓	Work opportunities/health promotion
Alaska					Safety from predators/mental health
Arizona	✓	✓			Recreation and programming
Arkansas	✓				Meaningful work/recreation
California		✓		✓	Medical services/overcrowding
Colorado	✓		✓	✓	Programme access/medical services
Connecticut	✓	✓			Safe environment/chronic health
Delaware					Medical services and costs
D.C.				✓	Health care issues/facility expansion
Florida	✓	✓	✓	✓	Appropriate structured programming
Georgia	✓	✓	✓	✓	Demand for assisted living space
Hawaii	✓	✓		✓	Separate housing and work needs
Idaho			✓		Medical services/limited facilities
Illinois	✓	✓		✓	Space/pre-lease issues/ADLs
Indiana	✓	✓		✓	Responding to ill/frail inmates
Iowa		✓			Personal safety/access to services
Kansas				✓	Discharge planning/activities for frail
Kentucky	✓	✓	✓	✓	Bed space/meaningful use of time
Louisiana	✓		✓	✓	Space/programmes for long-termers
Maine		✓	✓		Psychological needs/geriatric unit
Maryland		✓		✓	Housing/palliative care/programming
Massachusetts		✓			Health care services/mental health
Michigan	✓	✓		✓	Bed space/health services for frail

State	Recreation/programming/staffing	Social services/medical care/staffing	Service access, bed space, medical cost	Barrier free beds/geriatric unit	Special accommodations for frail	Health services/safe environment	Long-term medical conditions	Programming/space/caring for frail	Victimisation/medical services	Bed space/programming	Protective housing/medical care	Staff preparedness/programming	Community placement/medical needs	Staff training/geriatric facility/costs	Appropriate housing/medical care	Social isolation/programme accessibility	Social programmes/mental health needs	Work/therapeutic opportunities	Medical services/release concerns	Architectural barriers/programming	Safe environment/programmes/services	Medical problems/safe environment	Medical services/mental health issues	Depression/protection/inmate isolation	Health/support services/programming	Counselling/medical services/programmes	Chronic health problems/programming	Recreation/counselling/re-entry issues
Minnesota	✓																											
Mississippi	✓																											
Missouri	✓			✓																								
Montana	✓			✓																								
Nebraska																												
Nevada	✓																											
New Hampshire	✓				✓				✓																			
New Jersey																												
New Mexico	✓							✓																				
New York																												
North Carolina	✓									✓	✓																	
North Dakota	✓									✓	✓		✓															
Ohio	✓									✓			✓															
Oklahoma	✓												✓	✓														
Oregon	✓									✓					✓	✓												
Pennsylvania	✓									✓					✓	✓												
Rhode Island	✓															✓												
South Carolina	✓									✓						✓												
South Dakota	✓																	✓										
Tennessee	✓																		✓									
Texas	✓									✓									✓	✓								
Utah	✓									✓										✓								
Vermont																						✓	✓					
Virginia	✓																					✓	✓					
Washington	✓									✓														✓				
West Virginia	✓									✓														✓	✓	✓		
Wisconsin	✓									✓																✓		
Wyoming	✓																									✓		

Source: Corrections Compendium 2004

vision loss, and the inability to stand for long periods typically affect the type of work assignment that may be appropriate. The older prison population is frequently characterised as one with diverse interests and abilities. As a result, more individualised programming that reflects various functioning levels should be considered. Rather than placing an emphasis on vocational activities, the focus should also include leisure activities, a cottage industry or part-time work, volunteer activities within the institutions, or recreational activities such as gardening, woodworking, ceramics, and other craft activities (Anderson and McGehee 1991; Rosefield 1993). Despite their physical limitations, older prisoners need to stay physically active and mentally alert as long as possible.

Prisoners are also given information to assist them with pre-release planning on such relevant topics as social security, medicare/medicaid, estate planning and wills, advance directives, funeral planning, and community-based services. Additional recreational programmess are also offered that are better suited for ageing prisoners including low impact aerobics, power walking and team sports such as bowling and softball for inmates 55 and over. Outdoor horticultural activities are also offered in a number of facilities (Rosefield 1993). As these programmes demonstrate their effectiveness, other States will probably follow suit in designing more appropriate programming. A few facilities now employ psychologists and counsellors with professional training in geriatrics, so there is a greater awareness of the unique social, psychological, and emotional needs of these prisoners.

Educational programmes are also vital to individuals at any age. Prisoners as a group often require remedial assistance while in prison. Most State prison systems offer educational programming, which includes vocational education, literacy and coursework. Older prisoners, as a more settled group, derive a great deal of personal satisfaction and pride from education accomplishments. Many creative programmes have been developed in the educational arena. Most successful programmess blend elements of education and ageing awareness, family bonding health and end of life issues. The following activities (see below) for the older prison population (Wilkerson 1999) are examples taken from the Ohio Department of Rehabilitation and Corrections.

Aunt Jane's Story Book – Participants in this programme choose an age-appropriate book to share with a young member of their family. They read the story onto an audio tape, and send the book, tape and personal message to their young relative as a gift. This programme promotes literacy as well as family bonding.

Don't Forget! – Many older offenders experience memory loss due to ageing, substance abuse or other ailments. This loss can involve visual or auditory memory at immediate, short-term, and long-term recall levels. Following an assessment of their memory skills, the older-offender participants practice memory-improvement techniques. This programme uses audio tapes, note taking, handouts and mental exercises to retain and improve memory.

Medication Education – through lectures and discussions, older offenders who take psychotropic medications learn about the effects of the medications, the importance of taking them regularly, dosages, timing, etc.

Grandparenting – Using open discussion, lectures and handouts, these classes help older prisoners learn to deal with extended, blended and other family groupings, and help them support the family by being active and effective grandparents. Topics such as talking with children, toddlerhood and discipline are addressed.

Healthy, Well and Wise – These type of educational programmes discuss health and mental health concerns. Participants learn about dementia, confusion, vision, osteoporosis, depression, stroke, insurance issues, hospice and more. Participants are encouraged to learn how to use communication information and humour to cope with ageing issues. Counselling, assertiveness training, meditation and relaxation techniques are used to educate the older/medically fragile offender on ways to increase their coping skills for prison stressors.

Topic Talk – In this programme, offenders are afforded the opportunity to select and research a topic of interest to older women. They are required to give presentations, prepare to answer questions from their audience, and lead a discussion. The offenders benefit from learning about the topic they choose and from presenting to others. The programme creates self-worth and confidence and develops better working relationships with staff.

Life Beyond Loss – These programmes familiarises older offenders with the issues of death, dying and significant loss. Using the works of Elizabeth Kubler-Ross and other handouts, they explore the grieving process as they deal with the loss of family members and friends, the loss of physical health and the reality of their own eventual death.

Assertiveness Training – this programme teaches older/medically fragile offenders how to get their needs met in an assertive manner without conflict or confrontation. Older offenders often have different physical and mental needs in comparison to younger offenders. The programme empowers the offender to speak up in a productive and positive manner. An assertiveness training workbook is utilised with discussions, role-play, handouts and homework.

Exercise for Better Health – These programmes offer low impact, age-appropriate regular exercise for older and infirm prisoners. Exercising with others of their own age group encourages offenders to compete without fear of ridicule or worry about 'keeping up' with younger groups. Some programmes offer softball, basketball, bowling, pool, and other team sports for those over age 50 or 55.

Expressive Arts with the Aged – This programme uses art as a creative medium to encourage mobility and self-expression in older offenders regardless of their infirmities. Senses are stimulated through colour and texture and co-ordination is improved while using a variety of art supplies for self-expression. By displaying and explaining their art to fellow students, the participants develop better self-confidence.

Work assignments

Work provides a variety of latent functions in the prison setting. For the ageing prisoner, work is a very important activity. Many inmates have grown old while incarcerated and, for them, prison labour actually takes the place of a work career. Not only does work give inmates a sense of identity and purpose, it is also important for ageing prisoners' mental and physical health. When large segments of the day are filled with work-related activities, less time is left for prisoners to contemplate their situation, engage in self-pity, or for boredom to take over. Participating in work activities enables older prisoners the opportunity to stay in similar routines as younger prisoners, regardless of age. Work encourages inmates to remain engaged and physically active. In this regard, work can be considered a 'wellness' activity since older prisoners have to walk to work, walk to the dining room, to the commissary, and in some cases participate in physically demanding labour. According to Marquart *et al.* (2000), the most important aspect is the opportunity to work alongside men of varying ages. Maintaining a structured routine can serve as a stimulating experience for older inmates and perhaps slow down mental and physical decline.

Finding suitable work assignments for older prisoners poses significant challenges for prison officials. Prisoners have generally found the number of work opportunities available is rather limited (Caes 1990), and the big challenge is finding suitable work opportunities for all those who desire them. Older prisoners housed in the general prison population generally have much greater opportunity for prison employment than those in sheltered environments when compared to inmates living in special needs facilities. Older, frail prisoners who have been transferred from the general prison population to a special needs unit frequently complain about having to give up income-earning jobs (Marquart *et al.* 2000). For units that house up to 500 aged and infirm inmates to find appropriate jobs for every prisoner whose health permits is virtually impossible. The scarcity of prison industry jobs and other work or programming tends to result in the under assignment of inmates to work related activities. There are just so many light housekeeping jobs that can be manufactured for this special population. Of course, a significant number of ageing prisoners may work only a limited schedule and others are unable to perform any work activities.

Some older prisoners may work in a variety of cottage industries, which provide a legitimate community contribution as well as a limited income. Prison facilities also require a variety of maintenance tasks and services in order to function. These jobs include janitorial work, construction, food preparation, non-confidential clerical work, repair, laundering, landscaping, and serving as orderlies to mention a few. As the ageing prison population continues to increase, prison officials must be more creative in producing useful activities for this population. Currently, there are numerous activities that go on in most institutions as part of an illegitimate economy of the institution. For example, when permitted, prisoners provide services for each other such as tailoring, legal research, and correspondence. Cowles (1990) has suggested that if such activities could be legitimised and controlled, they could contribute to the smooth operation of the institution. At the same time, they would provide meaningful activities, and a viable occupation for long-termers and other ageing prisoners. For example, pushing prisoners' wheelchairs, helping other prisoners get dressed, carrying food trays, or assisting with bathing or feeding, writing letters, and making beds, have, in some cases, been defined as regular 'prison jobs'.

End of life issues

As a result of an increasing number of terminally ill prisoners, hospice programmes have found their way into the US prison system. As shown in Table 13.1, approximately 30 States now report some form of terminally ill service (*Corrections Compendium* 2004). Prison hospice programmes are governed by specific policies and procedures including criteria for admission, special privileges for terminally ill prisoners, requirements for housing in hospice settings, do not resuscitate orders, and the role of prison volunteers, among other issues. The decision to admit an inmate to a prison hospice programme is made in a variety of ways. In about half the States with hospice programmes, admission decisions are made jointly by medical and security staff or by medical staff and the hospice co-ordinator. In other States, the decision to admit an elder prisoner is made by medical staff and the hospice co-ordinator. Admission to most prison hospice programmes requires a doctor's certification that the patient has a terminal condition with an approximate life expectancy of six months or less. Hospice participants are required to sign informed consent statements, whose provisions vary by prison system.

Hospice patients have access to special privileges above and beyond those of a general prison population. The most common of these privileges is a relaxed visitation policy. For example, hospice patients at Angola Prison in Louisiana can designate up to ten people on a list and receive two visitors for up to two hours each seven days a week. Visitors may include non-family members and may include persons inside or outside the prison. Another hospice benefit is special food requests such as chocolates, fresh fruit or other culinary yearnings, which are provided to those in the final stages. Hospice patients often can keep additional personal property and, in some prison facilities, may have smoking privileges. The services of clergy and social workers as well as the opportunity to plan their memorial services are usually included in prison hospice services.

While some prisons in the US have been designated for elder prisoners or for the chronically ill, many sick prisoners remain in prisons that are unable to address their needs, medically or socially. Although hospice is becoming a more frequent service in the prison setting, pain management at the end of life is frequently under-utilised. Without such treatment protocols and programmes, sick and frail prisoners are left to their own resources to receive daily care, including, eating, grooming, socialising, and finding spiritual outlets. Frequently, other prisoners, not specifically trained in providing skilled nursing care, may care for a friend (Aday 1996).

Even with hospice patients, the care provided is typically not prisoner-centred, but prison-centred, and the prisoner's wishes are often not taken into account (Mezey *et al.* 2002). When sick prisoners are removed from the general prison population, they are frequently placed into even more restrictive medical units with their every movement highly monitored (Haney and Zimbardo 2001). Additionally, when they are transferred to another unit, they may not have the social supports they left behind and may now reside an even greater distance from family members. Prisoners fear spending their last hours in agony and separated from family on the outside. Frequently having suffered lifelong alienation from society, dying in prison is what prisoners dread most (Byock 2002).

Other issues complicate the assurance of quality of end of life care in prison. Programmes are needed encouraging inmates to employ the use of a living will to dictate their care when they are no longer capable of making medical decisions. Overcoming the lack of trust that many prisoners have for the medical staff who would make medical decisions on their behalf can be a major barrier. Selecting a proxy from the outside is not practical either, since the person would need to be present to discuss medical options and decisions with the treatment team. However, some States such as Ohio permit terminally ill prisoners to obtain advance medical directives including DNR (Do Not Resuscitate) orders. Generally, family input is sought when advanced directives are used (Anno 2001). Structured programmess that provide dying patients with the opportunity to receive spiritual and community support to reduce fears at the end of life should receive more consideration.

Compassionate release from prison is considered an important alternative to prison hospice care. While laws vary from State to State, 43 States have reported the availability of compassionate release (Anno *et al.* 2004). However, given the time required to process the paperwork and the political considerations that enter into the decision-making, only a few terminally ill prisoners are granted early release (Dubler and Heyman 1998). For example, when the State of Virginia abolished parole in 1994, it also created a possible loophole for older prisoners. Prisoners aged 60 or older who have served at least ten years of their sentence, or those 65 and older who have been incarcerated for at least five years are allowed to petition the parole board for geriatric release. Ten years later not a single geriatric prisoner has received an early release (Hammack 2004).

Conclusion

This chapter has presented some of the challenges of managing a growing ageing prison population held in State and federal institutions in the US. These prisoners of today are older and sicker than ever

225

before and have multiple chronic health concerns. As this population continues to increase, managing the special needs of this population will be a tremendous challenge. While it is obvious that prison officials and politicians are becoming more sensitive to the special needs of ageing prisoners, barriers will continue to interfere with the ability for States to respond effectively. Most States are faced with the rising costs of medical care and general overcrowding. There exists some public sentiment that providing special treatment or separate facilities in order to meet the needs of older prisoners is not necessary (Edwards 1998). Also, there is still disagreement regarding the ethical obligation to provide inmates with such acute care as heart by-pass surgery or kidney transplants when others in society may not have access to, or the money for, the same level of care.

To meet this challenging responsibility, professionally trained prison staff who can work comfortably with geriatric inmates will be essential. Prison staff need to be specifically trained to understand the social and emotional needs of the older adult population, dynamics of death and dying, procedures for identifying depression, and a system for referring older inmates to experts in the community. Functional assessment providing early and accurate identification of the complex needs of older prisoners will be critical for case management. Maintaining good communication between custody staff and health care providers will play an important role in the management process. Researchers should also continue to examine current prison conditions and programmes to recommend policies and procedures to standardise the management approach to the crisis.

Note

1   429 U.S. 97 (1976) 429 U.S. 97 Estelle, Corrections Director *et al. v* Gamble Certiorari to the United States Court of Appeals for the Fifth Circuit No. 75–929.

References

Aday, R.H. (1994) 'Golden Years Behind Bars: Programs and Facilities for the Geriatric Inmate', *Federal Probation*, 58 (2): 47–54.
Aday, R.H. (1995) *A Preliminary Report on Mississippi's Elderly Prison Population*. Parchment, MS: Mississippi Department of Corrections.

Aday, R.H. (1999) 'Golden Years Behind Bars: A Ten-year Follow-up'. Paper presented at the annual meeting of the Academy of Criminal Justices Sciences, Orlando, FL.

Aday, R.H. (2001) *A Comprehensive Health Assessment of Aged and Infirm Inmates*. Nashville, TN: Tennessee Department of Correction.

Aday, R.H. (2003) *Ageing Prisoners: Crisis in American Corrections*. Westport, CT: Preager Publishing.

American Correctional Association (2003) *Adult and Juvenile Directory*. Maryland: American Correctional Association.

Anderson, J.C. and McGhee, D. (1991) 'South Carolina Strives to Treat Elderly and Disabled Offenders', *Corrections Today*, 55 (5): 124.

Anderson, J.C. and Morton, J.B. (1989) 'Graying of the Nation's Prisons Presents New Challenges', *The Aging Connection*, 10: 6.

Anno, B.J. (2001) *Correctional Health Care: Guidelines for the Management of an Adequate Delivery System*. Chicago, IL: National Commission on Correctional Health Care.

Anno, B.J, Graham,C., Lawrence, J. and Shandsky, R. (2004) *Correctional Health Care: Addressing the Needs of Elderly, Chronically Ill, and Terminally Ill Inmates*. Washington, D.C.: National Institute of Corrections, US Department of Justice.

Beck, A.J. (1997) 'Growth, Change and Stability in the US Prison Population, 1980–1995', *Corrections Management Quarterly*, 1 (2) : 1–14.

Brunner, K. (2002) *Elder Inmates: An Analysis of Policy Options for the State of Florida*. Tallahassee, FL.: Florida Department of Corrections.

Byock, I.R. (2002) 'Dying Well in Corrections: Why Should we Care?', *Journal of Correctional Health Care*, 12: 27–35.

Caes, G. (1990) 'Long-term Inmates – A Preliminary Look at their Programming Needs and Adjustment Patterns' in *Long-term Confinement and the Ageing Inmate Population*, 120–41. Washington, D.C.: US Department of Justice.

Colsher, P.L., Wallace, R.B., Loeffelhotz, P.L. and Sales, M. (1992) 'Health Status of Older Male Prisoners: A Comprehensive Survey', *American Journal of Public Health*, 82: 881–84.

Corrections Yearbook (2003) South Salem, NY: Criminal Justice Institute.

Cowles, E.L. (1990) 'Program Needs for Long-term Inmates' in *Long-term Confinement and the Ageing Inmate Population*, pp. 15–27. Washington, D.C.: US Department of Justice.

Douglass, R.L. (1991) *Old-timers: Michigan's Elderly Prisoners*. Lansing, MI: Michigan Department of Corrections.

Dubler, N.N. and Budd, H. (1998) 'End-of-life Care in Prisons and Jails' in M. Puisis (ed.) *Clinical Practice in Correctional Medicine*, pp. 355–64. St. Louis, MO: Mosby.

Ebersole, P. and Hess, P. (1998) *Toward Healthy Ageing*. St. Louis, MO: Mosby.

Edwards, T. (1998) *The Ageing Inmate Population: SLC Special Series Report.* Atlanta, GA: The Council of State Governments.

Elderly Inmates: Survey Summary (2001). *Corrections Compendium*, 26 (5): 7–21.

Falter, R.G. (1999) 'Selected Predictors of Health Services Needs of Inmates Over Age 50', *Journal of Correctional Health Care*, 6: 149–75.

Flynn, E. (1992) 'The Graying of America's Prison Population', *The Prison Journal*, 16: 77–98.

Gallagher, E.M. (2001) 'Elders in Prison: Health and Well-being of Older Inmates', *International Journal of Law & Psychiatry*, 24 (2–3): 325–33.

Goetting, A. (1983) 'The Elderly in Prison: Issues and Perspectives', *Journal of Research in Crime and Delinquency*, pp. 291–309.

Hammack, B.W. (26 September 2004) 'Aging Prisoners Behind Bars', *Roanoke Times*, p. A1.

Haney, C. and Zimbardo, P. (2001) 'Twenty-five Years After the Stanford Prison Experiment' in P.G. Herman (ed.) *The American Prison System*, pp. 25–34. New York: H.W. Wilson Company. 'Inmate Health Care: Survey Summary (2004)', *Corrections Compendium*, 29 (6): 10–29.

Krebs, J.J. (2000) 'The Older Prisoner: Social, Psychological and Medical Considerations' in M.B. Rothman, B.D. Dunlop and P. Entzel (eds) *Elders, Crime and the Criminal Justice System*, pp. 72–84. New York: Springer.

Kratocoski, P. (2000) 'Older Inmates: Special Programming Concerns', in P. Kratcoski (ed.) *Correctional Counseling and Treatment*, pp. 23–35. Prospect Heights, IL: Waveland Press.

Marquart, J.W., Merianos, D.E. and Doucet, G. (2000) 'The Health-related Concerns of Older Prisoners: Implications for Policy', *Ageing and Society*, 20: 79–96.

Mezey, M., Dubler, N.N., Mitty, E. and Brody, A.A. (2002) 'What Impact do Setting and Transitions Have on the Quality of Life at the End of Life and Quality of the Dying Process?' *The Gerontologist*, 42, Special Issue III, pp. 54–67.

Moritz, J. (21 March 2004) 'Elderly Inmates Costing Millions', *Ft. Worth Star– Telegram*, p. 1, 1A.

Morton, J.B. (1992) *An Administrative Overview of the Older Inmate*, Washington, D.C.: US Department of Justice.

National Institute of Corrections (1997) *Prison Medical Care: Special Needs of Populations and Cost Control in Special Issues.* Longmont, CO: US Department of Justice, National Institute of Corrections Information Centre.

Neffe, J. (1997) 'The Old Folks' Slammer', *World Press Review*, 44 (2): 30–4.

Rosefield, H.A. (1993) 'The Older Inmate – "Where Do We Go From Here?"', *Journal of Prison & Jail Health*, 13: 51–58.

Shimkus, J. (2004) 'Corrections Copes with Care for the Aged', *Correct Care*,18 (3):1, 16.

Vega, M. and Silverman, M. (1988) 'Stress and the Elderly Convict', *International Journal of Offender Therapy and Comparative Criminology*, 32: 153–62.

Vito, G.S. and Wilson, D.G. (1985) 'Forgotten People: Elderly Inmates', *Federal Probation*, 49 (1): 18–24.

Walsh, C.E. (1989) 'The Older and Long-term Inmate Growing Old in the New Jersey Prison System', *Journal of Offender Counselling, Services and Rehabilitation*, 13: 215–48.

Wilkerson, R.A. (1999) *A Comprehensive Approach to Addressing the Needs of Ageing Prisoners.* Columbus, OH: Ohio Department of Rehabilitation and Correction.

Williams, G.C. (1989) *Elderly Offenders: A Comparison of Chronic and New Offenders*, Unpublished Thesis. Murfreesboro, TN: Middle Tennessee State University.

Wilson, D.G. and Vito, G.F. (1986) 'Imprisoned Elders: The Experience of One Institution', *Criminal Justice Policy Review*, 1: 399–421.

Yates, J. and Gillespie, W. (2000) 'The Elderly and Prison Policy', *Journal of Ageing & Social Policy*, 11 (2–3): 167–76.

Chapter 14

Older offenders and community penalties: a framework for thinking

Gaynor Bramhall

Introduction

After agreeing to contribute a chapter on older offenders and community penalties for this collection I began to consider what the chapter might include and what the main focus of the piece of work should be. My last piece of detailed research in this area with my colleague Helen Codd (Codd and Bramhall 2002) was now three years old and at that time there seemed to be a growing awareness and concern about the interactions between elders and crime. I naively assumed that there would be a larger and growing body of research and was optimistic that others would have taken up this neglected area and have pushed forward our knowledge and understanding of the interactions of older offenders with community penalties. My first task then was to undertake a thorough literature search, familiarise myself with the material, and then reflect on the purpose, shape and content of the chapter. This proved to be a rather thankless task as although there are some committed and enterprising researchers determined to give the voices and experiences of older offenders, particularly those in prison, a space to be heard, within the field of older offenders and community penalties in the UK there was little new work.

The emerging literature on older offenders and imprisonment highlights the lack of concern about the interactions of older offenders with community penalties and poses the question 'why?' I began to reflect on the growing awareness of age and ageing in a society where elders form an ever increasing proportion of the population and consider how concern for elders in terms of quality of life, health, social care, access to resources, ethnicity, and gender differences are well established and have begun to have a presence in criminological debates on imprisonment – but not those on community penalties. This chapter provides a new way of thinking about older offenders and community penalties. It considers a number of inter-related aspects and issues within criminal justice and explores how they have contributed to a continuing lack of concern about and invisibility of older offenders being supervised in the community.

Recent concern about elders as offenders has resulted in a growth of research and publications related to the experiences of elders as prisoners, in particular in relation to their health and social care needs. This growing body of knowledge has highlighted the negative impact and often inappropriateness of imprisonment for older offenders (Codd 1994; Wahidin 1999, 2004; Ware 2001). However this focus on imprisonment has not been matched by a comparable growth of interest in and concern about elders' experiences or interaction with community penalties, or indeed the appropriateness of community penalties for this group (Codd and Bramhall 2002). To enable a more comprehensive and theoretically informed understanding of the interactions of older offenders with the criminal justice system researchers have to examine all aspects of elders' interactions with the criminal justice process, from arrest to prosecution and sentencing. Widening this debate to incorporate community penalties will contribute to a greater understanding of the interactions of older offenders with criminal justice agencies and shed further light on possible points of discriminatory decision making or processes of ageism. Prior work with other areas of social divisions and crime, such as class, gender and 'race' have shown that there are often contradictory patterns that need to be explained to begin to understand the complex processes and interactions that are taking place, thus a stronger focus on older offenders and community penalties is timely.

The research and published material concerning older offenders and community penalties is sparse: much of it relates to North America and whilst it provides indicators that we can consider, its application or generalisability to the UK must be evaluated with caution, given our different cultural, political and socio-economic contexts. This chapter questions why this situation continues against a background context of an emerging body of research that focuses on older offenders and imprisonment (Codd 1994; Wahidin 1999, 2004; Ware 2001), a growth in the number of elders in the prison population (Brogden and Nijhar 2000; Howse 2003) and official public policy concern about the growing number of elders in the population (Midwinter 2005). There is an identifiable lack of focus or interest amongst practitioners, academics and policy makers on the issue of community penalties and older offenders.

This chapter identifies and examines a number of inter-related issues that contribute to the continuing invisibility and neglect of older offenders and community penalties. Firstly, the nature or understanding of 'community penalties' in comparison with 'imprisonment' is problematic: it is not clear what they are (Raynor 2002). They tend to be defined as what they are not, not imprisonment, *alternatives* to custody, rather than what they are. In an age of populist punitive measures prison is seen as the only real punishment which leaves community penalties as a vague punishment that only makes sense as a comparison to prison. This has led Worrall and Hoy (2005) to argue 'We simply cannot think about punishment without thinking about prison because we do not have the words with which to do it' (p. xv). This lack of clarity is further compounded in relation to community penalties as they are historically identified in terms of probation policy and practice with youth (Mair 1997). Age in terms of elders is rarely discussed and is absent from debates about difference or discrimination within community penalties.

Secondly, our commonsense understanding and perception of the elderly as 'vulnerable' or 'victims' rather than as offenders is explored. This is an ageist assumption in itself and contributes to the deeply ambivalent views we hold about older offenders. These assumptions are examined in relation to sex offenders who form a significant and highly visible proportion of older offenders (Brogden and Nijhar 2000; Codd and Bramhall 2002; Howse 2003), the possibility of stereotypical views of sex offenders impacting on commonsense perceptions of the elderly as offenders is considered. The third pair of issues to be addressed is how our ambivalent views of older offenders relate to sentencing practices and their implications for older offenders and community penalties. The chapter will conclude with a discussion of how consideration of these inter-related issues can provide a framework for an agenda of continuing research that will contribute to a theoretically informed discussion of policy initiatives relating to community penalties from an elders' perspective.

Before moving on it is pertinent to pause and consider where in the lifespan and criminological literature does an offender become an 'older offender'? This remains a problem for researchers on both sides of the Atlantic as a range of ages from 50 to 65+ is used, making comparison between studies and data difficult (Brogden and Nijhar 2000; Wahidin 2004). Whatever the age at which an offender is considered 'older' is inevitably an arbitrary decision, and an ageist one. Selecting a chronological age for defining 'older' neglects the concept of ageing … because social ageing – that is, the roles which society casts us into at different ages – is getting more and more out of step with biological ageing' (Young 1990, cited in Midwinter 2005, p. 10). There are some strong arguments in support of choosing the younger threshold of 50. Firstly, research indicates that older prisoners tend to have a biological age about ten years in advance of their contemporaries (Howse 2003; Wahidin 2004). Secondly, choosing a threshold of 50 means that women will not be excluded as there are so few women aged 60 or older at present either in prisons (Wahidin 2004) or subject to community penalties (Codd and Bramhall 2002). The majority of studies use 50, and in line with existing research 'older' is interpreted here as meaning aged 50 or more (Codd 1996; Brookes-Gunn and Kirsch 1984; Midwinter 1990; Pilcher 1995; Wahidin 2004).

Community penalties

It is perhaps understandable that concern about older offenders as prisoners has emerged in both the UK and North America prior to any serious consideration of older offenders' experiences of community penalties. Societal attitudes are generally sympathetic towards elders facing physical decline and the possibility of a diminution of their mental capacities, what Midwinter (1990) refers to as the 'sympathy syndrome'. This sympathy translates itself into shared views and attitudes about the appropriate places for elders to be, which generally exclude prison. Elders are expected to be with families and friends, and, if they have significant health or social care problems, in residential or nursing homes. Such views are reinforced by the ever present social policy debates about the rising number of the 'third age' in our population (Midwinter 2005), underpinned by successive governments from the 1970s onwards promoting the concept of 'community' as the right place for the elderly to be; to keep and maintain their community contacts.

The majority of existing research on older prisoners is in broad agreement with Brogden and Nijhar (2000) when they argue that: 'In most institutions older prisoners decay without a realistic personal future and without appropriate facilities' (p. 150). It seems inevitable then that the thrust of criminological concern about older offenders is that they should be 'outside' of prison facing a different kind of punishment. Conversely, if the community is considered an appropriate place for older offenders to be, this has helped contribute to a lack of concern about older offenders and community penalties as they are already outside of prison, resulting in the interactions between ageing, crime, and supervision in the community remaining neglected. Despite community penalties being the most frequently used sentences in modern penal systems they, 'have not received the degree of criminological interest that has been accorded to the study of custodial penalties' (Hughes 2001, p. 258). They remain in comparison to prison an under researched area in general, and for older offenders in particular. Less is known about interactions between older offenders and community penalties, either where they are sentenced directly to a community penalty, or where supervised as part of post-release conditions (Codd and Bramhall 2002), than about older offenders sentenced directly to custody.

The lack of interest in older offenders and community penalties is further compounded by the '… contested and imprecise nature of the concept of "community penalties"' (Raynor 2002, p. 1168). The term community is vague and can be used to describe a number of things from local neighbourhoods to national identity, communities of people with shared interests such as the 'traveller community', or a geographical identity. With the rise of neo-liberalism in the late 1970s the term became associated with rolling back the boundaries of the nanny-state, enabling voluntarism or privatisation. The concept of community has two underpinning assumptions. Firstly, that there is some common or shared sense of social solidarity, identity or understanding. Secondly, that this shared sense of community results in a form of mutual responsibility, where citizens are willing to deal with, or look after, the problems or needs of community members: care by and within the community (Worrall and Hoy 2005). These assumptions are present in both 'new right' and 'new labour' discourse, but emphasis has increasingly been laid on the individual's responsibility to the community. There is a well developed critique of the contentious nature of the concept of 'community' and how this concept can be used in debates on crime (Hughes 2001; Worrall and Hoy 2005). For crime, the idea of community raises issues of whether the offender should be excluded or reintegrated, whether belonging to a community is available to all, whether the community itself is the cause of crime through social and economic deprivation, whether the community has the capacity to prevent crime, and concerns over whether the community has broken down and no longer holds any moral sanction or deterrence value for the offender (Worrall and Hoy 2005).

Combine 'community' with 'penalties' and you have a phrase that is widely used, but often misunderstood. Technically, community penalties are all punishments that are imposed in the community, such as the fine which is the most widely used example. However, what is generally meant in criminal justice discourse when community penalties are referred to is a penalty with some element of supervision such as probation: now a Community Rehabilitation Order (CRO); and Community Service: now a Community Punishment Order (CPO), (following the Criminal Justice and Court Services Act 2000), and other forms of penalties such as tagging and curfews (Raynor 2002). Whilst supervision following release from custody on licence has generally been excluded from discussions of community penalties, this distinction is gradually being eroded with the development of new penalties such as 'custody plus' and 'intermittent custody'. The current Labour Government has acted to erode this distinction further with the creation of the new National Offender Management Service (NOMS) that effectively merges the Prison and National Probation Services and introduces the concept of seamless sentences (being phased in at the time of writing). Further changes to probation provision are planned following the implementation of the Criminal Justice Act 2003. The most significant changes are the re-naming and structuring of current community penalties. For the purposes of this discussion, the term community penalties is taken to mean all types of supervision in the community whether directly sentenced or post-release.

It is beyond the scope of this chapter to discuss in detail management and structural changes to the organisation that provides community penalties. However, it is crucial to understand that probation services have been subject to rapid change in the era of the new penology (see Worrall and Hoy 2005). One of the most ironic outcomes of these changes is that the term 'probation', a well known feature of the criminal justice landscape over the last century, has all but disappeared and been replaced with terminology that reflects the new penology and focus on punishment, 'risk', and 'what works'. Such a rapid period of transition and change raises concerns about how a focus on social divisions in policy and practice can be maintained within the new managerialist culture that probation services now operate in. Chouhan (2002), argues that probation services were amongst the first agencies to develop anti-discriminatory policies and practice and makes the pertinent point that progress in areas of diversity is not a matter of understanding or resources but '… one of leadership and political and individual commitment' (p. 115). Whilst it is a difficult time for probation services to take on board and develop concerns for older offenders as a new and emerging area of social divisions, a more positive stance is to recognise how well probation services have withstood the pace and change of the past two decades. Codd and Bramhall (2002), argue that older offenders are currently not perceived as a marginalised or excluded group and that within the research exploring 'race', gender and class in relation to community penalties, ageing remains an invisible dimension (Masters 1979; Worrall 199). Youth and young offenders are a dominant theme within current discourse on crime and criminal justice; the dominance of youth as an issue has led Phillips, Worrall and Brammer (2000) to argue that 'the relationship between age and criminal behaviour has been constructed almost exclusively as a problem of youth' (p. 253). A paradigm shift in terms of ageism and a subsequent willingness to examine all areas of policy and practice for inherently ageist practices is required.

There are two key areas of contemporary debate within community penalties: 'what works' and 'risk'. Within each of these there are implications for older offenders. 'What works' is a cognitive behavioural approach that currently shapes the nature and content of supervision work with offenders in the community, directly sentenced or post-release. Specific named programmes must be well structured and effective to receive accreditation. Therefore making community penalties a more attractive or default sentencing option for older offenders requires careful attention to social and cultural differences, knowledge of pathways into and out of crime, and an understanding of offending patterns and life course histories. Gelsthorpe (2001), warns of the dangers of introducing generic programmes without prior research to inform detailed sensitivity to social and cultural differences, warning that offender alienation can occur and the potential for effectiveness can be lost. Experience and knowledge gained from research and practice concerning the marginalisation of women and minority ethnic offenders demonstrates that early attempts that viewed minority issues as an 'add on' feature to existing practices have a history of failure or achieving the opposite outcome to that intended (Bowling and Phillips 2002; Gelsthorpe 2002).

Any consideration of older offenders and community penalties must also address 'risk'. The meaning of the term risk changed within probation discourse during the last two decades of the twentieth century: from the 1980s where risk meant the risk of an offender receiving a custodial penalty, to the 1990s where following the Criminal Justice Act 1991 risk began to mean the risk the offender posed to the public, with offenders themselves becoming the 'repository of risk' (Kemshall 2002). Penal policy has moved towards control through family and community networks, through responsibilisation. With hindsight it is possible to reflect on this change and the prominence of risk and to see that older offenders were unlikely to benefit from this changing discourse as any concerns about lack of family ties and community networks would render them 'bad risks' for a community penalty and thus exclude them further by increasing the potential use of custody. The growing prominence of risk has been matched by the introduction of successive generations of predictive assessment of 'risk' tools. Risk assessment mechanisms have been introduced into probation practice to help to predict risk of future offending and to indicate appropriate sentencing options. Risk assessment tools are viewed as neutral. However there has been a growing disquiet about the 'neutrality' of risk assessment with evidence from other marginalised groups indicating that discriminatory patterns occur. Third generation risk assessments contain subjective factors as part of the assessment, and it is how these are perceived by those assessing risk that is at issue. Hudson and Bramhall (2005), argue that Asian offenders suffer disproportionately from poorly written and thought out pre-sentence reports that lack a clear recommendation for a community penalty. Subjective risk factors are being interpreted differently for minority ethnic offenders, making them more likely to receive a custodial sentence despite having lower risk scores than comparable white offenders. Worrall (2002), effectively demonstrates that the current population of women prisoners does not pose a great 'risk' and argues that probation is often a missed opportunity for women. Kemshall (2002) has called for probation agencies and government to consider moving away from the pursuit of the 'perfect risk assessment tool' in a society where all risk can not be predicted, and to consider taking 'a risk with risk' (p. 110).

Images of older offenders

The image we hold of elders is not as offenders, as Midwinter (1990) so aptly comments:

> Such is the strength of the association of older people with being victims of crime, that the raised eyebrow, even the incredulous smile, greets any attempt to discuss criminal activity by elderly people. (Midwinter 1990, p. 55)

Whilst this response is likely to be a shared experience for those who have embarked on research in this area, Midwinter's comment captures the strength of our commonsense perceptions and attitudes. 'As a society, we are unaccustomed to thinking about elderly people as criminal offenders' (Wahidin 2004, p. 9). Our dominant societal view of elders is as physically frail with diminishing mental capacities. This is extended to incorporate elders who offend as frail, confused, or lacking in agency. The stereotype of older offenders committing petty theft, minor fraud and motoring offences for socio-economic or deteriorating health reasons is strongly held with serious crime being viewed as the preserve of younger, male offenders (Midwinter 1990).

This leaves elders who commit crimes who are not physically frail, do not have reduced mental capacities, or are not in dire economic circumstances as different or 'other'. They do not fit within our commonsense explanations of crime, age and criminality and thus challenge and lie 'outside' of our received wisdom or understanding. Confronting the rationality, intent, culpability or aggression of older offenders is uncomfortable for us, their actions contradict our stereotypical views and it is easier to view them as 'other' than to challenge our dominant images. The difficulties we experience in developing a discourse on older offenders that views them as rational and possessing a sense of agency demonstrates the deeply ambivalent views we hold about them as offenders. If they are frail and confused they receive the 'sympathy syndrome'; if they are rational and culpable what then? Jewkes (2004), argues that our images of offenders are increasingly becoming 'binary oppositions', that our frameworks of understanding result in categories of 'good' or 'evil', 'normal' or 'sick': and that this process of simplification results in polarised extremes that neglect an understanding of the complex realities of social situations. Jewkes (2004), applies this framework to children and demonstrates how they have become 'evil monsters' or 'tragic victims' in the world of crime. This framework is also applicable to older offenders. Women over 50 in prison represented only 4 per cent of the total female prison estate in 2005 and out of the total prison population for both men and women 13 per cent are over the age of 50. (Wahidin and Aday 2005; data provided by the Research, Development and Statistical Department and Statistics Directorate of the Home Office). Men in prison constitute 94.22 per cent of the total prison population and men over 50 represent 8 per cent of the male estate. In terms of actual numbers, there were 170 women and 4,513 men in prison who were over the age of 50 in January 2005 (see Wahidin 2005b). Male (aged 60 and over) prison receptions in England and Wales doubled in the decade 1986–1996, from 299 to 699 (Brogden and Nijhar 2000, p. 126). This trend continues with the number of male (aged 60 and over) prison receptions rising to 774 in the year 2000: and for women (aged 60 and over) from 14 in 1990, to 34 in the year 2000, more than doubling in a six-year period (Howse 2003, p. 7). By 2003 the number of males (aged 50 and over) in prison in England and Wales and under sentence was 4,227; with 155 women (aged 50 and over) in the same category (Wahidin 2004, pp. 205–6). The actual numbers of older offenders (aged 50 and over) in prison warrant consideration, but they are subsumed by a system that caters for the young and able bodied male. An alternative way of thinking about the numbers of older offenders in prison is to reflect on the fact that by 2003 the numbers of male and female older prisoners: 4,382 (aged 50 or more) is greater than the total number of women of all ages imprisoned: 3,396 (calculated from Wahidin 2004, p. 205–6). Much concern has been expressed by practitioners, academics and policy makers about the rise in the women's prison population (Gelsthorpe 2002). This has not been matched by a rising concern about the growing number of older offenders within prison, or the wider criminal justice system.

Discussions thus far have referred to the marginalisation or invisibility of older offenders, there is however one group of older offenders which is highly visible: sex offenders. Sex offenders are identified throughout the criminal justice system by offence rather than age. Howse (2003, p. 11) comments on the disproportionately high numbers of older sex offenders, with one third of adults (aged 60 or over) being sentenced to imprisonment in the year 2000 for a sexual offence compared with approximately 3 per cent of all adults received into prison that year. This is particularly so for males, with sexual offences being the most significant offence for older males in prison (Brogden and Nijhar 2000). This is also commented on by Codd and Bramhall (2002) in their study of the records of offenders contained in the database of a large urban probation agency, with sexual offences accounting for contact with 53 per cent of male offenders aged 50 and over. The most common offences for older women (aged 50 and over) to be sentenced to imprisonment are violence against the person, drug-related offences and fraud (Wahidin 2004). The increase in the significance of sexual offences for older male offenders may reflect growing awareness of child abuse, the increase in numbers of children reporting abuse many years after the event leading to convictions of older men who were younger when the offences were committed (Sampson 1994), and changing patterns of sentencing practices leading to increased periods of custody and post-release supervision under section 58 of the Crime and Disorder Act 1998 (NACRO 1998). But it is the significance of sexual offences when considering images of older offenders and community penalties that may be problematic.

Older, male sex offenders are at odds with the arguments developed so far, but it is their 'visibility' and 'difference' from other older offenders (male and female) that may have negative consequences on policy and practice concerning older offenders and community penalties. They are highly visible in terms of the attention they receive in penal and criminal justice policy and practice and the social condemnation they attract (Bramhall 2004). The terms sex offender and paedophile have become conflated and interchangeable in commonsense discussions about sex offenders, ignoring differences between those who 'look' and those who 'abuse'. Jewkes (2004) argues that sex offending has become regarded as the most 'heinous' crime of our age. They are perceived as the most intractable group of offenders with two key elements to this strongly held view. Firstly, attempts at reform or rehabilitation are limited and secondly, that they get worse as they get older: though there is little evidence to support either assumption (Jewkes 2004; Worrall and Hoy 2005). Both these aspects have implications for community penalties. Worrall and Hoy (2005) argue that the 'sex offender has been constructed as morally, socially and politically irredeemable' (p. 175), and that this group of offenders has become a '... socially excluded offender group' (Thomas and Tuddenham 2001, p. 16, cited in Worrall and Hoy 2005, p. 175). For older male sex offenders this presents a forceful image of exclusion based explicitly on offender group and implicitly on age. Negative images of age and offending are re-inforced with official discourse on sex offenders rejecting rehabilitation in favour of surveillance (Worrall and Hoy 2005). Images interact with current penal policy concerns about 'risk' and 'what works' to contribute to a context where there is little impetus or interest in developing community penalties that focus on other offence groups committed by older male offenders, and a neglect of the potential of community penalties for older female offenders. The impact of the dominance of sex offenders as a central concern in the criminal justice system is to mask and obscure other patterns and interactions of age, class, gender, 'race' and offending.

Sentencing and older offenders

Our ambivalent views about older offenders are further reflected in attitudes to sentencing and their implications for older offenders in an era of populist punitive attitudes. Hudson (2003) argues that within such a climate there is support for a more retributive sentencing approach, thus distancing offenders from benefiting from a more rehabilitative, reformative or restorative justice approach. Brogden and Nijhar (2000), outlined a jurisprudential framework in relation to older offenders and argued that both retributive and utilitarian principles can be used to justify a more severe or more lenient approach to sentencing. For example, from a retributive position older offenders can be seen as more culpable or blameworthy due to their life experience, and from a utilitarian position their capacity to learn can be seen as decreasing with age: justifying a harsher response. However, from a retributive position the punishment should be proportionate to the offence and a longer or harsh sentence could mean an older offender spending a greater part of their remaining life being punished: 'Time for older offenders is more likely to be seen as a diminishing, exhaustible resource in which the future becomes increasingly valuable' (Steffensmeier and Motivans 2000, S143).

Like children, older offenders are the only other group to be appraised on the basis of age rather than on individual attributes (Steffensmeier and Motivans 2000). Generally, ageist assumptions about older offenders suggest that they should be sentenced more like children. From a retributive perspective the moral guilt of older offenders decreases with declining mental capacities, thus it makes no sense to punish those who can not be morally guilty. From a utilitarian perspective if older offenders lacked the mental capacity of rational action and they could not understand the principle of deterrence then punishment would be unlikely to be successful and could not be justified (Brogden and Nijhar 2000).

The physical infirmity and diminished mental capacity approach underpins the case for differential treatment for older offenders (Howse 2003). US studies on the sentencing of older offenders present them as less of a danger or threat to society. Elders in prison are less aggressive and less able to use force, with prison placing greater physical and psychological demands on elders (Steffensmeier and Motivans 2000). There is however a strong argument for disaggregating the concept of age and ageing and considering instead individual aspects of each older offender: an age-neutral approach (Brogden and Nijhar 2000; Howse 2003). The significance of vulnerability then becomes a determining factor in sentencing in individual cases with evidence of dementia or physical incapacity being used in the same way as any defendant of any age could use evidence of mental illness (Brogden and Nijhar 2000). The age-neutrality approach is a forceful argument for not developing special procedures, or a sentencing framework, for older offenders. An age-neutrality approach is further supported by a more informed understanding of the ageing process whereby the group identified as older offenders would have an 'age cohort' of 50 or more years in common, but the defining characteristic of this group as a whole would not be their age but their differences, or lack of homogeneity as the older we get the more different we become. Age should not be a synonym for physical frailty and mental incapacity, rather it should just be used to indicate seniority without the attachment of other attributes (Midwinter 1990). An age-neutral approach to sentencing requires a wider, more open and unstructured approach to sentencing older offenders.

Whilst the study of sentencing practices concerning older offenders is quite well established within North America, in the UK there is little work that informs our discussion. Within the UK there are many studies of other marginalised groups, particularly women and minority ethnic groups, informing and enabling discussion and contributing to the development of feminist and anti-racist critiques of sentencing practices (Bowling and Phillips 2002; Gelsthorpe 2002), enabling critics and commentators to monitor the impact of new legislation and policies on recognised marginalised groups and to lobby, petition and actively challenge, shape and inform new priorities and agendas.

Conclusion

The use of community penalties for marginalised groups such as women or minority ethnic groups has a well developed research literature that contributes to evolving theoretical critiques. This work has undoubtedly benefited from the inclusion and prioritisation of the voices of women and ethnic minorities who have actively challenged discriminatory attitudes, assumptions and policies. Emerging work on older offenders and community penalties has much to learn from the developmental paths of feminist critiques and anti-racist strategies. The voices and experiences of older offenders must be incorporated to help ensure that ageist stereotypes and assumptions are exposed and challenged as they are recognised. More comprehensive research that focuses on decision-making processes that affect older offenders from arrest to prosecution and sentencing is required. Attempts to understand decision-making processes, policies and practices that affect older offenders can benefit from contemporary research in other areas of social divisions by considering the disaggregation of the large mass of other adult offenders they are being compared with to match the current offence and offending history of the older offender/s under scrutiny. Alongside quantitative studies of trends and patterns which tend to give snapshot pictures across a cohort there need to be in-depth qualitative analyses of older offenders' experiences to develop an informed and sensitive understanding of the interaction between older offenders, crime, and community penalties through their life course.

In each of the inter-related issues explored above the consideration of their implications for older offenders and community penalties has been highlighted and links formed across the issues to demonstrate the complexity of exploring the processes that contribute to the invisibility or marginalisation of older offenders and their interactions with community penalties. In general they present a rather pessimistic view, but as a group of inter-related arguments they do begin to address why, despite emerging research and literature elsewhere in the criminal justice system on older offenders and their experiences, community penalties have attracted so little attention from practitioners, researchers, academics or policy makers.

There are some key issues that emerge from this discussion for probation services staff. Whilst evidence and research is rather thin, what has emerged from this discussion is a pattern of older offenders being more likely to receive a direct sentence of custody and less likely to receive a community penalty than other adult offenders (Phillips and Brown 1988, cited in Howse 2003). The challenge is to address what role community penalties can play in this changing context that is appropriate and effective for older offenders. Besides a discussion of conceptual issues there are some very real pragmatic issues for probation services staff to consider. The first is that the numbers of older offenders are small, but as this discussion has argued, not insignificant. Older offenders are not located in any one centre or locality, but randomly throughout the UK, which means that where they are encountered they are in a numeric minority as well as a part of a minority group. The current focus on youth and younger males tends to take precedence and contributes to masking the needs and realities of older offenders. A concerted effort is required to focus on older offenders as a group with diverse needs, rather than on the one offence category where older males are more prevalent, sex offenders. The new sentencing framework for community penalties introduced under the Criminal Justice Act 2003 may be an opportunity to rethink and reconsider the nature of community penalties, to re-appraise the content of approved programmes, and to re-assess what is effective or good practice from existing work with older offenders, particularly from post-release supervision where most older offenders are currently likely to be found. The new sentencing framework has the potential to enhance the role of community penalties as a sentencing option, perhaps placing them as an automatic sentence of choice rather than as an alternative to custody in cases assessed as appropriate. The challenge is to keep a focus on the offending patterns, histories and interactions of older offenders to enable a more sensitive and informed approach to their potential for supervision in the community in an organisation that is being subjected to rapid change from penal policy and management re-structuring.

We must learn from the experience gained from researching other areas of discrimination which have shown that acknowledgement of subjectivity has highlighted the dangers of viewing marginalised or minority groups as uniform categories (Bowling and Phillips 2002; Williams 1991). They show us clearly the danger of reducing policy initiatives to simplistic minority related factors. In terms of older offenders and community penalties this is a warning not to take a knee-jerk reaction and introduce initiatives that are based on simplistic age related factors that may themselves be imbued with ageist assumptions. Finally, in many ways the most fascinating thing about ageing is the different responses and paths we all take as we all become more 'different'. Incorporating and integrating an anti-ageist approach to offending will not be a simple task, but demands that we place a clear focus on the needs, experiences and voices of older offenders and place them at the centre of our thinking (Andersen and Collins 1995).

References

Andersen, M.L. and Collins, P.H. (eds) (1995) *Race, Class and Gender: An Anthology*, 2nd edn. New York: Wadsworth.

Bowling, B. and Phillips, C. (2002) *Racism, Crime and Justice*. Harlow: Pearson.

Bramhall, G. (2004) 'Older Offenders and Community Penalties', paper presented to the Ageing, Crime and Society Conference, for the British Society of Criminology and Better Government for Older People, March 2004, London.

Brogden, M. and Nijhar, P. (2000) *Crime, Abuse and the Elderly*. Cullompton: Willan Publishing.

Brookes-Gunn, J. and Kirsch, B. (1984) 'Life Events and the Boundaries of Midlife for Women' in G. Baruch and J. Brookes-Gunn (eds) *Women in Midlife*, pp. 11–30. New York: Plenum.

Chouhan, K. (2002) 'Race Issues in Probation' in D. Ward, J. Scott, and M. Lacey (eds) *Probation: Working for Justice*, 2nd edn, pp. 111–27. Oxford: Oxford University Press.

Codd, H. (1994) 'White Haired Offenders', *New Law Journal*, 144 (No. 6672), pp. 1582–83.

Codd, H. (1996) 'Feminism, Ageing and Criminology: Towards an Agenda for Future Research', *Feminist Legal Studies*, IV:2, pp. 179–94.

Codd, H. and Bramhall, G. (2002) 'Older Offenders and Probation: A Challenge for the Future?', *Probation Journal*, Vol. 49, No. 1, pp. 27–34.

Gelsthorpe, L. (2001) 'Accountability: Difference and Diversity in the Delivery of Community Penalties' in A. Bottoms, L. Gelsthorpe and S. Rex (eds) *Community Penalties: Changes and Challenges*, pp. 146–47, Cullompton: Willan Publishing.

Gelsthorpe, L. (2002) 'Feminism and Criminology', in M. Maguire, R. Morgan and R. Reiner (eds) *The Oxford Handbook of Criminology*, 3rd edn, pp. 112–143. Oxford: Oxford University Press.

Howse, K. (2003) *Growing Old in Prison: A Scoping Study on Older Prisoners*. London: Prison Reform Trust.

Hudson, B. (2003) *Justice in the Risk Society: Challenging and Re-affirming Justice in Late Modernity*. London: Sage.

Hudson, B. and Bramhall, G. (2005) 'Assessing the "Other": Constructions of "Asianness" in Risk Assessments by Probation Officers', *British Journal of Criminology*, 45 (5): 721–40.

Hughes, G. (2001) 'The Competing Logics of Community Sanctions: Welfare, Rehabilitation and Restorative Justice' in E. McLaughlin and J. Muncie (eds) *Controlling Crime*, 2nd edn, pp. 257–301. London: Sage.

Jewkes, Y. (2004) *Media and Crime*. London: Sage.

Kemshall, H. (2002) 'Risk, Public Protection and Justice' in D. Ward, J. Scott and M. Lacey (eds) *Probation: Working for Justice*, 2nd edn, pp 95–110. Oxford: Oxford University Press.

245

Mair, G. (1997) 'Community Penalties and the Probation Service' in M. Maguire, R. Morgan and R. Reiner (eds) *The Oxford Handbook of Criminology*, 2nd edn, pp. 1195–232. Oxford: Oxford University Press.

Masters, G. (1997) 'Values for Probation, Society and Beyond', *Howard Journal of Criminal Justice*, 36 (3): pp. 237–47.

Midwinter, E. (1990) *The Old Order: Crime and Older People*. London: Centre for Policy on Ageing.

Midwinter, E. (2005) 'How Many People are there in the Third Age?', *Ageing and Society*, 25: 9-18.

NACRO (1998) *Sex Offenders: Reducing the Risk*. London: NACRO.

Phillips, J., Worrall, A. and Bramner A. (2000) 'Elders and the Criminal Justice System in England' in Rothman M. B., Dunlop B.D. and Entzel, P. (eds) *Elders, Crime and the Criminal Justice System*, pp 253–72. New York: Springer.

Pilcher, J. (1995) *Age and Generation in Modern Britain*. Oxford: Oxford University Press.

Raynor, P. (2002) 'Community Penalties: Probation, Punishment and "What Works"' in M. Maguire, R. Morgan, and R. Reiner (eds) *The Oxford Handbook of Criminology*, 3rd edn, pp. 1168–98. Oxford: Oxford University Press.

Sampson, A. (1994) *Acts of Abuse: Sex Offenders and the Criminal Justice System*. London: Routledge.

Steffensmeier, D. and Motivans, M. (2000) Older Men and Older Women in the Arms of Criminal Law: Offending Patterns and Sentencing Outcomes', *The Journal of Gerontology*, 55B, 3; ProQuest Nursing Journals, S141-S151.

Wahidin, A. (1999) 'The Hidden Minority: The Needs of an Ageing Female Prison Population', paper presented to the British Criminology Conference, Liverpool, July 1999.

Wahidin, A. (2004) *Older Women in the Criminal Justice System: Running Out of Time*. London: Jessica Kingsley Publishers.

Wahidin A. (2005) 'Older Offenders, Crime and the Criminal Justice System' in C. Hale, K. Hayward, A. Wahidin and E. Wincup (eds) *Criminology*, pp. 403–23. Oxford: Oxford University Press.

Wahidin, A. and Aday R. (2005) The Needs of Older Men and Women in the Criminal Justice System: An International Perspective, *Prison Service Journal*, July: 160: 13–22.

Ware, S. (2001) 'Alone, Elderly and Still Banged Up', *Howard League Magazine*, 19 (2): 8.

Williams, F. (1991) 'Somewhere Over the Rainbow: Universality and Selectivity in Social Policy', paper presented to 25th Annual Conference of the *Social Policy Association*, 9–11 July, University of Nottingham.

Worrall, A. (1997) *Punishment in the Community*. London: Longman.

Worrall, A. (2002) 'Missed Opportunities? The Probation Service and Women Offenders' in D. Ward, J. Scott, and M. Lacey (eds) *Probation: Working for Justice*, 2nd edn, pp 134–48. Oxford: Oxford University Press.

Worrall, A. and Hoy, C. (2005) *Punishment in the Community: Managing Offenders, Making Choices.* Cullompton: Willan Publishing.

Chapter 15

Towards a better government for older people and the policy implications in the criminal justice system

Mervyn Eastman

Setting the scene

As a social worker on call during the early 1970s in Newham, East London, I received a referral from Brentwood police (Essex). They were holding in custody one of our residents from an older people's home who had earlier that morning viciously attacked another resident, resulting in her hospitalisation.

The police considered that Mr Brown, who was 80 years old, was suffering from a mental disorder, thus explaining the attack on another resident. I was called to undertake a mental health assessment. Notwithstanding the multiple injuries sustained by the victim and the failing health of the alleged perpetrator, I was initially struck by the police response. They knew Mr Brown had attacked her (there were several witnesses), endangering her life, but they were reluctant about placing Mr Brown within the criminal justice system, finding it initially more comfortable that he should be dealt with via the health and social care processes in place at that time.

As it turned out Mr Brown *was* charged, taken before Shenfield Magistrates, and subsequently remanded to Brixton Prison to await trial. His performance in court was worthy of a BAFTA! He did indeed have minor mobility difficulties, was somewhat hard of hearing, and had a chronological age of 80+. His age, however, was irrelevant to the offence, and the magistrates were not fooled by his performance as a 'frail, confused, elderly gentleman'. In light of the seriousness of the offence they considered that custody was the appropriate disposal. During the course of the following year Mr Brown died whilst still on remand.

Almost 30 years ago, whether in the field of gerontology, criminology, social care, or social policy, the only serious academic attempt to develop a theoretical understanding of the relationship between crime and older people was that of Aday (1976). Fifteen years later Midwinter again picked up the baton (1990). They made the first tentative steps towards integrating two disparate disciplines – gerontology and criminology. My own practice-based experience highlighted in the above anecdote failed to register on my practice radar, remaining a rather interesting aberration until the intervention of Sir David Ramsbotham in the late 1990s (he was then HM Chief Inspector of Prisons (HMCIP)). Sir David wrote to the Association of Directors of Social Services (ADSS) requesting advice on how to address the social care needs of older prisoners (Eastman 2002). For me, that letter changed everything.

As with Gaynor Bramhall (Chapter 14 of this book) I felt a degree of 'self concern and panic' when invited to contribute to this publication. My research for the Inspectorate/ADSS remains unpublished, and thus five years out of date. Moreover, although this is a concluding note, I am anxious not to summarise all the preceding contributions. Instead I wish to offer a personal perspective, thus adding to the editors' desire to 'mine the riches from the fields of criminology and gerontology'. In writing this piece my growing unease developed from the possibility that by integrating criminological and gerontological perspectives we might inadvertently reinforce the possibility that criminologists researching 'age' and 'crime' would simply turn older people into 'someone else' – others to be patronised/infantilised, turned into objects to be tested and researched, whilst gerontologists would continue to posit older people in the context of their welfare needs rather than discussing the positive contributions that come with age and ageing.

Furthermore, to draw upon the experience of older people at risk of abuse, even the enabling guidance of the *No Secrets* (Department of Health 2000) or *In Safe Hands* (Welsh Assembly 2000) policy frameworks will not in and of themselves meet the needs and aspirations of older people in relation to the criminal justice system (see Penhale; Manthorpe; and Fitzgerald, in this book). To use explicit labels such as 'vulnerable' in the elder abuse guidance discourse is yet again to reinforce the separateness and engage in 'othering' of older people in society. This leads to older people's experiences (whether as criminal and/or as victim) being regarded as 'abnormal', and to older people themselves being regarded as people to be protected, pitied, or imprisoned!

Not only should we rethink criminology and ageing studies (Powell and Wahidin, pp. 20–8), but in addition we need to rethink elder abuse, the notion of fear of crime (Burnett, pp. 130–32), and vulnerability to distraction burglary (Lister's and Wall's fascinating contribution, p. 118), as well as health and social care within and outside of prisons (Aday, pp. 213–5). The evidence offered in this book on accelerated ageing in prison, ongoing challenges in health care, and the current, almost negligent, non-strategic approach to the problems of older prisoners forces attention to the policy implications of older offenders in the criminal justice system and provides an engaging and critical analysis of them. This book has argued that in rethinking *ageing, crime and society* research has to be strategic and foundational for policy. The purpose of this concluding chapter is to put forward such a framework. It is by placing older people as perpetrators and victims of crime within the context firstly of citizenship and secondly 'whole systems approaches'[1] to public services that this can be achieved. To start the debate I intend primarily to draw upon the UK government's own strategy to meet the challenges of ageing in the twenty-first century (Home Office 2005) together with the Thematic Review by the Chief Inspector of Prisons (HM Inspectorate of Prisons 2004) and secondly to incorporate the lessons from Better Government for Older People, an initiative established at the outset of the Labour Government in 1997.

Assumptions

I need now to make explicit the assumptions on which I am basing this final chapter. Whilst having sympathy with Foucauldian gerontology (Powell and Wahidin, p. 29) and sharing Phillips's preference for ageing life course approaches (Chapter 4 of this book), I hold the following position:

1. Age and ageing continue to be viewed within a medical (deficit) model in public policy! This is also the case for older people in the criminal justice system.

2. That model emphasises deficit, dependency, and sickness.

3. Older people are broadly stereotyped as victims, powerless and vulnerable.

4. Thus the social construction of ageing has reinforced 'dependency'

(the basis of much public policy and provision) until quite recently.

5. Older people are viewed within either a so called third or fourth age construct which re-enforces people 50+ as somebody else!

6. Elder abuse continues to be dominantly construed within the health and social care dependency construct.

7. Human rights legislation has failed to have any significant impact on the experience of older people generally and prisoners specifically.

8. How policy makers, academics, and practitioners think about older people is the central blockage to achieving effective public policy towards older people.

9. Closed organisations (ie prisons and also residential and nursing homes) are breeding grounds for potential abuse.

10. The effective engagement of older people with the criminal justice system is yet to be a reality.

11. The lack of a strategic approach reflects at best poorly articulated thinking between government departments and at worst the 'avoidance of ministerial embarrassment' (attention therefore to punishment!).

12. Instead it is necessary to engage effectively with older people in overcoming the worst aspects of ageist social policy and hence practice. This approach will lead to citizenship-based approaches.

13. A broader whole systems approach therefore reflects the fact that older people live 'joined up' lives and are not simply health and social care challenges (inside or outside the criminal justice system).

The question has surely to be how these axioms and insights apply to older *prisoners*.

From Ramsbotham to Owers

Sir David Ramsbotham, the charismatic former Chief Inspector of Prisons (1996–2001) published an account of his time at the prison inspectorate called *Prison Gate* (Ramsbotham 2003). He identified five separate minority groups within prisons, and older prisoners constituted one of the cohorts. As the Chief Inspector of Prisons he wished to work in partnership with the statutory and voluntary sectors which would include a review of the prison service areas of responsibility. In writing to the ADSS in October 2002 he said:

> As I go around the prison estate I am finding an increased number of elderly prisoners, all of whom are classified as being retired, which means that they do not qualify for work. Without qualifying for work they do not get wages, and therefore they live in pretty impoverished circumstances ... (cited in Eastman 2002)

The study, carried out jointly by the Inspectorate and the ADSS, was completed in 2000 and to date remains unpublished. Despite Ramsbotham's desire to confront punitive regimes in penal institutions, this present book reveals the continuing plight of older male and female prisoners. Moreover, as the number of older people in prison increases this will presage a multiplication of needs and challenges, for which there is little systematic planning of provision. This book contextualises ageing and crime, and addresses why this cohort has not as yet been the object of explicit policy intervention. This absence of such policy has been highlighted by Anne Owers, David Ramsbotham's successor. The thematic review entitled *No Problems – Old and Quiet: Older Prisoners in England and Wales* (HMCIP 2004) found that:

> few prisons take seriously the special needs of older prisoners; there is a lack of any meaningful engagement with them and that activities and offending behaviour programmes were not taking place. (HMCIP 2004, p. xi).

The review in addition commented that the National Probation Service has no better strategy for dealing with older offenders than does the Prison Service! The key recommendation not surprisingly was for a national strategy for 'older and less able prisoners that conforms to the requirements of the Disability Discrimination Act and the National Service Framework for Older People' (HMCIP 2004, p. 24).

What is interesting from the approaches of both Ramsbotham and Owers is how the prison service and inspectorate think about older prisoners. Both, however, acknowledge that the majority of older prisoners are neither disabled nor infirm. A strategic policy would necessitate a 'whole systems/citizenship' approach to underpin any specific proposals regarding older prisoners. In fact, however, older prisoners are discriminated against and are seen as 'less deserving' than the non-older people in the community. The *No Problems – Old and Quiet* Thematic Review rightly alludes to the need to include Social Services (now Adult Social Care) and NHS departments, but fails nonetheless to reflect the wider social policy agenda and the developing policy framework evident at the time of the 2004 publication.

The policy agenda

Until recently, the role of social policy in relation to older people was rooted in a health and social care model. Let that be our starting point. The debate (enshrined in the Department of Health (2001) National Service Framework for Older People) defines age and ageing in traditional and hence outdated terms:

1. entering old age – those who have completed their career in paid employment: namely active and independent;
2. transitional phase – those between healthy, active life and frailty;
3. frail older people – vulnerable as a result of health problems.

This construct could arguably reinforce the notion that people 50+ (and certainly post 60 years) are best seen in terms of dependency and sickness. The evidence is, however, that older people (defined 50+) remain active well into later years. Previous contributors have rightly emphasised the ongoing productivity of older people. Nevertheless not only do the challenges of ageing in prison accelerate not just the so-called ageing processes, but the very physical environment and the lack of facilities increase the risk and vulnerability of older prisoners.

The moral authoritarianism of successive governments where social policy is predicated on rights and responsibilities has been successful in reshaping the probation service but has failed, according to McTernan (2002) fundamentally to change how politicians review and alter public opinion about crime and punishment. From Harold Shipman[2] to Lord Archer[3], older prisoners are defined on the basis of their crimes rather than their 'well-being'.

'Prison *is* punishment, *not* for punishment,' once said Lord Britton (cited in Ramsbotham 2003, pp. 63–4). Public opinion often leads the policy agenda, but scant attention is given to understanding public attitudes or to encouraging the public to enter a meaningful engagement in penal reform (Roberts and Hough 2002). Certainly over the past 20 years ill informed public opinion has dominated the crime and punishment debate, and the focus has turned to the rights of victims of crime. One may feel uncomfortable seeing a very sick bedridden ex-train robber in a prison cell, but who considered the well-being of Shipman[2] or the hell and purgatory that Jeffrey Archer[3] found himself in?

Whilst prison policy is becoming 'welfare' based for older prisoners (let's support the frail and increase systems and responses to those in transition from health to ill health), who is publicly debating the 'citizenship and well-being' of older prisoners?

A number of common themes have been emerging over the past five years with regard to older people outside the criminal justice system. These have increasingly challenged the health and social care construct (welfare and dependency models) preferring listening to and engaging with older people and developing deliberate strategic approaches based on choice, control and well-being.

The critical dimensions now for policy and practice are about:

1. promoting a holistic approach which embraces the concept of 'citizenship' and recognises the broad set of partners that need to be engaged to promote social inclusion for older people;

2. promoting older people's priorities which need to be reflected in the structures and forums that are key in deciding resource allocation and community planning;

3. resulting in a community-based whole systems framework for commissioning universal and specialist services involving community members and a range of organisations;

4. moving away from choice and independence to control and interdependence.

These dimensions have influenced and informed two important policy papers from Central Government during the Spring of 2005. Firstly, the UK-wide strategy for an ageing population, *Opportunity Age* (Home Office 2005) and the Green Paper *Adult Social Care – Independence, Well-Being and Choice* (Department of Health 2005). The

Welsh Assembly Government has already published the first national older people's strategy in 2000. The important messages in all these papers are as follows:

1. ensuring older people remain actively employed;
2. older people playing a full and active role in society and their communities;
3. older people retaining independence and control of their lives even if constrained by health problems;
4. greater focus on well-being;
5. stronger strategic and leadership role for local government;
6. encouraging the development of new and exciting models of service delivery and harnessing technology to deliver outcomes.

And what are the strategic outcomes that are to apply to all older people?

1. Improved quality of health.
2. Improved quality of life.
3. Making a positive contribution.
4. Exercise of choice and control.
5. Freedom from discrimination or harassment.
6. Economic well-being.
7. Personal dignity.

Are these strategic outcomes applied to older prisoners or those placed in secure settings? If not, do these outcomes apply only to the so called 'deserving' older people? Do the crime(s) for which one is serving a period of imprisonment mean that one is excluded from these outcomes? Indeed, the above strategic outcomes should apply to all prisoners regardless of age, but given these are specific policy outcomes for older people the prison service has an enormous task ahead.

What is important to note, however, is that neither paper – *Opportunity Age* (Home Office 2005) and the *Vision for the Future of Social Care for Adult Services* (Department of Health 2005) – made any reference to older people within, or to those entering, the criminal justice system. What was even more worrying was that when Azrini Wahidin, Sir David Ramsbotham and I questioned the Prison Service at a conference in 2005 (discussing the Thematic Review about *Opportunity Age*) the senior civil servant knew 'nothing about the strategy'! All government departments were invited to contribute to the White Paper. One has to ask, where was the Prison Service? Presumably viewing older prisoners as 'somebody else'.

Perhaps as Lumby (2002) states:

> ... prisoners are dehumanised in the popular consciousness. They are rarely presented as individuals, and when they are it's only their crimes and their scarred backgrounds which are brought to light. Prisons are places beyond the community, places few of us wish even to imagine. (Cited in Brown and Wilkie 2002, pp. 103–12.)

Let me be clear. Harold Shipman and Lord Archer were older prisoners up until the suicide of the former and the discharge of the latter. In the twenty-first century under the Declaration of Human Rights, one has a right to expect that human dignity and human rights should be the underpinning priority during any period of imprisonment, including the imprisonment of high profile offenders (see Archer 2003; 2004; 2005).

Towards citizenship

The whole systems and citizenship approach underpinning the present government policy (including Wales) highlighted above must apply to the convicted prisoner, in spite of his/her imprisonment. Health care must be of the same standard as found in the community. There exists today the notion of a 'healthy prison' (Stern 2004) in which:

1. every prisoner is safe;
2. every prisoner is treated with respect as a fellow human being;
3. every prisoner is encouraged to improve him or herself, and given the opportunity to do so;
4. every prisoner is enabled to maintain contact with their family.

Under Article 10 of the International Covenant on Civil and Political Rights (ICCPR) prisoners are to be treated with the inherent dignity of the human person. The findings of the Thematic Review clearly demonstrate that many older prisoners' dignity is compromised by the inadequate physical environment, the lack of facilities, lack of regimes tailored to the expectations of the age group, unsuitable health and healthcare provision, and the failure to prepare elders for release and post release care.

One male offender of 62 years of age, serving a life sentence states:

> It is not clear to me what can be achieved at my current prison for the resettlement of a person of my age when clearly the structure which I would take to be common to all resettlement prisons and units is overwhelmingly geared towards those prisoners of much younger years. (Wahidin 2005, p. 12)

It is ironic that, whilst the Prison Service can and will prepare a younger prisoner for release, it is often thought to be a waste of resources to provide the same preparation for the individual needs of the aged offender who might in any event have come to the end of his or her working life, and therefore, in the view of some staff, have no value to the community (Wahidin 2005).

Such compromises are regularly challenged in residential and in nursing home provision. A glance at the voices of older prisoners quoted throughout the Thematic Review is depressing. Many older prisoners do indeed continue to live in impoverished circumstances. A mark of citizenship is (i) that older people, including prisoners, have the right to access public services and institutions which are accountable to them, the service users; (ii) that their civil and human rights are met; (iii) that they have access to appropriate specialist provision and are able to contribute actively to their 'community'. Brown and Wilkie (2004) discuss the contradiction between prisoners and citizenship. They argue that full citizenship is unlikely, but nevertheless state that prisoners should be able to participate in and challenge legal processes, and that their immediate and surrounding communities should reflect what the 'healthy prison' should embrace. Prisoners have rights, and the fact that they have become the 'least meritorious of human rights claimants' (ibid. 25) should not allow the public sector to collude with public sentiment, which is based primarily on a total ignorance of 'life in prison'. Older prisoners face multiple jeopardies, such as ageism in society at large; the social construction of older people as predominantly the victims of crime rather than the perpetrators of crime; that older people are somehow different from everybody else; and that growing old is a time of decline and dependency. Our present ideas of human rights and democratic citizenship and of ageing must surely be debated in the context of the older prisoner.

This publication is a significant step forward, and I feel privileged to be the final contributor. Before concluding, however, there remains one last task: to share a perspective on what a whole system citizenship approach to older prisoners could look like. Drawing on the Audit Commission/Better Government for Older People Study (2000), I offer such a framework: one that seeks to reflect the themes outlined in the Thematic Review *No Problems – Old and Quiet* (HMCIP 2004), with the *UK Older People's Strategy (Opportunity Age)* (Home Office 2005), and hopefully picks up upon a number of issues raised by the contributors in this book.

In addition, the framework seeks to be a spur to the Prison Service and to government generally to take forward their aspirations for creating better government for all older people, including older prisoners.

The adoption of such a framework may go some way to integrating national policy intentions into the commissioning and delivery of the prison service, meeting human and civil rights obligations, and addressing the arguments raised by the contributors throughout this book. Current sentencing policy, images of older offenders, and current thinking in relation to community penalties evidence the distance we have to travel before rendering older prisoners truly visible and having a joined up whole system approach to meeting their needs.

Policies now are in place. English and Welsh local councils and their partners are increasingly being required via performance assessment processes to demonstrate and give evidence of strategies in relation to older people, of engagement processes with all older people, and of what impact such strategies and processes are having. Measures have yet to be put in place to ensure that older prisoners are included in this policy in order to prevent older people within the criminal justice system from being excluded from one of the most basic of human rights – the protection of their dignity and humanity.

Notwithstanding the apparent lack of any serious thinking about older prisoners, there are three 'developments in the framework of law, policy and practice which will shape the use of prisons and alternatives over the coming years' (Esmee 2004). This report 'Rethinking Crime and Punishment' identifies the measures contained in the Criminal Justice Act 2003, *Custody Minus, Custody Plus,* and *Intermitted Custody*. These are attempts to reduce the overall prison population and reduce the impact of imprisonment on individual offenders. Secondly, the merging of the Prison and Probation Services seeks to ensure a more integrated and hence joined up approach at a regional level. The final measure in reducing re-offending is the adoption of strategies to improve the prospects of offenders leaving prison. These are encouraging developments, but as the Esmee Fairburn Report (2004) clearly states:

> How these developments work in practice will depend on the climate of opinion. There is a danger of an increasingly tough political rhetoric ... when elections preoccupy government and opposition thinking. (Esmee Fairburn Report 2004 p. 68)

For readers familiar with the disciplines of criminology and gerontology, the need to involve the community and the public in criminal justice, addressing social exclusion and health inequalities which contribute to crime, and using prisons as a 'genuine last resort' are imperative. If *better government for older people* means anything – it means better government for *all* and as the late Professor Bernard Isaas wrote:

> design for the young and you exclude the old; design for the older and you include the young. (Better Government for Older People 2005)

As we seek a society for all ages we need to create a criminal justice system which does not view older people as a growing problem. This book has provided you, the reader, with the opportunity to rethink our attitude towards age and ageing, and to re-evaluate the relationship between ageing, crime, and society. This indeed is a welcome addition to the literature.

Appendix 1

A Strategic Approach: Whole Systems Citizenship (Older Prisoners)

Involving all prisons, including ex-prisoners over 50+.	• All prisons with older prisoners (50+) have processes in place that engage with older prisoners on a regular basis.
	• Older prisoners are supported to participate fully, for example by offering induction or training sessions to prison staff.
	• Older prisoners are involved in a range of ways, including planning services, governance

259

	structures, and responses within the prison for the quality and delivery of services.
A picture of the local older prisoners population.	• That local authorities work alongside the prison service in identifying ethnicity, housing status, and income levels, as well as health inequalities, in the composition of the local population. • Projections of likely future changes in the older prisoner population are available.
A strategic approach	• Local authorities alongside their partners (and including the Prison Service) publish their strategic approach, with clarity about the improvement in the lives of older prisoners as part of their overall ageing strategies. This approach is to be underpinned by the principles of independence and Opportunity Age strategic outcomes. • Local Strategic Partnerships with prisons in their locality (if including older prisoners) take responsibility alongside the Prison Service to explicitly link to community and social inclusion strategies and partnership working.
Commitment and leadership	• The local authority identifies an elected member to lead on older people's issues across the authority. To liaise with prisons in the locality and to ensure that older prisoners are included within their portfolio. • Each prison with older prisoners to appoint at senior Governor level an older people's officer. All policies and procedures to be age sensitive.
Partnership/whole systems working	• All key agencies outside the Prison Service/ local authority, including the NHS, Link Age Service, Pension Service, voluntary organisations, are committed to a strategic approach. To include the probation service as a key contributor.

Communication and information	• There is information for older prisoners that signposts them not only to prison-related issues, but that are part of the wider older people's strategic services (where relevant, e.g. leisure, education, *et al.*) which should be the responsibility of the local community, not a parallel service.
	• Updates on progress on the strategic approaches relating to older prisoners.
	• Staff within the prison service, probation services, and across the local authority/ partnership agencies are well informed about the strategic approach and their role in contributing to change.
Evaluation and impact	• The community has systems in place, built in from the outset, to measure the impact of the strategic approach across the system, including surveys of older prisoners' views and voices.
	• The evaluation process includes outputs and outcome on older people (including prisoners) playing a central role.

Source: Audit Commission/BGOP 'Older People – Building a Strategic Approach' 2004, pp. 42–3).

Notes

1 The Whole Systems approach is defined as the integration of all policy and practice related to older people's public services underpinned by an infrastructure that reflects older people's wants and aspirations (see Better Government for Older People (2000), pp. 2–4).

2 Harold Shipman was Britain's most prolific serial killer. The doctor killed at least 250 of his elderly patients over 23 years. He was found dead in his cell at Wakefield prison on 13 January 2004, having hanged himself. The 57-year-old was serving 15 life sentences.

3 Lord Archer was found guilty of perjury and perverting the course of justice. He was sentenced to four years' imprisonment.

References

Aday, R.H. (1979) *Institutional Dependency: A Theory of Aging in Prison,* unpublished PhD thesis, Oklahoma University.

Archer, J. (2003) *Prison Diary – Vol 1.* Basingstoke: Macmillan.

Archer, J. (2004) *Wayland – Purgatory – Prison Diaries – Vol 2,* Basingstoke: Macmillan.

Archer, J. (2005) *Heaven – Prison Diary Vol 3,* Basingstoke: Macmillan.

Audit Commission – Better Government for Older People (2004) *Older People: Building a Strategic Approach,* pp. 42–3.

Better Government for Older People (2000) *All Our Futures: The Report of the Better Government for Older People Steering Committee.* London: Better Government for Older People.

Better Government for Older People (2005) *Summary of Adult Social Care Vision.* London: Better Government for Older People.

Brown, D. and Wilkie, M. (eds) (2004) *Prisoners as Citizens: Human Rights in Australian Prisons.* Sydney: The Federation Press.

Department of Health and Home Office (2000) *No Secrets: Guidance on Developing and Implementing Multi-Ageing Policies and Procedures to Protect Vulnerable Adults from Abuse.* London: Home Office.

Department of Health (2001) *National Standard Framework for Older People,* London: Department of Health.

Department of Health (2005) *Adult Social Care: Independence, Wellbeing and Choice* (Green Paper). London: Department of Health.

Eastman, M. (2002) *Discovering the Older Prisoner: Meeting the Social Care Needs of Older Prisoners,* unpublished by the Association of Directors of Social Services and HM Inspectorate of Prisons.

Esmee Fairbairn Foundation (2004) *Rethinking Crime and Punishment,* Policy Document.

Her Majesty's Chief Inspector of Prisons (2004) *No Problems – Old and Quiet: Older Prisoners In England and Wales.* London: The Home Office.

Home Office (2005) *Opportunity Age: Meeting the Challenges of Ageing in the 21st Century.* London: The Home Office.

Lumby, C. (2002) 'Televising the Invisible: Prisoners, Prison Reform and the Media' in D. Brown and M. Wilkie (eds) *Prisoners as Citizens: Human Rights in Australian Prisons,* pp. 103–114. Sydney: The Federation Press.

McTernan, J. (2000) 'Future Drivers for Change' in L. Kendall and L. Harker (eds) *From Welfare to Wellbeing – the Future of Social Care.* London: Institute for Public Policy Research.

Midwinter, E. (1990) *The Old Order: Crime and Older People.* London: Centre for Policy of Ageing in association with Help the Aged.

Ramsbotham, D. (2003) *Prison Gate.* London: Free Press.

Roberts, J.V. and Hough, M. (2002) *Changing Attitudes to Punishment: Public Opinion, Crime and Justice.* Cullompton: Willan Publishing.

Stern, V. (2004) 'Prisoners and Citizens: A view From Europe' in D. Brown and M. Wilkie (eds) *Prisoners as Citizens: Human Rights in Australian Prisons*, pp. 154–173. Sydney: The Federation Press.

Wahidin, A. (2005) 'Managing the Needs of Older Male and Female Offenders', *'Preventing Crime and Promoting Justice – Voices for Change'*, International Society of Criminology, 14th World Criminology Congress, 7– 11 August 2005, University of Pennsylvania. Unpublished paper.

Welsh Assembly Government (2000) *In Safe Hands: Guidance on Protecting Vulnerable Adults*. London and Cardiff: Home Office and Welsh Assembly.

Index

abuse *see* elder abuse
accelerated ageing 172
Action on Elder Abuse 90–1, 98,
    102, 142
administrative criminology 39, 44,
    48
adult protection
    after *No Secrets* 143–4
    before *No Secrets* 141–3
    citizenship framework 95
    committees 148
    communication and negotiation
        144–8
    coordinators 146
    need for multi-layered strategies
        103
    pressure group politics 142
    prevention 150–1
    small group level 148–9
    term 140, 142
Adult Social Care – Independence,
    Well-Being and Choice 254
advance medical directives 225
age
    as classificatory tool 22
    and crime 53
    in criminology 1, 18, 20, 23
    distraction burglary 115, 117–18

and gender 26–8
NSF definition 253
victimisation 43
vulnerability 9
age-neutral approach, sentencing
    242
age-related behaviour, societal
    expectations 233
aged *see* older people
ageing
    accelerated 172
    NSF definition 253
    studies *see* gerontology
    wider theories of 58–9
'ageing in place' 62
ageism
    distraction burglary 120–1
    images of older offenders 60
    prison resources 182
    sentencing older prisoners 241
    and sexism 28
    targeting, distraction burglary 115
agency, denial of 9
Alchemy Limited 36–7, 38
ALMA France 161–2
ALMA Wallonie-Bruxelles 164
Americans with Disabilities Act
    (1990) 214